读总统故事学英文

英汉双语对照

传奇人生

——美国历任总统的那些事儿

苏宗文　龙金顺 编译

北京航空航天大学出版社
BEIHANG UNIVERSITY PRESS

图书在版编目（CIP）数据

传奇人生：美国历任总统的那些事儿：英汉对照 / 苏宗文，龙金顺编译 .-- 北京：北京航空航天大学出版社，2013.10

ISBN 978-7-5124-1242-2

Ⅰ.①传… Ⅱ.①苏… ②龙… Ⅲ.①英语－汉语－对照读物 ②总统－生平事迹－美国 Ⅳ.① H319.4:K

中国版本图书馆 CIP 数据核字 (2013) 第 206221 号

传奇人生——美国历任总统的那些事儿

苏宗文　龙金顺　编译

责任编辑　江小珍

*

北京航空航天大学出版社出版发行

北京市海淀区学院路 37 号(邮编 100191）　http://www.buaapress.com.cn

发行部电话：(010)82317024　传真：(010)82328026

读者信箱：bhpress@263.net　邮购电话：(010)82316936

涿州市新华印刷有限公司印装　　各地书店经销

*

开本：710×960　1/16　印张：15.5　字数：341 千字

2013 年 10 月第 1 版　2013 年 10 月第 1 次印刷

ISBN 978-7-5124-1242-2　定价：39.80 元（含光盘 1 张）

前言

美国自开国独立以来，从筚路蓝缕开创母邦的乔治•华盛顿到一脸灿烂、意气风发的巴拉克•奥巴马，迄今共产生了44任总统。尽管出身不同，经历各异，但他们都通过自己不凡的天赋、坚韧的个性与不懈的努力，在美国历史或世界历史的长河里留下或深或浅、或是或非的印记。

毋庸讳言，由于时代的不同和历史的局限，这44任美国总统的政绩并非皆出类拔萃。有些总统的立场、思想、行为与做派，我们亦不敢恭维。然而，长期以来，这44任总统深深地吸引了世人的目光。华盛顿的人格之伟大、杰斐逊的学识之广博、林肯的思想之开放、小罗斯福的性格之刚毅、里根的言谈之幽默以及奥巴马的身世之独特，一直不停地被人们所渲染并传扬。或许我们可以说，回溯这些美国总统的生命历程，他们所铸就的传奇，宛如一曲曲跌宕起伏且韵味无穷的歌，回荡在美国政坛和欧美社会的芸芸众生之中。随着中美关系的日益发展，又在中国人的心中发出了深沉的回声。

本书编录了美国历任总统的逸闻趣事、传奇历程、其任期内的著名演说以及当时所发生的一些重大事件。书中不少趣闻轶事使人忍俊不禁或拍案叫绝；不少传奇经历令人肃然起敬或唏嘘不已；不少重大事件叫人掩卷沉思或感慨万千；不少著名演说则让人为之振奋或深受启迪。全书所采用的英语原文语言纯正流畅、精炼简洁，令人叹服；文采绚丽多姿、酣畅淋漓，难出其左。

书中每一节里的“总统及第一夫人简介”部分分别对每位总统与夫人进行了简明扼要的介绍，使读者能更为便捷地对历任总统及其夫人有一个基本的了解，在扩展知识的同时，进一步有效地提升阅读的乐趣和效果。书中每篇文章都配有热点词汇注释、背景知识注释、精美译文，以加深读者对原文的理解，使他们的英语水平在不知不觉间有较大的提高。值得一提的是，书中详尽的“背景知识注释”，与相应的译文相互补充，相得益彰，形成了有机链接，是一道道亮丽的风景线。因此，本书是一本上乘的英语读物。仔细加以研读对于学习地道英语、开阔视野、锤炼思想、了解美国政治、历史和文化都有着不可估量的积极作用。

本书由龙金顺、苏宗文、景天宽和陈敦波四位老师合力编译。在编写的过程中，曾参考并借鉴了国内外大量中外文电子或纸质资料。由于所涉及的范围甚广，受篇幅的局限，难以逐一列举与彰显，特此说明，并向原编著者表示深切的歉意和诚挚的感谢。与此同时，编译者向美国友人William Walsh先生，Barbara Toews女士，Tennant Wright先生，James Pongrass先生，Whitney夫妇以及英国友人Melville夫妇，德国友人Nolte夫妇致以由衷的敬意。由于他们伸出无私的援手，为我们答疑解惑、指点迷津，有力地保证了本书的编译质量。值此本书付梓之际，编译者深感这段情谊的令人难忘与弥足珍贵。

编译者

2013年6月

目录

1 George Washington as a Soldier 身为士兵的乔治·华盛顿

乔治·华盛顿 总统及第一夫人简介

乔治•华盛顿(George Washington, 1732.2.22～1799.12.14)，首任美国总统，美国独立战争大陆军总司令。1789年，当选为美国第一任总统(1789～1797)，1793年连任，在两届任期结束后，由于厌倦政治加之感觉年龄偏大，他自愿放弃权力不再续任，隐退于弗农山庄；在那里他享受了不到3年的退休生活便于1799年12月14日因咽喉感染去世，举国为他哀悼了数月。他由于在美国独立战争和建国中扮演了最重要的角色，故被尊称为“美国国父”。

玛莎•丹德里奇•柯蒂斯•华盛顿(Martha Dandridge Custis Washington, 1731.6.2～1802.5. 22)，美国开国总统乔治•华盛顿的妻子，大农场主的女儿。独立战争期间，华盛顿是大陆军总司令，玛莎深知丈夫责任重大，她独自在家抚养孩子，毫无怨言。玛莎还十分体谅士兵们生活上的疾苦，常常探望并照料军中的病号，安抚想家的士兵。她的举动深深感动了官兵们，增强了他们战胜敌人的信心，玛莎也因此成为官兵们爱戴的对象。1789年4月，华盛顿当选为美国第1任总统，玛莎无法回避社交活动，但她从不参政，她依然生活简朴、举止含蓄，保持一个受人爱戴的“国母”形象。

经典原文
Original Text

1 At 16, Washington helped survey and plot the lands of Lord Fairfax, who owned more than 5 million acres in northern Virginia and the Shenandoah Valley. After surveying for a few years, he was commissioned a Lieutenant Colonel in 1754 and fought in the French and Indian War. In 1755, he was serving as an aide to British General Edward Braddock at a fateful battle in Pennsylvania on July 9. That day the British made an attempt to capture *Fort Duquesne*①.

2 George Washington had been sick during most of the month of June but he insisted on joining the battle. The British suffered a terrible defeat that day. Out of 1,459 soldiers, almost 1,000 were killed or wounded. The French and their Indian allies routed the British who were not accustomed to the guerrilla warfare style of combat. General Braddock was killed, and Washington had to help lead the Virginians and British in retreat to safety. Do you think this experience was frightening to the young cavalry officer?

3 Washington kept a record of his life, in letters and journals. Ten days after the battle he wrote a letter to his mother, Mary Ball Washington. He said that he had escaped uninjured but "I had four bullets through my coat, and two Horses shot under me."

4 No doubt Mrs. Washington was worried about her son, but he proved to be an excellent soldier. Washington was made commander of all Virginia troops. Due to difficult circumstances and hardships in the wild, Washington became very ill and his doctor insisted he go home to his estate in Virginia to recover.

Words & Expressions

plot [plɔt] *vt.* 把…分成小块

acre [ˈeikə] *n.* 英亩，土地，耕地

commission [kəˈmiʃn] *vt.* 委任，使服役 *n.* 委员会

Lieutenant Colonel （美军)中校

aide [eid] *n.* 副手，副官

fateful [ˈfeitful] *adj.* 重大的；决定性的，命中注定的

capture [ˈkæptʃə] *vt.* 夺取，俘获

ally [ˈælai] *n.* 同盟者，同盟国；联盟

rout [raut] *vt.* 击溃 *vi.* 搜寻

guerrilla [gəˈrilə] *n.* 游击战，游击队员

combat [ˈkɔmbæt] *n.* 战斗，格斗

cavalry [ˈkævəlri] *n.* 骑兵，装甲兵

commander [kəˈmaːndə] *n.* 指挥官

troop [truːp] *n.* 军队

estate [iˈsteit] *n.* 房地产，财产

5 Washington recovered from his illness, and then returned to lead the Virginia army. He attained the rank of Brigadier General and was a major factor in Britain's defeat of the French and capture of Fort Duquesne (renamed Fort Pitt by the British) in 1758. Immediately after his return to Virginia, Washington married Martha Dandridge Custis on January 6, 1759.

6 Wilderness fighting had made Washington a trained military man. This training helped prepare him for his greatest military challenge — leading the American revolutionary forces as commander in chief during the fight for independence that began in 1775 with the *Battles of Lexington and Concord* ②.

attain [ə'tein] *vt.* 获得，实现

Brigadier General （美军）准将

wilderness ['waildnəs] *n.* 野生，野蛮

military ['militri] *n.* 军人，军队，军事

背景知识注释
Background Notes

1. Fort Duquesne 杜魁斯要塞，位于美国的俄亥俄河谷。
2. Battles of Lexington and Concord 莱克星顿和康科德战役，又被译为“莱克星顿的枪声”，是美国独立战争中发生的第一场军事冲突。1775 年 4 月 19 日，这场战役发生在马萨诸塞州米德尔塞克斯县，波及城镇包括莱克星顿、康科德、林肯、阿灵顿以及毗邻波士顿的剑桥。这场战役意味着英国与其北美 13 个殖民地正式爆发了战争。

中文译文
Suggested Translation

1 16岁时，华盛顿就帮助裴尔费克斯勋爵 (Lord Fairfax) 测量及划分其所属土地，裴尔费克斯勋爵的土地分布在弗吉尼亚北部及谢南多厄河谷 (Shenandoah Valley)，占地超过500万英亩。做了几年的测量工作后，华盛顿于1754年被授予中校 (Lieutenant Colonel) 军衔，并参加了法国–印第安人战争。1755年，华盛顿升任英国将军爱德华•布雷多克 (Edward Braddock) 的副官，于7月9日参加了一场在宾夕法尼亚州进行的重大战役，那天英国人试图攻下杜魁斯要塞。

2 几乎整个6月，乔治•华盛顿都处于生病状态，但他仍坚持参加了这场战役。当天，英国遭受了一场惨烈的败仗；出战的1,459位士兵中，有将近1,000名士兵战死或受伤。法军及其印第安盟友利用游击战术将英军打得溃不成军，布雷多克将军也阵亡。因而华盛顿必须带领弗吉尼亚州人及英军撤至安全地带。您认为这位年轻的骑兵军官是否被这次的经历吓坏了呢？

3 华盛顿用日记和信件的形式记录了他的生活。此次战役后的第十天，在一封写给他母亲玛莉・鲍尔・华盛顿 (Mary Ball Washington) 的信中，华盛顿表示他毫发未伤地成功突围，但“我身上的外套有四个子弹弹孔，且有两匹战马在我胯下遭射杀”。

4 毫无疑问，华盛顿的母亲很担心她儿子的安危。但事实证明他是个极为杰出的军人。华盛顿后来成为弗吉尼亚部队的司令官，但由于荒野的艰难状况及困苦环境，华盛顿的病情十分严重，他的医生坚持认为华盛顿必须返回他位于弗吉尼亚州的庄园内静养。

5 病愈后，华盛顿马上返回去指挥弗吉尼亚部队。他获颁陆军准将的军衔并成为1758年英国击败法国并攻下杜魁斯要塞（英国人将其重新命名为“匹特要塞”）的关键因素。1759年1月6日，刚返回弗吉尼亚州的华盛顿即与玛莎•丹德里奇•柯蒂斯 (Martha Dandridge Custis) 结婚。

6 荒野的战斗使华盛顿成了一名训练有素的军人。这样的锻炼也为华盛顿军事生涯中的最大挑战做了准备，使得他在1775年爆发的独立战争中，有能力以总司令的身份带领美国革命军打响莱克星顿及康科德战役的枪声。

2 President John Adams' Duty —"Remember the Ladies"

约翰·亚当斯总统的"任务"——"记住女士们"

约翰·亚当斯 总统及第一夫人简介

约翰•亚当斯 (John Adams, 1735.10.30～1826.7.4)，曾是第1任美国副总统(1789～1797)，后接替乔治•华盛顿成为第2任美国总统（1797～1801）。亚当斯出生在马萨诸塞海湾殖民地。他是一位受过哈佛教育的律师，与一些爱国者达成了共识；作为美国独立运动最重要的领导人之一，亚当斯在独立战争后被选为第一和第二届国会议员。他是《独立宣言》的起草人和签署者之一。1778年参加了美国宪法的起草工作。他被美国人视为最重要的开国元勋之一，他的长子约翰•昆西•亚当斯后来当选为美国第6任总统。

阿碧格尔•史密斯•亚当斯(Abigail Smith Adams, 1744.11.22～1818.10.28)是第2任美国总统约翰•亚当斯的妻子，她不仅捍卫妇女的权利，而且反对奴隶制。早年，约翰•亚当斯热心于社会活动，为美国的独立而奔走，这期间全家的生活均靠夫人经营农场支撑着。阿碧格尔不仅相夫教子，而且还积极参与当时的政治活动。美国革命战争时期亚当斯在费城出席新大陆会议时，阿碧格尔曾通过许多信件向丈夫提供了对政府和政治方面的建议，提醒他在开会时注意妇女的社会地位和权益的保护，否则可能引发美国的第二次革命。这件事在美国历史上被传为佳话。他们是入住白宫的第一对主人。

经典原文
Original Text

Abigail Adams read a lot of history books mainly through self-study. Engaged in official business away from home year in and year out, John Adams maintained a correspondence with Abigail. On March 31, 1776, when the Continental Congress was contemplating the declaration of independence, Abigail Adams wrote to her husband, reminding her husband to "remember the Ladies" when the new Code of Laws was enacted. On April 14, 1776, in his reply to his wife, he treated the extraordinary Code of Laws which she had mentioned as a little joke. The following were their letters.

Abigail to John

1 I long to hear that you have declared an Independency — and by the way in the new Code of Laws which I suppose it will be necessary for you to make I desire you would Remember the Ladies, and be more generous and favourable to them than your ancestors. Do not put such unlimited power into the hands of the Husbands. Remember all Men would be tyrants if they could. If particular care and attention is not paid to the Ladies we are determined to foment a Rebellion, and will not hold ourselves bound by any Laws in which we have no voice, or Representation.

2 That your Sex are Naturally Tyrannical is a Truth so thoroughly established as to admit of no dispute, but such of you as wish to be happy willingly give up the harsh title of Master for the more tender and endearing one of Friend. Why then, not put it out of the power of the vicious and the Lawless to use us with cruelty and indignity with impunity. Men of Sense in all Ages abhor those customs which treat

Words & Expressions

code of laws 法典

tyrant [ˈtairənt] *n.* 暴君

foment [ˈfəument] *vt.* 煽动，挑起

harsh [hɑːʃ] *adj.* 严厉的，严酷的，刺耳的，粗糙的

tender [ˈtendə] *adj.* 温柔的，柔软的，脆弱的

vicious [ˈviʃəs] *adj.* 恶毒的，恶意的，堕落的

impunity [imˈpjuːnəti] *n.* 不受惩罚，无患，免罚

abhor [əbˈhɔː] *vt.* 痛恨，憎恶

vassal ['væsəl] n. 诸侯，封臣
providence ['prɔvidəns] n. 远见，节俭，天佑，天意，天道
supreme being 上帝，至高无上的力量
cannot but 不得不，禁不住
turbulent ['tə:bjulənt] adj. 骚乱的，狂暴的，吵闹的
insolent ['insələnt] adj. 无礼的
intimation [ˌinti'meiʃən] n. 暗示，告知
coarse [kɔ:s] adj. 粗糙的，粗俗的，下等的
compliment ['kɔmplimənt] n. 恭维，称赞，问候，致意
saucy ['sɔ:si] adj. 俏丽的，活泼的，莽撞的
blot… out 抹掉，忘却
know better than 很懂得（而不至于），明白事理而不至于…
repeal [ri'pi:l] vt. 废除，放弃
exert [ig'zə:t] vt. 运用，发挥，施以影响
be obliged to (do sth.) 不得不做，有义务做，被迫做
subject (sb.) to… 使某人服从于，使某人经受
despotism ['despətizəm] n. 专制，独裁，专制政治
petticoat ['petikəut] n. 衬裙子
oligarchy ['ɔligɑ:ki] n. 寡头政治
ochlocracy [ɔk'lɔkrəsi] n. 暴民政治
landjobber 土地投机商
trimmer ['trimə] n. 机会主义者
bigot ['bigət] n. 盲信者

us only as the vassals of your Sex. Regard us then as Beings placed by providence under your protection and in imitation of the Supreme Being make use of that power only for our happiness.

John to Abigail

1 ... As to your extraordinary Code of Laws, cannot but laugh. We have been told that our Struggle has loosened the bands of Government every where. That Children and Apprentices were disobedient—that schools and Colleges were grown turbulent—that Indians slighted Their Guardians and Negroes grew insolent to Their Masters. But your Letter was the first Intimation that another Tribe more numerous and powerful than all the rest were grown discontented. This is rather too coarse a Compliment but you are so saucy; I won't blot it out.

2 Depend upon it, We know better than to repeal our Masculine systems. Although they are in full Force, you know they are little more than Theory. We dare not exert our Power in its full Latitude. We are obliged to go fair, and softly, and in Practice you know We are the subjects. We have only the Name of Masters, and rather than give up this, which would completely subject us to the Despotism of the Petticoat, I hope General Washington, and all our brave Heroes would fight. I am sure every good Politician would plot, as long as he would against Despotism, Empire, Monarchy, Aristocracy, Oligarchy, or Ochlocracy. A fine Story indeed. I begin to think the Ministry as deep as they are wicked.

3 After stirring up *Tories*①, Landjobbers, Trimmers, Bigots, Canadians, Indians, Negroes, *Hanoverians*②, *Hessians*③, Russians, Irish Roman Catholics, Scotch

Renegades, at last they have stimulated the Ladies to demand new Privileges and threaten to rebel.

renegado ['renigeid] n. 叛教者，背叛者

背景知识注释 Background Notes

1. Tories ['tɔ:ris] 英国托利派，王党保守党。托利党这个政党名称起源于1688年的光荣革命，一般认为他们是最早出现的资产阶级政党之一。“托利”(Tory) 一词起源于爱尔兰语，意为“不法之徒”。托利党人是指那些支持世袭王权、不愿去除国王的人。
2. Hanoverian ['hænəu'viəriən] n. （德国）汉诺威城居民；汉诺威人。
3. Hessian 黑森人（士兵），（美国独立战争时期英国招募的）德国佣兵；雇佣兵；（泛指）佣兵，炮灰。

中文译文 Suggested Translation

John and Abigal

A Life in Letters

阿碧格尔•亚当斯主要通过自学阅读了大量历史书籍。在约翰•亚当斯常年离家忙于公务的岁月里，这对夫妇一直保持通信。1776年3月31日，当大陆议会正在认真考虑宣布独立时，阿碧格尔•亚当斯写信给她丈夫约翰•亚当斯。在描述了马萨诸塞春天到来的情景后，她提醒她丈夫约翰•亚当斯在制定新法典时要“记住女士们”。在亚当斯1776年4月14日给他妻子的回信中，他把她提到的“特别法典”视做他爱妻的一个小小的玩笑。以下是他们信件的内容。

阿碧格尔写给约翰的信

1 我盼着听到你们宣布独立的消息。顺便说一下，我想你们需要立个新法典，在此新的法典中，我们希望你们能记住女士们，而且要比你们的先辈们对她们更宽厚、更释怀。不要让丈夫们掌握如此无限制的权力。要记住，所有的男士只要有可能都会成为暴君。如果对女

士没有给予特别的照顾和重视，我们就决心煽动大家造反，我们不会让那些我们没有发言权或没有代表资格参与制定的法律来约束我们。

2 你们男士天生霸道，这是确定无疑的事实，毋庸争辩。但是，像你这样希望得到幸福的人，是很愿意放弃“主人”这个刺耳的称号而换上“朋友”这个更温柔亲切的称号的。那么，你们为什么不让那些邪恶之徒和违法者不能以残忍和侮辱的手段来对待我们且逍遥法外？任何时代，通情达理的人都憎恶那些只把我们当做你们男人的奴仆的陋习。请把我们当做是天意置于你们保护之下的生灵，效法上帝，使用那种权力，仅仅是为了给我们造福。

约翰写给阿碧格尔的回信

1 ……至于你所谓的特别法典，我只能一笑置之。我们已经获悉，我们的斗争已经使各地都放松了政府的管束。孩子和学徒都变得违拗不顺，中小学和大学滋生骚乱，印第安人蔑视监护人，黑奴对主人粗暴无礼。但是，你的来信第一次正式宣告又有一个族群在滋生不满，而且这群人比其他所有族群人数更多，力量更大。你这是给我提出了一个相当棘手的建议，但既然你敢这样提出，我也不会置之不理。

2 可以肯定地说，我们是明白事理的，不至于将我们的男性制度完全废除。虽然这些男性制度现在具有充分的威力，但你知道它们只不过是理论而已。我们并不敢全面行使我们的权力。我们必须公正温和，实际上你知道我们都是庶民。我们仅有主人之名，而且宁可放弃这个名分，这样就使我们完全服从于妇女的专制。我希望华盛顿将军以及我们所有勇敢的英雄都来战斗，我肯定每一个善良的政治家都会终身谋划反对专制、帝国、君权、贵族、寡头政治或暴民政治。这的确是个动听的故事。我开始认为牧师们既精明又邪恶。

3 在煽起托利党人、土地投机商、骑墙派、盲信者、加拿大人、印第安人、黑人、汉诺威人、黑森人、俄国人、爱尔兰罗马天主教徒、苏格兰叛教者之后，最后他们又激起女士们来要求新的特权，而且还威胁说要造反。

3 President Thomas Jefferson and Cooking 托马斯·杰斐逊总统与烹饪

托马斯·杰斐逊 总统及第一夫人简介

托马斯•杰斐逊 (Thomas Jefferson, 1743.4.13～1826.7.4)，第3任美国总统(1801～1809)，美国政治家、思想家、哲学家、科学家、教育家。他是美国独立战争期间的主要领导人之一，1776年，作为一个包括约翰•亚当斯和本杰明•富兰克林在内的起草委员会的成员，起草了美国《独立宣言》。此后，他先后还担任了美国第1任国务卿、第2任副总统。他在任期间保护农业，发展民族资本主义工业。从法国手中购买路易斯安那州，使美国领土近乎增加了一倍。他被普遍视为美国历史上最杰出的总统之一。

玛莎•斯格尔顿•杰斐逊(Martha Skelton Jefferson, 1748.10.30～1782.9.6)，第3任美国总统托马斯•杰斐逊的妻子。1772年元旦，两人在玛莎娘家结婚，结婚后十年，相亲相爱。玛莎受过良好的教育，举止大方，能弹琴、弹吉他，还能绣花，还在庄园里指导人自酿啤酒。杰斐逊出任弗吉尼亚首任州长后，她也积极参与独立运动。玛莎自成为杰斐逊夫人后健康就开始走下坡路，1782年33岁时，她生下第六个孩子几个月之后就去世了。杰斐逊和玛莎的爱情虽然称不上惊天地泣鬼神，可是也到了几乎影响美国独立的地步。

经典原文
Original Text

1 Thomas Jefferson was a man of many interests. While serving as the American minister to France in the 1780s, he developed quite a taste for European cooking. When he returned to the U.S. from France, he brought with him a French cook and many recipes from France and Italy. One of the Italian foods he ate was pasta. In his drawing of a macaroni machine you can see that Jefferson was figuring out how the dough was made. What do you think some of Jefferson's favorite foods were?

2 Some of Jefferson's favorite dishes to serve guests included macaroni, macaroons, peach flambé (flaming peaches), and ice cream! While in France, Jefferson collected many French recipes for things such as sauces, fruit tarts, French fries, blood sausages, pigs' feet, rabbit, and pigeon. One of the recipes he brought home has since become an American favorite: vanilla ice cream. This was one of the most popular dishes at his home in Monticello, and this recipe was written by Jefferson himself. On the back is his recipe for *Savoy*① cookies to go along with the ice cream.

3 Jefferson had to have a nice place to invite his friends and serve them delicious food. His home in Charlottesville, called Monticello ("little mountain"), was known as one of the finest estates in Virginia. He designed his home himself and he included a series of rooms where he entertained guests. He also created a room just for his books and an office with a copy "machine". Some of his public rooms displayed things he had collected: Native American artifacts, fossils discovered by *Lewis and Clark*②, and images of

Words & Expressions

minister [ˈministə] *n.* 部长；大臣；牧师

recipe [ˈresipi] *n.* 食谱，处方，秘诀

pasta [ˈpɑːstɑː] *n.* 意大利面食，面团（用以制意大利通心粉）

macaroni [ˌmækəˈrəuni] *n.* 通心粉，通心面条

dough [dəu] *n.* 生面团

macaroon [ˌmækəˈruːn] *n.* 蛋白杏仁饼，小杏仁饼

peach flambé 酒汁樱桃（用桃子制成的食物，在食物上浇上白兰地并点燃后端出）

sauce [sɔːs] *n.* 调味汁，（俚）烈酒

tart [tɑːt] *n.* 果馅饼

vanilla ice cream 香草冰淇淋

delicious [diˈliʃəs] *adj.* 美味的

fossil [ˈfɔsl] *n.* 化石

people he admired. Today you can visit Monticello, which is recognized as a national treasure.

背景知识注释
Background Notes

1. Savoy [sə'vɔi] 萨瓦（法国东部地区，与瑞士、意大利接壤，1860年后并入法国）[法语为Savoie]。
2. Lewis and Clark (expedition) 刘易斯与克拉克（远征），发生于1804年～1806年，是美国国内首次横越大陆西抵太平洋沿岸的往返考察活动。领队为美国陆军的梅里韦瑟•刘易斯上尉(Meriwether Lewis)和威廉•克拉克少尉 (William Clark)，该活动是由杰斐逊总统发起的。

中文译文
Suggested Translation

1 托马斯•杰斐逊兴趣非常广泛。在18世纪80年代，身任美国驻法外交使节的杰斐逊对欧洲烹调情有独钟。当他回国时，他还带了一位法国厨师及许多法国和意大利食谱。其中一样他吃过的意大利食品就是意大利面食。从杰斐逊所绘的通心粉制作机的素描中，可以看出他在揣测面团的做法。您猜杰斐逊的爱食有哪些？

2 杰斐逊最爱用来招待宾客的食物包括通心粉、蛋白杏仁饼干、酒汁樱桃及冰淇淋！在法国期间，杰斐逊收集了许多法式食物的烹调方法，如：酱汁、水果塔、薯条、血肠、猪脚、兔肉及鸽子肉。他带回来的其中一份食谱从此以后成了美国人的最爱：香草冰淇淋。这是他在蒙蒂萨罗家中最受欢迎的一道菜，而且这道食谱是由杰斐逊本人亲笔写下的，食谱的背面则是搭配冰淇淋的萨瓦饼干的做法。

3 杰斐逊拥有一个体面的居所用来招待他的朋友，品尝他的食物。他位于夏洛茨维尔的家被称为“蒙蒂塞罗”(意为“小山”)，是弗吉尼亚州境内最优美的庄园之一。这个家是由他本人亲自设计规划的，里面建有一系列用来招待客人的厅室。此外，他还建了一个专门用来放书的房间及一间放有复印“机”的办公室。他的一些公共房则放有他的收藏品，如：美国原住民手工艺品、路易斯和克拉克探险队所发掘的化石以及他所敬爱的人物的肖像。如今，你也可以前去造访这座被视为国家宝藏的蒙蒂塞罗庄园。

4 A Great Friendship — James Madison and Thomas Jefferson 伟大的友谊——詹姆斯·麦迪逊和托马斯·杰斐逊

詹姆斯·麦迪逊 总统及第一夫人简介

詹姆斯·麦迪逊(James Madison, 1751.3.16～1836.6.28)，第4任美国总统 (1809～1817)。他担任总统期间曾领导进行第二次美英战争，保卫了美国的共和制度，为美国赢得彻底独立建立了功勋。1776年，他参加了弗吉尼亚宪法的制定，被认为是“美国宪法之父”。他还是出席大陆会议的代表，是制宪会议的主要人物；他是北部联邦党人文件的起草人之一，与约翰·杰伊及亚历山大·汉密尔顿共同编写《联邦党人文集》。他是最后一位去世的美国开国之父。

多莉·派恩·托德·麦迪逊(Dolley Payne Todd Madison, 1768.5.20～1849.7.12)是第4任美国总统詹姆斯·麦迪逊的妻子。他们于1794年结婚，多莉具有很出色的社交能力，帮助界定了“第一夫人”的角色，使麦迪逊总统更加受人们欢迎。多莉还以热情好客和拯救白宫而流芳至今。多莉入住白宫时，开创了白宫女主人负责检查和修缮白宫的先例。多莉视白宫和国家的利益高于一切，甚至超过她的生命。1814年8月24日，英军部队占领华盛顿，随着英军向白宫逼近，多莉不顾个人安危，在朋友的帮助下，将总统文件、书籍和一些白宫珍品装载到一辆马车上，免于被英军掠夺，这其中就包括现在仍挂在白宫墙上那张价值连城的乔治•华盛顿画像。多莉以临危不惧和舍身忘我的精神为她的后来者们树立了榜样。

经典原文 Original Text

1 Thomas Jefferson and James Madison met in 1776. Could it have been any other year? They worked together starting then to further the American Revolution and later to shape the new scheme of government. From that work sprang a friendship perhaps incomparable in intimacy and the trustfulness of collaboration and indurations. It lasted 50 years. It included pleasure and utility but over and above them, there were shared purpose, a common end and an enduring goodness on both sides. Four and a half months before he died, when he was ailing, debt-ridden, and worried about his impoverished family, Jefferson wrote to his long-time friend. His words and Madison's reply remind us that friends are friends until death. They also remind us that sometimes a friendship has a bearing on things larger than the friendship itself, for has there ever been a friendship of greater public consequence than this one?

2 "The friendship which has subsisted between us now half a century, the harmony of our political principles and pursuits have been the sources of constant happiness to me through that long period. It's also been a great solace to me to believe that you're engaged in vindicating to posterity the course that we've pursued for preserving to them, in all their purity, their blessings of self-government, which we had assisted in acquiring for them. If ever the earth has beheld a system of administration conducted with a single and steadfast eye to the general interest and happiness of

Words & Expressions

further [ˈfəːðə] *vt.* 促进，助长

scheme [skiːm] *n.* 计划，组合，体制，诡计

spring [spriŋ] *vt.* 产生，发源

intimacy [ˈintiməsi] *n.* 亲密

induration [ˌindjuˈreiʃən] *n.* 坚固

ail [eil] *v.* 使受病痛

debt-ridden [ˌdetˈridn] *adj.* 债务缠身的

impoverished [imˈpɔvəriʃt] *adj.* 穷困的，无创造性的

have a bearing on… 与…有关系，对…有影响

subsist [səbˈsist] *vi.* 存在，维持生活

solace [ˈsɔləs] *n.* 安慰，慰藉

vindicate [ˈvindikeit] *vt.* 维护，证明…无辜，证明…正确

posterity [pɔsˈteriti] *n.* 子孙，后裔，后代

steadfast [ˈstedfəst] *adj.* 坚定的，不变的

those committed to it, one which, protected by truth, can never know reproach, it is that to which our lives have been devoted. Myself, you have been a pillar of support throughout life. Take care of me when dead and be assured that I shall leave with you my last affections." (Feb. 17, 1826)

reproach [riˈprəutʃ] *n.* 责备，耻辱

indulge [inˈdʌldʒ] *vt.* 满足，纵容，使高兴，使沉迷于

withhold [ˈwiðˈhəuld] *vt.* 保留，隐瞒，抑制

3 A week later Madison replied —

4 "You cannot look back to the long period of our private friendship and political harmony with more affecting recollections than I do. If they are a source of pleasure to you, what aren't they not to be to me? We cannot be deprived of the happy consciousness of the pure devotion to the public good with which we discharge the trust committed to us and I indulge a confidence that sufficient evidence will find its way to another generation to ensure, after we are gone, whatever of justice may be withheld whilst we are here."

中文译文 Suggested Translation

1 托马斯·杰斐逊和詹姆斯·麦迪逊相识于1776年。为什么恰好是这一年呢？当时他们开始共同努力推动美国革命，后来又一道为政府拟订新计划。在这些合作中孕育出的友谊是亲密无间、信诚以托、坚不可摧的。这份友谊维持了50年。当中包含有欢乐、协作，而超越这些之上的便是他们志同道合地朝着共同的目标迈进，历经多年从不间断地令彼此受益。在离开人世前四个半月时，杰斐逊重病在身，债台高筑，并为家庭的贫困感到忧心如焚，于是他提笔给这位知交好友写了封信。从他的信以及麦迪逊的回复中，我们可以看出：这两个朋友是一生之交；并且有时候，他们之间的友情意义之大更超越了友情本身，这份友谊给大众带来的深远影响是前所未有的。

2 "你我之间的友谊迄今已经维持了半个世纪，我们在政治原则与追求上取得的协调在过去的漫漫岁月中为我带来了源源不断的快乐。我感到一大安慰的是，我相信你还在执著地

致力于造福子孙后代的事业——这份事业我们曾为他们争取过，我们也曾参与为他们获取一种自治体制，我们希望这种体制的恩惠能纯洁无瑕地留存给他们。坚信世界上有一种治理体制，执行时能对大众的利益和为之奋斗者的福祉给予坚定不移的监护，得到真理的庇护并将永远与责难无缘，这正是我们一生所致力的事业。我自己，还有你，毕生都为此鼎力支持。请你照顾我的身后之事，也请相信，我的友情永远和你同在。”(1826年2月17日)

3 一个星期后，麦迪逊写了回信——

4 “在过去的漫长岁月中，你我的友谊与一致的政治观，总令我在回想时心中无比感动。它们为你带来欢乐，对我又何尝不是如此？我们肩负人民的信任，为大众福祉鞠躬尽瘁，从中获得的幸福感是难以泯灭的。我坚信，无论当前对我们所做的一切评判如何，我们身后的一代人必将依据事实给予公断。”

5 Things to Know about President James Monroe

詹姆斯·门罗总统传奇事迹

詹姆斯·门罗 总统及第一夫人简介

詹姆斯·门罗(James Monroe, 1758.4.28～1831.7.4)，第5任美国总统 (1817～1825)，美国著名政治家、外交家，早年参加过独立战争。他是《邦联条例》的制定者之一，也是《权利法案》的有力支持者，并与杰斐逊等人共同创建了共和党。门罗任总统时，正值美国结束连年战争进入和平建设时期，他对内强调国家意识，对外大力开拓疆土，为美国的发展创造了有利条件。门罗是一位技艺娴熟的外交家，1823年门罗提出的美国外交政策方针，著名的“门罗主义”，是与他的名字联系在一起的，对美国外交产生了深远的影响。门罗老境凄凉，病逝在女儿家中，享年73岁。

伊丽莎白•科特莱特•门罗(Elizabeth Kortright Monroe, 1768.6.30～1830.9. 23)是美国第5任总统詹姆斯•门罗的夫人。1785年，27岁的门罗与17岁的伊丽莎白•科特莱特结婚，育有一子二女，但只有两个女儿长大成人。门罗夫人是个传统的淑女型女性，不善言谈和交际，又患有严重的慢性病，这大大限制了她社交活动的范围。在门罗入主白宫期间，第一夫人体弱多病，所以很少参加官方活动。她未能很好地行使白宫女主人的角色，因此在美国第一夫人的发展史中，她未能留下什么痕迹，但这并没有影响她与门罗的感情。

经典原文
Original Text

1 James Monroe was born on April 18, 1758 in Westmoreland County, Virginia. He was elected the fifth president of the United States in 1816 and took office on March 4, 1817. Following are some key facts that are important to understand when studying the life and presidency of James Monroe.

◆ Only Concurrent Secretary of State and War

2 When James Madison became president, he appointed Monroe to be his Secretary of State in 1811. In June, 1812, the U.S. declared war on Britain. By 1814, the British had marched on Washington, D.C.. Madison decided to name Monroe Secretary of War making him the only person to hold both posts at once. He strengthened the military during his time and helped bring about the end of the war.

◆ Easily Won the Election of 1816

3 Monroe was extremely popular after the War of 1812. He easily won the Democratic-Republican nomination and had little opposition from Federalist candidate Rufus King. Extremely popular and easily won both the Dem-rep nomination and the election of 1816. He won the election with almost 84% of the electoral votes.

◆ Had No Opponent in the Election of 1820

4 The Election of 1820 was unique in that there was no contender against President Monroe. He received all electoral votes save one. This began the so-called "*Era of Good Feelings*[①]."

◆ The *Monroe Doctrine*[②]

5 On December 2, 1823, during President Monroe's

Words & Expressions

concurrent [kən'kʌrənt] *adj.* 同时发生的，共存的，共同起作用的，合作的

nomination [ˌnɔmi'neiʃən] *n.* 提名，任命，被提名，被任命，提名权，任命权

Dem-rep *n.* 民主共和党

unique [juː'niːk] *adj.* 唯一的，独特的

contender [kən'tendə] *n.* 争夺者，竞争者

save [seiv] *prep.* 只是，要不是，除了…以外

doctrine ['dɔktrain] *n.* 教义，声明，法律原则

seventh annual message to Congress, he created the Monroe Doctrine. This is without question one of the most important foreign policy doctrines in U.S. History. The point of the policy was to make it clear to European nations that there would be no further European colonization in the Americas or any interference with independent states.

◆ First *Seminole War* ③

6 Soon after taking office in 1817, Monroe had to deal with the First Seminole War which lasted from 1817 — 1818. Seminole Indians were crossing the border of Spanish-held Florida and raiding Georgia. General Andrew Jackson was sent to deal with the situation. He disobeyed orders to push them back out of Georgia and instead invaded Florida, deposing the military governor there. The aftermath included the signing of the Adams-Onis Treaty in 1819 which gave Florida to the United States.

◆ *The Missouri Compromise* ④

7 Sectionalism was a recurring issue in the U.S. and would be until the end the Civil War. In 1820, the Missouri Compromise was passed as an effort to maintain the balance between slave and free states. The passage of this act during Monroe's time in office would hold off the Civil War for a few more decades.

annual message 年度咨文，年度报告

raid [reid] *vt.* 突然袭击，行凶，抢劫，搜捕

depose [di'pəuz] *vt.* 免职，罢免，废黜

aftermath ['ɑːftəmæθ] *n.* 结果，后果

sectionalism ['sekʃənəlizəm] *n.* 地方主义，本位主义

recurring [ri'kəːriŋ] *adj.* 循环的，再发的，反复的

hold off 拖延，不接近，抵挡

背景知识注释 Background Notes

1. Era of Good Feelings （1817～1825年门罗当美国总统时的）善意的时代。

2. Monroe Doctrine (=Monroeism) 门罗主义，1822 年～ 1823 年，当欧洲“神圣同盟”企图干涉拉丁美洲的独立运动时，美国积极推行起“美洲事务是美洲人事务”的政策。1823 年，美国总统门罗向国会提出咨文宣称：“今后欧洲任何列强不得把美洲大陆已经独立自由的国家当做将来殖民的对象。”他又称：美国不干涉欧洲列强的内部事务，也不容许欧洲列强干预美洲的事务。

这项咨文就是通常所说的“门罗宣言”。它包含的原则就是通常所说的“门罗主义”。门罗主义的含义主要有三个：(1) 要求欧洲国家不在西半球殖民。这一原则不仅表示反对西欧国家对拉美的扩张，也反对俄国在北美西海岸的扩张；(2) 要求欧洲不干预美洲独立国家的事务；(3) 保证美国不干涉欧洲事务，包括欧洲现有的在美洲的殖民地的事务。从某种意义上讲，门罗主义在客观上起到了防止已独立的拉美国家再沦为欧洲列强的殖民地的作用。

3. Seminole War　塞米诺尔战争。

4. the Missouri Compromise　密苏里妥协案；密苏里妥协。它是1820年美国南部奴隶主同北部资产阶级在国会中就密苏里地域成立新州是否采取奴隶制问题通过的妥协议案。该妥协案虽使南北之间的尖锐矛盾暂时缓和，但是北方工业制度和南方种植园制度之间的冲突仍是不可避免的，并最终导致了美国内战。

中文译文
Suggested Translation

1 詹姆斯•门罗于1758年4月18日出生在弗吉尼亚州的威斯特摩兰县。他1816年被选为美国第5任总统，并于1817年3月4日就职。以下是了解詹姆斯•门罗总统生涯的几个重要事件。

◆ 国务卿与战争部长双肩挑

2 詹姆斯•麦迪逊当选为总统后，于1811年任命门罗为他的国务卿。1812年6月,美国向英国宣战。到1814年，英军已经推进至华盛顿特区，麦迪逊决定任命门罗为战争部长，使他成为唯一同时肩挑双职的人。任职期间他加强军事，并协助促使战争的结束。

◆ 轻松赢得1816年选举

3 1812年战争后，门罗深受民众的欢迎。他轻松赢得了民主共和党的提名，几乎没有受到联邦候选人鲁弗斯•金(Rufus King)的反对。由于极受民众欢迎且轻松赢得了民主共和党的提名和1816年的总统选举，他赢得的选票几乎达到84%。

◆ 1820年选举时没有对手

4 1820年的选举是独一无二的，因为门罗总统没有竞争对手。他赢得了除一票之外的所有选票。这开启了所谓的“善意的时代。”

◆ 门罗主义

5 1823年12月2日，在门罗总统给国会的第7个年度咨文期间，他创立了门罗主义。这无疑是美国历史上最重要的外交政策理论之一。该政策旨在向欧洲列强表明，不得把美洲大陆各国当做将来进一步殖民的对象和不容许其干预美洲已独立国家的事务。

◆ 第一次塞米诺尔战争

6 1817年上任后不久，门罗总统就不得不应付从1817年持续到1818年的第一次塞米诺尔战争。塞米诺族印第安人越过西班牙人控制的佛罗里达边境并突袭了佐治亚。安德鲁•杰克逊将军被派去对付这一局面。他违背了将他们赶出佐治亚的命令，而是入侵了佛罗里达，废黜了那里的军事总督。其结果就是在1819年签署了《亚当斯-奥尼斯条约》，佛罗里达从此由美国管辖。

◆ 密苏里妥协案

7 在南北战争结束之前，地方主义在美国曾是一个反复出现的问题。1820年，门罗总统通过了《密苏里妥协案》，试图维持奴隶州与自由州之间的平衡。该法案在门罗就职期间的通过将美国内战推迟了几十年。

6 Several Anecdotes about President John Quincy Adams
约翰·昆西·亚当斯总统的几件轶事

约翰·昆西·亚当斯 总统及第一夫人简介

约翰•昆西•亚当斯 (John Quincy Adams, 1767.7.11～1848.2.23)，第6任美国总统(1825～1829)。他是第2任总统约翰•亚当斯及第一夫人阿碧格尔•亚当斯的长子，是美国历史上第一位继其父亲之后成为总统的人。他20岁就成了有名的外交官，曾出使欧洲多年，熟悉欧洲事务。他在詹姆斯•门罗时期担任国务卿，曾协助起草《门罗宣言》，并发展“门罗主义”，解决了与英国的许多纠纷，还从西班牙手中取得佛罗里达。因此，他被认为是美国历史上“最有成就的国务卿之一”。他也是唯一一位当选美国众议院议员的卸任总统。

路易莎·凯瑟琳·约翰·亚当斯 (Louisa Catherine Johnson Adams, 1775.2.12 ～ 1852.5.15) 是第6任美国总统约翰·昆西·亚当斯的妻子，两人一见钟情，于1797年结婚。路易莎时年22岁，身材窈窕，气质高雅。路易莎出生在英国伦敦，是美国历史上唯一一位出生于外国的第一夫人。二人感情甚笃，婚后生活可谓幸福美满，但这一婚姻并非没有经历考验。路易莎长期患病，跟不上丈夫快节奏的生活步伐，两人的生活方式也有很大差异，因此她常常郁郁寡欢，极为敏感，甚至有时产生幻觉。但他们最终超越了这些障碍，恩恩爱爱生活了五十多年，养育了四个孩子。其中小儿子查尔斯·弗朗西斯·亚当斯是他们的骄傲，后来成为著名的废奴战士和外交家，在使英国对美国内战保持中立立场上发挥了重要的作用。

经典原文 Original Text

Words & Expressions

skinny dipping 裸泳

spot [spɔt] n. 地点，场所，职务

strip down 拆开，脱去

sneak [sni:k] vi. 溜，鬼鬼祟祟做事

shiver [ˈʃivə] vi. 哆嗦；颤抖

staunch [stɔ:ntʃ] adj. 坚定的，忠诚的，坚固的

advocate [ˈædvəkeit] n. 提倡者，支持者，（辩护）律师

cause [kɔ:z] n. 原因，动机

kidnap [ˈkidnæp] vt. 绑架，诱拐，拐骗

1 John Quincy Adams was also a very honorable man. But he enjoyed skinny dipping in *the Potomac River*[①]. One day, a female reporter, Ann Royall, who had tried to get an interview with President Adams and failed, heard about his morning "dips" into the Potomac. So she went to his favorite spot and waited for the President to strip down and get into the water. She then sneaked out from behind the bushes and sat on his clothes. She was very patient waiting for the President to return.

2 When *JQA*[②] turned toward the shore, he saw her sitting there. Being a Gentleman, he wouldn't come out of the water as long as she was sitting there. So she finally got the interview she wanted (while the President was shivering in the water!).

3 After his term as President, JQA did not leave government service — he became a representative from Massachusetts. He was the only ex-president to serve in the House of Representatives.

4 As a representative, "Old Man Eloquent", as JQA was nicknamed, became a staunch advocate of the anti-slavery cause.

5 This lead to one of his most famous cases. JQA argued before the Supreme Court for the cause of *the Amistad*[③]. The ship Amistad had illegally (it was at that point against international law to kidnap anyone to sell into

slavery) kidnapped Africans, men, women and children, to sell into slavery. The kidnapped people overpowered their captors and took control of the ship, wanting to return to Africa, but they didn't know the way and were led astray by their captors.

6 Despite the political climate at the time (pre-Civil War) JQA won the case and the Amistad Blacks were given the choice of staying in the U.S. as free people or of returning to Africa. 35 of them were returned to Africa.

7 A few months short of his 81st birthday, JQA was preparing to address the House of Representatives (in which he was still serving) when he suffered a cerebral hemorrhage. He died a few days later with his family by his side. His last words were reported to be "This is the last of Earth. I am content."

overpower [ˌəuvəˈpauə] *vt.* 压倒，克服，使无法忍受

captor [ˈkæptə] *n.* 捕获者，俘虏

astray [əˈstrei] *adj.* 误入歧途地，迷途地

cerebral hemorrhage (内科) 脑出血

背景知识注释
Background Notes

1. the Potomac River 波多马克河，是美国东部的主要河流之一，全美第21大河流。波多马克河有两个源头，北源发源于西弗吉尼亚州普雷斯顿县、格兰特县和塔克县交界处，南源发源于弗吉尼亚州海兰德县，两者在汉普夏县境内汇合后东流，后折向东南，成为马里兰州和西弗吉尼亚州、弗吉尼亚州和华盛顿哥伦比亚特区的边界，最终注入切萨皮克湾。
2. JQA 这里是约翰•昆西•亚当斯名字的缩写。
3. the Amistad (Mutiny) "雅米斯泰德号"(暴动)，1839年，西班牙帆船"雅米斯泰德号"船上的非洲黑人为了人身自由而进行的暴动。暴动的领导者约瑟夫 • 辛格说："我已经下定决心，宁死也绝不变成白人的奴隶。"1840年联邦最高法院对此案进行了审理，辛格及其暴动者与当时的范•布伦总统之间的争执并没有因此而解决。前总统约翰 • 昆西 • 亚当斯 (John Quincy Adams) 在最高法院上诉中表示"雅米斯泰德号"上的非洲人被非法奴役。因此"应该被赋予所有来自人类与基督教国家应有的仁慈与调解"。法院赞同亚当斯的说法，"雅米斯泰德号"暴动的生还者于1841年3月9日被释放，而这场暴动的胜利也对后来废除奴隶制度的运动具有很大影响。这个真实事件已被拍成电影《雅米斯泰德号》。

中文译文
Suggested Translation

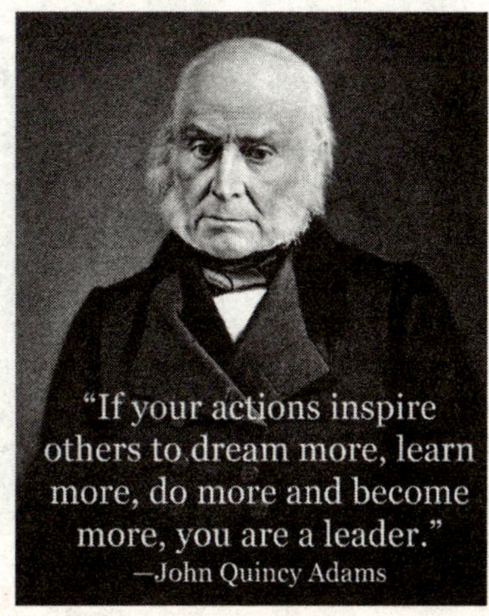

"If your actions inspire others to dream more, learn more, do more and become more, you are a leader."
—John Quincy Adams

1 约翰·昆西·亚当斯是一个值得尊敬的人，但他喜欢在波托马克河里裸泳。一位名叫安·罗亚尔的女记者曾试图采访亚当斯总统但并未取得成功。一天，她听说总统早晨又要去波托马克河“裸泳”。于是，她就到总统最常去的地方等着他脱衣进入水中。然后她偷偷溜到灌木丛后坐在他的衣服上。她非常耐心地等待总统上岸穿衣服。

2 当约翰·昆西·亚当斯转身上岸时，他看见女记者坐在那里。作为一位绅士，只要她坐着不走他是不会出水的。因此，她终于得到了她想要的采访（而总统却在水中被冻得瑟瑟发抖呢！）

3 在约翰·昆西·亚当斯的总统任期结束后，他并未停止为政府服务——他成了马萨诸塞州的一位代表。他是唯一一位在众议院效力的前总统。

4 作为代表，这位被昵称为“雄辩的老将”成了一位坚定地反对奴隶制事业的倡导者。

5 这就导致了约翰·昆西·亚当斯最著名的经历之一。他在最高法院前为“雅米斯泰德号”船暴动的起因辩护。这艘“雅米斯泰德号”船非法(绑架任何人将其贩卖为奴隶这点正是违反国际法的行为)绑架非洲人，包括男人、女人和孩子，并将他们贩卖为奴隶。这些被绑架的人们制服了贩奴者并控制了该船。他们想返回到非洲，但他们不熟悉航线，因而被贩奴者们引入了歧途。

6 在当时的政治气候（美国内战前夕）下，约翰·昆西·亚当斯还是赢得了这场官司。“雅米斯泰德号”船上生还的黑人被给予了要么作为自由人留在美国，要么返回非洲的选择。其中有 35 人返回了非洲。

7 离 81 岁生日只差几个月的某一天，约翰·昆西·亚当斯正准备在众议院（当时他还在为之效力）的发言，这时他突遭脑出血。几天之后他就辞世了，他的家人陪伴在他身边。据报道，他的临终遗言是：“末日已到，我心满意足。”

7 A Crusty Old Soldier — President Andrew Jackson 安德鲁·杰克逊总统——一位脾气火爆的老兵

安德鲁·杰克逊 总统及第一夫人简介

安德鲁·杰克逊 (Andrew Jackson, 1767.3.15 ~ 1845.6.8)，第 7 任美国总统 (1829 ~ 1837)。杰克逊是美国总统中，最后一位参与独立战争的，也是唯一一位曾为战俘的总统。他是首任佛罗里达州州长、新奥尔良之役中的战斗英雄、民主党创建者之一，"杰克逊式民主"也是因他而得名。在美国政治史上，1820 年代与 1830 年代的第二党体系 (Second Party System) 以他为极端的象征。因行动强硬而著称的杰克逊，绰号为"老山胡桃" (Old Hickory) 及"印第安人杀手"。杰克逊始终被美国的专家学者视为美国最杰出的 10 位总统之一。

瑞秋•唐尼尔森•罗巴兹•杰克逊(Rachel Donelson Robards Jackson, 1767.6.15～1828.12. 22)是美国第7任总统安德鲁•杰克逊的妻子，于安德鲁•杰克逊就职总统两个月后身故，原因不明。许多人声称她死于严重的心脏病，但无从证实。鳏居的杰克逊后来邀瑞秋的外甥女爱米莉•唐尼尔森(Emily Donelson)作为白宫的女主人，以及非正式的第一夫人，履行白宫女主人的职责。 莎拉•约克•杰克逊(Sarah Yorke Jackson)，自1834年起与爱米莉一起担任白宫的女主人。有两名女士同时担任非正式的第一夫人，这在美国历史上是唯一一次。爱米莉于1836年去世后，莎拉接管了第一夫人的所有职责。

经典原文
Original Text

Words & Expressions

pay one's respects 向某人致意，向某人致敬

rotunda [rə(u)ˈtʌndə] *n.* 圆形大厅，圆形建筑

malice [ˈmælis] *n.* 恶意，怨恨，预谋

drifter [ˈdriftə] *n.* 流浪汉，漂流物

pistol [ˈpistl] *n.* 手枪，信号枪

lunge [lʌndʒ] *vi.* 刺，突进

pull the trigger 扣动扳机，开枪

misfire [misˈfaiə] *n.* 失败，卡弹

crusty [ˈkrʌsti] *adj.* 易怒的，执拗的，有壳的

squeeze [skwi:z] *vt.* 挤，紧握，勒索

flail [fleil] *vt.* 鞭打，抽打

cane [kein] *n.* 手杖

would-be assassin 谋杀未遂犯

whisk [hwisk] *vt.* 拂，掸，搅拌，挥动

dodge [dɔdʒ] *vt.* 躲避，避开

in a row 连续，成一长行

1 It was a cold day in Washington on January 30, 1835, as President Andrew Jackson made his way from his White House office to the U.S. *Capitol* ① building to pay his respects at the funeral of a congressman who had passed away. The Capitol rotunda held a crowd, gathered in hopes of getting a glimpse of the President. One of the onlookers, however, held malice in his heart.

2 *Richard Lawrence*②, a young drifter, had two pockets full of pistols. As people made way for President Jackson to pass, Lawrence lunged out of the crowd while pulling one of the pistols. Lawrence pulled the trigger and a loud explosion echoed through the rotunda. For a tense moment, everything fell silent—nothing happened. The bullet never left the gun. A misfire.

3 Jackson, a crusty old soldier with quick instincts, went after Lawrence with his walking cane. Lawrence managed to back away and produced the second pistol. At close range, aiming for the President's heart, Lawrence squeezed the trigger. Nothing. Another misfire!

4 Some men from the crowd, including Davy Crockett, the Tennessee Congressman, tackled Lawrence and held him to the ground. Jackson continued flailing his cane, trying to crack the would-be assassin's skull. His aides had to pull him away and whisk him back to the safety of the White House. The President was safe. The attempt had failed. Andrew Jackson dodged the bullet—twice. Firearms experts figure the chance against two misfires in a row is about a lottery-sized 125,000 to 1.

5 At his trial, Richard Lawrence, an unemployed house

painter, was deemed insane. His motive for attacking President Jackson, he said, was that he, as rightful heir to the British throne, wanted to punish the President for killing his father three years before. The story made absolutely no sense. A jury found Lawrence not guilty of attempted murder for being "under the influence of insanity." Richard Lawrence spent the rest of his life in an insane asylum.

insane [in'sein] *adj.* 疯狂的，精神病的
heir [eə] *n.* 继承人，后嗣
jury ['dʒuəri] *n.* 陪审团，评判委员会
insane asylum 疯人院，精神病院

背景知识注释
Background Notes

1. Capitol ['kæpitəl]（美国）国会大厦。
2. Richard Lawrence 理查德·劳伦斯（1800？~ 1861.6.13），是美国历史上已知的第一位试图刺杀总统的人。劳伦斯成年时被认为患有精神病，曾当过油漆工。据分析，正是由于长期接触油漆中的化学物质导致了他的精神错乱。1830 年代他失业了，同时产生他是英国理查三世国王的幻想，并认为美国政府欠了他一大笔钱，而安德鲁·杰克逊总统阻止他领取这笔钱，他还责怪杰克逊就是杀死他父亲的凶手，于是萌生了要暗杀总统的念头。

中文译文
Suggested Translation

1 1835年1月30日的华盛顿市，天气寒冷。就在这天，安德鲁•杰克逊总统离开了白宫的办公室，前往国会大厦。他是去参加一位刚去世议员的遗体告别仪式的。国会大厦的圆形大厅里，一群人朝他聚拢过去，他们想要一睹总统的风采。然而，这群人中却混着一个居心叵测的人。

2 这个人名叫理查德·劳伦斯（Richard Lawrence），是个年轻的流浪汉。他在衣服的两个口袋里都藏着手枪。当围观者们为杰克逊总统让出一条路来的时候，劳伦斯突然冲出人群，掏出手枪。他扣动了扳机，紧接着，一声巨响回荡在大厅之中。在这紧张的时刻，大厅里鸦雀无声——然而什么也没有发生。子弹没有离开枪膛。枪支卡弹了！

3 作为一位脾气火爆的老兵，杰克逊总统的反应敏捷，他立即举起手杖向劳伦斯冲去。劳伦斯往后一退，掏出了第二把手枪。他近距离地瞄准总统的心脏开了一枪。什么事也没有。枪支再次卡弹！

4 这时，人群中有人出来扭住了劳伦斯的胳膊，把他按倒在地上，这其中包括田纳西

州的议员戴维·克罗克特（Davy Crockett）。而杰克逊仍然挥舞着他的手杖，试图敲碎这个谋杀未遂犯的头盖骨。他的助手只好急忙把他拉开并送到白宫的安全场所。总统安全了。谋杀的企图失败了。安德鲁·杰克逊两次躲开了子弹。火器专家指出，枪支连续两次出现卡弹的概率大约等于12,500:1的中彩几率。

5 理查德·劳伦斯，这个失业的油漆工，在法庭上被视做精神失常。据他说，他本人是英国王位的合法继承人，而之所以想杀杰克逊总统，是因为总统三年前杀了他的父亲（英国国王），他要报仇。他讲的这个故事完全是无稽之谈。陪审团认定劳伦斯试图谋杀罪名不成立，因为他是“在精神错乱的情形下”作案的。于是，理查德·劳伦斯在精神病院中度过了他的余生。

8 Several Interesting Facts on President Martin Van Buren
马丁·范·布伦总统趣闻

马丁·范·布伦 总统及第一夫人简介

马丁·范·布伦（Martin Van Buren, 1782.12.5 ～ 1862.7.24），第 8 任美国副总统（1833 ～ 1837）及第 8 任总统（1837 ～ 1841）。他是荷兰人的后裔，是《美国独立宣言》正式签署后出生的第一位总统。他为人圆滑，善于权术，是一位出色的政党组织者，有“魔术师”和“红狐狸”之称，是前总统安德鲁·杰克逊最得力的助手。1837 年上台后，加拿大爆发了边界争端，他灵活处理。美国又爆发了第一次经济危机，虽然这不是他的错，但人民对范·布伦失去信心了。1840 年他竞选连任时，败给威廉·亨利·哈里森。后来又两度参加竞选，都遭到失败，从此退出政坛，归隐故乡。

汉纳·豪斯·范·布伦（Hannah Hoes Van Buren, 1783.3.8～1819.2.5）是第8任美国总统马丁·范·布伦的妻子，也是他的远亲表妹，是一位漂亮女子。在童年的交往中这对表兄妹关系甚好。1807 年2月21日，他们举行了婚礼。婚后，他们共生了五个儿子，有四个长大成人。从1812 年马丁·范·布伦被选为纽约州议员时起，汉娜除了要照顾四个孩子外，还要常常关照范·布伦一家，她还喜欢社交活动。1819 年2 月5 日，汉娜因染肺病去世。此后，第一夫人的职责就由他的大儿媳安吉莉卡·辛格里顿·范·布伦(Angelica Singleton Van Buren)承担。汉娜去世后，为怀念汉娜，范·布伦未再结婚。

经典原文 Original Text

Words & Expressions

be credited with 归功于，认为某人有某事物

stature ['stætʃə] n. 身高，身材，（精神、道德等的）高度

uncanny [ʌn'kæni] adj. 神秘的，离奇的，可怕的

come down on 申斥，惩罚，索取

controversy ['kɔntrəvə:si] n. 公开辩论，论战

undertone ['ʌndətəun] n. 低音，浅色，小声，潜在的含意

snub [snʌb] vt. 冷落，严厉斥责，掐灭

scandal ['skændl] n. 丑闻，丑事，耻辱

1 Martin Van Buren was a colorful political figure of his time. He was a small man who stood only 5 feet, 6 inches tall, but had a commanding presence no matter what the situation.

2 Martin Van Buren is credited with giving us several things — among them the expression "OK" (meaning all right). Van Buren was from Kinderhook, New York, which was sometimes called "Old Kinderhook." "OK" clubs were formed in support of Van Buren's political campaigns, and somehow the expression "OK" came to be a substitute for the term "all right."

3 The nickname "the Little Magician" was given to Van Buren because of his small stature and his uncanny ability to come down on the winning side of every political controversy. In 1828, Van Buren was elected governor of New York State, but he resigned the post after he was offered the position of secretary of state by then — President Andrew Jackson.

4 Van Buren was happy to be secretary of state, but that post wasn't the height of his political ambitions. He had his eye fixed on becoming vice president. He did become the vice president by beating out John C. Calhoun in a political struggle with social undertones.

5 Then, Vice President Calhoun's wife publicly and privately snubbed the secretary of war's (John Eaton) wife, because there were rumors that she had started her romance with Eaton while her previous husband was still alive. This was a real scandal of the times. But Van Buren openly and

publicly supported Eaton's wife, Peggy. Andrew Jackson's wife, Rachel, had suffered a similar stigma that Jackson never forgave nor forgot, and he was determined that Peggy would not suffer the same fate.

6 Van Buren helped Jackson by resigning his Cabinet post and paving the way for Jackson to ask the other members of his Cabinet (whose wives had snubbed Peggy) to resign. Jackson then made Van Buren his running mate in the 1832 election and Van Buren went on to become the president (albeit a one-term president) in 1836.

stigma [ˈstigmə] *n.* 柱头，耻辱，污名，烙印

pave the way for 为…做好准备，为…铺平道路

albeit [ɔːlˈbiː it] *conj.* 虽然；即使

中文译文
Suggested Translation

1 马丁•范•布伦是他那个时代一位丰富多彩的政治人物。虽然个子矮小，身高只有5英尺6英寸，但无论在什么情况下他一贯都是威风凛凛的。

2 马丁 • 范 • 布伦被公认为赠送了我们几样礼品，其中之一就有"OK"这个词语(意为"行")。范 • 布伦来自纽约的肯德胡克，而纽约有时被称为"老肯德胡克"(Old Kinderhook)。"OK"俱乐部的成立是为了支持范 • 布伦的政治竞选，不知怎么的，"OK"逐渐成为了"all right"这个词语的替代语。

3 范•布伦之所以赢得"小魔术师"的绰号，是因为他身材矮小以及他不可思议的才能使他总能站在每场政治争议的胜利一方。1828年，范•布伦当选为纽约州州长，但当他被时任美国总统的安德鲁•杰克逊提出任命为国务卿之后，他便辞去了州长一职。

4 范•布伦很乐于担任国务卿一职，但这个岗位并不是他最大的政治抱负。他的眼光已经瞄准了副总统一职。后来，他在具有社会意味的政治斗争中击败了约翰•C•卡尔豪，也的确实现了担任副总统的夙愿。

5 当时，副总统卡尔豪的妻子公开和私下都冷落战争部长(约翰•伊顿)的妻子佩吉(Peggy)，因为有传言称，佩吉(Peggy)在她的前夫还活着时就开始与伊顿有风流韵事。

这在当时是一条十足的丑闻。但范•布伦坦率并公开支持伊顿的妻子佩吉（Peggy）。安德鲁•杰克逊的妻子瑞秋(Rachel)也曾遭受过类似的耻辱，以至于杰克逊无法原谅她且一直耿耿于怀。范•布伦断定佩吉将不会遭受同样的命运。

6 范·布伦通过辞去内阁职位帮助杰克逊，并为杰克逊要求他的内阁其他成员（其妻子曾冷落过佩吉）辞职铺平了道路。杰克逊于是在1832年的选举中成了范·布伦的竞选伙伴。1836年，范·布伦当选为总统（虽然只担任了一届总统）。

9 America's Shortest Serving President William Henry Harrison 美国历史上任职时间最短的总统——威廉·亨利·哈里森

威廉·亨利·哈里森 总统及第一夫人简介

威廉·亨利·哈里森（William Henry Harrison, 1773.2.9 ~ 1841.4.4），第9任美国总统（1841.3.4 ~ 1841.4.4），出身于弗吉尼亚种植者贵族家庭。哈里森是一位军事家，曾在与印第安人的战斗中获得胜利，人称“提帕卡农英雄”；在第二次美英战争中有过显赫功绩。他就职时年已68岁，也是美国历史上执政时间最短的总统，宣誓就职不久即患肺炎，1个月即告去世。他的孙子是美国第23任总统本杰明·哈里森。

安娜·西姆斯·哈里森（Anna Symmes Harrison, 1775.7.25 ~ 1864.2.25）是第9任美国总统威廉·亨利·哈里森的妻子，两人于1795年结婚，共有六儿四女。1841年，哈里森从俄亥俄州奔赴白宫就任总统时，其夫人安娜·西姆斯由于身体不好，加上舍不得离开家乡，因此没有同行，打算推迟到5月再去。于是哈里森便邀请他儿媳简·欧文·哈里森（Jane Irwin Harrison）暂时充当白宫女主人。然而，哈里森总统宣誓就职刚满1个月就因病去世，安娜·西姆斯也就成了美国历史上第一位在其丈夫任职总统期间未正式成为第一夫人的总统夫人。

经典原文 Original Text

Words & Expressions

aide-de-camp [ˌeiddəˈkɔmp] n. 副官，侍从武官，助手

encroachment [inˈkrəutʃmənt] n. 侵入，侵犯，侵蚀

succumb to 屈服于

strip [strip] vt. 剥夺；剥去；脱去衣服

intertribal [ˌintəˈtraibəl] adj. 部族间的，种族间的

uprising [ˈʌpraiziŋ] n.起义，暴动

seasoned regulars 老练的正规军

militia [miˈliʃə] n. 民兵组织；自卫队

brigadier [ˌbrigˈdiə] n. （美）旅长，（英）陆军准将

1 At age 18 Harrison enlisted as an army officer, serving as an aide-de-camp to General Anthony Wayne, who was engaged in a struggle against the Northwest Indian Confederation over the westward encroachment of white settlers. Harrison took part in the campaign that ended in *the Battle of Fallen Timbers* ① (August 20, 1794), near present-day Maumee, Ohio. The following year, on November 25, he married Anna Tuthill Symmes. As her father objected to the match, the couple married in secret.

2 In subsequent years Harrison held several government positions. President John Adams named Harrison secretary of the Northwest Territory, a vast tract of land encompassing most of the future states of Ohio, Indiana, Michigan, Illinois, and Wisconsin, in 1798, and he was sent to Congress as a territorial delegate the following year. In May 1800 Harrison was appointed governor of the newly created Indiana Territory, where, succumbing to the demands of land-hungry whites, he negotiated between 1802 and 1809 a number of treaties that stripped the Indians of that region of millions of acres. Resisting this expansionism, *the Shawnee* ② intertribal leader Tecumseh organized an Indian uprising. Returning to military service, Harrison led a force of seasoned regulars and militia that defeated the Indians at *the Battle of Tippecanoe* ③ (November 7, 1811), near present-day Lafayette, Indiana, a victory that largely established his military reputation in the public mind. A few months after *the War of 1812* ④ broke out with Great Britain, Harrison was made a brigadier general and placed in command of all federal forces in the Northwest Territory. On October 5,

1813, troops under his command decisively defeated the British and their Indian allies at *the Battle of the Thames*[5], in Ontario, Canada. Tecumseh was killed in the battle, and the British-Indian alliance was permanently destroyed; thus ended resistance in the Northwest.

alliance [lains] *n.* 结盟，同盟

destroy [dis'trɔi] *vt.* 破坏，摧毁，消灭

背景知识注释 Background Notes

1. Battle of Fallen Timbers　鹿寨之战，（发生于1794年8月20日）是西北印第安战争中最后一场战斗，这是隶属于西部联盟的美洲印第安部落与美国之间为争夺西北领地控制权的斗争。安东尼•韦恩率领久经沙场的1,000人的部队在莫米河畔的迈阿密堡将2,000印第安人士兵彻底击溃，1795年8月韦恩与印第安人签订《格林维尔条约》，迫使印第安人将俄亥俄州大部及印第安纳、伊利诺斯、密歇根大片土地割让给美国。这场战斗对于美国是一个决定性的胜利，结束了该地区存在的主要敌对状态。

2. the Shawnee　肖尼族。肖尼族是属于阿尔昆冈语族的北美印第安部落，原先定居在今天的俄亥俄河谷中部地区。17世纪时，肖尼人被依洛魁人驱逐出了自己的土地，被迫分散迁徙到各地。肖尼人中的一部分迁到了现在的伊利诺伊，一部分则在坎伯兰谷落户，另有一支继续向东南迁徙。1725年后，肖尼人又在俄亥俄重聚，组成了抗击殖民者的中坚力量。1794年，他们在鹿寨之战中被安东尼•韦恩将军击败。其后，特库姆塞酋长(Chief Tecumseh)与英军的联盟也宣告破产，未能保住他们在俄亥俄河谷的家园。肖尼人又分成三个独立的分支(Absentee，Eastern，Cherokee)散居在俄克拉荷马州各地。

3. the Battle of Tippecanoe　蒂珀卡努河之战。蒂珀卡努河是美国印第安纳州北部河流。1811年在印第安纳的蒂珀卡努战役中，哈里森击败了肖尼部落印第安人，他的昵称“蒂珀卡努”——1840年总统竞选中的口号“蒂珀卡努再加上泰勒”——由此而得名。

4. the War of 1812　1812年战争，又称第二次独立战争，是美国与英国之间发生于1812至1815年的战争，也是美国独立后第一次对外战争。这场战争是第一次、到目前为止也是唯一一次使美国首都曾经被外国军队占领的战争。这场逼和大英帝国的战争为美国赢得了国际声望。

5. the Battle of the Thames　泰晤士河战役（1813），此处泰晤士河是指加拿大安大略省南部的一条河流，全长260公里。泰晤士河战役是美英战争中两国军队在泰晤士河地区进行的一次战役，英军攻陷底特律及密歇根领地，从而控制了大湖区周围一带，此后，美国的目标就是夺回底特律和西北地区。美将哈里逊在托莱多附近建立梅格斯堡，英将普洛克特一再进攻，未能得手。英军在伊利湖战斗中失败后，美军以优势兵力穷追不舍，普洛克特遂在泰晤士维尔以东数英里

处陷入绝境。伊利湖和泰晤士河之战使美国恢复了对西北地区的控制。

中文译文
Suggested Translation

1 18岁时，哈里森入伍当了一名军人，作为安东尼·韦恩将军 (General Anthony Wayne) 的副官，哈里森参与了一场对抗西北印第安人联盟入侵西部白人移民者的斗争。哈里森参加了发生于现在的俄亥俄州莫米市附近以鹿寨之战（1794年8月20日）的胜利而告结束的那场战役。次年的11月25日，他和安娜•西姆斯(Anna Tuthill Symmes)结婚。由于安娜的父亲反对他们结合，因此他们的婚事是秘密进行的。

2 在随后的几年中，哈里森担任了数个政府职位。1798年，约翰•亚当斯总统任命哈里森为西北领地秘书。西北领地是一块广袤的土地，涵盖了大部分的未来几个州，如俄亥俄州、印第安纳州、密歇根州、伊利诺伊州和威斯康星州。第二年，他作为领地代表被派往国会。1800年5月，哈里森被任命为新建的印第安纳领地的总督。由于屈从于该地区渴望土地的白人需求，1802年至1809年期间，哈里森通过谈判达成了若干条约，剥夺了该地区印第安人的数百万公顷的土地。为了抵制这种扩张，肖尼部落领袖特库姆塞组织了一次印第安人起义。重返军队服役后，哈里森领导了一支身经百战的正规军和民兵武装，在今天的印第安纳州拉斐特地区附近进行的蒂珀卡努河之战(1811年11月7日)中击败了印第安人。这场胜利很大程度上在公众心目中确立了他的军事声誉。与英国冲突的1812年战争爆发后的数月中，哈里森擢升为准将，并统帅西北领地的所有联邦军队。1813年10月5日在哈里森的指挥下，英军及其印第安人盟友在今天的加拿大安大略省进行的泰晤士河之战中被打得一败涂地。特库姆塞酋长战死沙场，英国–印第安联盟受到永久性破坏；因此，西北部战事尘埃落定。

10 President John Tyler Who Died a Traitor to the United States
死时“背叛”了美国的约翰·泰勒总统

约翰·泰勒 总统及第一夫人简介

约翰·泰勒 (John Tyler, 1790.3.29～1862.1.18)，第10任美国总统(1841～1845)，也是第一个因在任总统逝世后由副总统继任为总统的人。在他的坚持下，副总统得在继任总统之后取得和总统一样的地位。约翰·泰勒继任总统后，迅速巩固了手中的权力。在任期间，他改组美国海军，建立美国气象局，结束了佛罗里达州的第二次塞诺米尔战争；1861年初，主持华盛顿和平会议以调解南北方分歧。南北战争爆发后，他支持南方的分裂行动，加入“南部联盟”的议会。北方各州对他十分憎恨。他1862年去世时，联邦政府毫无悼念的表示。值得一提的是，1844年，约翰·泰勒任职期间，美国还同中国签订了第一个不平等条约——《中美望厦条约》，美国通过这一条约获得了协定关税、五口通商、领事裁判、最惠国待遇等特权，中国向美国开放港口通商。

利蒂西亚·克里斯蒂安·泰勒(Letitia Christian Tyler, 1790.11.12～1842.9.10)是第10任美国总统约翰·泰勒(John Tyler)的第一任妻子。1813年两人结婚，生有三儿五女，夫人利蒂西亚有残疾，其第一夫人一职由儿媳普里西拉·库珀·泰勒(Priscilla Cooper Tyler)充当。1842年9月10日，利蒂西亚病故，成为美国历史上第一位在白宫去世的总统夫人。1844年6月26日，泰勒总统与年龄比他小30岁的朱莉亚·加德纳(Julia Gardiner)结婚，成为美国历史上第一位在任期间结婚的总统。朱莉亚是一位大地主的千金。他们生了五儿两女。朱莉亚成为泰勒担任总统最后八个月期间的第一夫人。泰勒去世后，她靠儿女和总统遗孀补助金生活，于1889年去世。

经典原文
Original Text

1 After Tyler's tumultuous presidency ended, his political career was pretty much short. His 1862 obituary in The *New York Times* described Tyler as "the most unpopular public man that had ever held any office in the United States," and even that depiction might have been a bit charitable. Tyler did manage to maintain some popularity throughout the South, though, so when the Confederacy broke away at the start of the Civil War, Tyler found himself elected to the Congress of the Confederate States of America.

2 Tyler died in 1862 before he could take his seat, but running for a Confederate office severely hurt his stock in Washington. President Lincoln didn't issue a proclamation mourning Tyler's passing, and flags didn't dip to half-staff on federal properties. The Confederacy, on the other hand, threw a lavish funeral for Tyler in *Richmond* ①, including a 150-carriage procession.

3 Just how reviled in the North was Tyler when he died? Check out the penultimate paragraph of the aforementioned *Times* obit: "He ended his life suddenly, last Friday, in Richmond — going down to death amid the ruins of his native State. He himself was one of the architects of its ruin;

Words & Expressions

tumultuous [tju'mʌltjuəs] *adj.* 吵闹的，骚乱的，狂暴的

obituary [əu'bitʃuəri] *n.* 讣告

depiction [di'pikʃən] *n.* 描写，叙述

charitable ['tʃærətəbl] *adj.* 慈善事业的，慷慨的，仁慈的，宽恕的

take one's seat 就座，就职

stock [stɔk] *n.*（对人或事物的）估计，声望，信任

proclamation [ˌprɔklə'meiʃən] *n.* 公告，宣布，宣告，公布

half-staff ['hɑ:fstɑ:f] *vt.* 降半旗

lavish ['læviʃ] *adj.* 浪费的，丰富的，大方的

revile [ri'vail] *v.* 辱骂，斥责

penultimate [pi'nʌltimət] *adj.* 倒数第二的，倒数第二音节的

aforementioned [ˌəfɔ:'menʃənd] *adj.* 上述的，前面提及的

and beneath that melancholy wreck his name will be buried, instead of being inscribed on *the Capitol* [2]'s monumental marble, as a year ago he so much desired."

melancholy [ˈmelənkəli] *adj.* 忧郁的，使人悲伤的

monumental [ˌmɔnjuˈmentəl] *adj.* 不朽的，纪念碑的，非常的

背景知识注释 Background Notes

1. Richmond 里士满。美国南北战争时南方的首都，现为弗吉尼亚州首府。
2. the Capitol 美国国会大厦。

中文译文 Suggested Translation

1 泰勒总统动荡的任期结束后，他的政治生涯是相当短暂的。1862 年在《纽约时报》上登载的讣告将泰勒描述为“美国历史上曾经任职的最不受欢迎的公众人物，”甚至这种描述也还算是有点慷慨的。泰勒在整个南方一直都成功地受人爱戴。因此，在内战爆发初南方联盟宣布独立时，泰勒仍然当选为南部联盟的国会议员。

2 泰勒还来不及就职就于1862年去世了，但竞选南部邦联的职位严重伤害了他在华盛顿的声望。林肯总统没有发出哀悼泰勒去世的公告，联邦大楼上的国旗也没有下半旗志哀。相反，南部联盟却在里士满为泰勒举行了一个盛大的葬礼，其中有包括一支150 辆马车的送行队伍。

3 泰勒去世后他在北方究竟受到怎样的谩骂呢？不妨看看先前提到《时代周刊》登载的讣告上的倒数第二段：他上周五在里士满突然结束了自己的生命——死于他故乡所在州的废墟中。他本人就是其废墟的建造者；他的名字将埋葬在忧郁的残骸下，而不是如一年前他所渴望的那样镌刻在国会大厦不朽的大理石上。

11 A "Dark Horse" Candidate James K. Polk
"黑马"候选人詹姆斯·K·波尔克

詹姆斯·诺克斯·波尔克 总统及第一夫人简介

詹姆斯·诺克斯·波尔克 (James K. Polk, 1795.11.2 ~ 1849.6.5)，第 11 任美国总统(1845 ~ 1849)。詹姆斯·波尔克是安德鲁·杰克逊的忠实门徒，有"小山核桃"之称，他在 1844 年大选成僵局时，异军突起，成为第一位"黑马"总统。在短短的四年任期内，他完成了对选民的四大承诺：降低关税；恢复独立国库制；解决俄勒冈边界问题；取得加利福尼亚地区。把美国领土向北扩张到北纬 49° 线，向西扩张到太平洋，向南几乎兼并了墨西哥一半领土。今天美国领土的 1/4 是他取得的。他每天工作 18 个小时以上，而且没有休闲活动，以至于未老先衰，离开白宫三个多月就病逝了，终年 53 岁。他被历史学家评为美国最勤奋最有效率的总统。

萨拉·奇尔德雷斯·波尔克 (Sarah Childress Polk, 1803.9.4 ~ 1891.8.14) 是第 11 任美国总统詹姆斯·波尔克的妻子。萨拉 20 岁时与 28 岁的詹姆斯·波尔克结婚，婚后 25 年一直没有生育。虔诚著名的萨拉把全部时间和精力都献给了丈夫的事业。波尔克总统在离任的次日就染上慢性腹泻，离开白宫不久就病逝了。萨拉把田纳西的家收拾干净，并将它命名为"波尔克之家"，过着清贫孤独的日子。南北战争彻底摧毁了萨拉赖以维生的密西西比庄园，她失去了经济来源，只得变卖庄园的土地换取一次性的微薄收入。1882 年，美国国会批准每年补助 5,000 美元养老金给她，萨拉的生活才有了保障。1891 年萨拉逝世，终年 88 岁。

经典原文 Original Text

1 When James K. Polk accepted the Democratic Party's nomination for the presidency, he was not very well known. The Whig opposition party played on his obscurity, sniping, "Who is James K. Polk?" An experienced speaker, Polk surprised everyone when he campaigned vigorously and won the presidency on November 5, 1844. He was called a "dark horse" candidate because he was not expected to beat his opponent, Henry Clay of *the Whig Party*[①], to become the 11th president of the United States.

2 Winning by a narrow margin, Polk campaigned on his strong support for westward expansion, a hotly debated issue that was dodged by other candidates. After taking office, Polk acted swiftly to fulfill his campaign promises, as he intended to serve only one term. In four years, he oversaw the addition of Texas, the reestablishment of an independent treasury system, and the acquisition of territory from Mexico. This new land from Mexico eventually became California, New Mexico, Arizona, Utah, and parts of Colorado and Wyoming. This new land came just in time for the discovery of gold in California in 1848.

3 But Polk's considerable political accomplishments took their toll on his health. Full of enthusiasm and vigor when he entered office, Polk left the White House at the age of 53, exhausted. He died less than four months later at his new home, "Polk Place," in Nashville, Tennessee, the state he had served as governor. Polk's wife, Sarah

Words & Expressions

obscurity [əbˈskjuriti] *n.* 朦胧，阴暗，晦涩，身份低微

snipe [snaip] *vi.* 狙击，伏击，抨击，猎鸟，诽谤

campaign [kæmˈpein] *n.* 运动，战役

vigorously [ˈvigərəsli] *adv.* 精神旺盛地，活泼地

by a narrow margin （比分）相差不大地

dodge [dɔdʒ] *vt.* 躲避，避开

oversee [ˌəuvəˈsiː] *vt.* 监督，审查，俯瞰，偷看到

take one's toll on… 给…敲响警钟，使…付出代价，给…带来害处（影响）

pilgrimage [ˈpilgrimidʒ] *n.* 漫游，朝圣之行
neutral [ˈnjuːtrəl] *adj.* 中立的
legacy [ˈlegəsi] *n.* 遗赠，遗产

Childress Polk, lived there another 42 years, hosting many visitors. During the Civil War, she welcomed both Union and Confederate leaders. “Polk Place” became a pilgrimage destination and was respected as neutral ground, even during the bloody *Battle of Nashville*②. James and Sarah Polk left an important legacy to a greatly expanded United States.

背景知识注释 Background Notes

1. the Whig Party　辉格党，历史党派名称，有英国辉格党和美国辉格党。英国辉格党产生于17世纪末，19世纪中叶演变为英国自由党。美国辉格党始创于19世纪30年代，后于19世纪50年代瓦解，存续约26年。美国辉格党党员中有许多杰出的全国性政治人物。
2. Battle of Nashville　那什维尔之战。在田纳西州的那什维尔成为现在的音乐之都前，在内战期间，这里曾经发生过死伤惨重的战争。

中文译文 Suggested Translation

1 当詹姆斯·波尔克接受民主党的提名，成为总统候选人时，许多人对他还相当陌生。反对党“辉格党”(Whig) 就曾拿这点来做文章说：“谁是詹姆斯·波尔克呀？”但是波尔克是一个经验丰富的演说家，他卖力地参与竞选，并且在 1844 年 11 月 5 日赢得了总统选举，让许多人都跌破眼镜。他被称为是“黑马”候选人，因为一般人都没预期到他会击败他的对手——辉格党的亨利·克雷 (Henry Clay)，而成为美国的第 11 任总统。

2 波尔克在选举中险胜，而他在竞选时大力支持美国应该向西部扩张，虽然这是相当热门的话题，但是其他候选人似乎都刻意回避。因为并不想竞选连任，所以波尔克就任总统之后立刻展开行动以实践竞选承诺。在四年任内，他领导美国取得了得克萨斯州的土地，重建了独立的财政制度，并且还从墨西哥取得了部分领土。这一大片从墨西哥取得的领土，也就是现在的加利福尼亚州、新墨西哥州、亚利桑那州、犹他州，以及一部分的科罗拉多州与怀俄明州。1848年加利福尼亚州发现了金矿，所以这片土地的取得可以说正是时候。

3 但是波尔克却因为忙于政治事业，而忽略了自己的身体健康。他满怀壮志、精力充沛地就任总统，但在他 53 岁离开白宫时却显得筋疲力尽。就在他卸任总统之后，他回到曾经

担任州长的田纳西州的家中。不到四个月的时间，波尔克就在那什维尔的“波尔克之家”去世。后来，他的妻子萨拉·奇尔德雷斯·波尔克（Sarah Childress Polk）在那里独自生活了42年之久，并招待了许多访客。在内战期间，萨拉曾迎接过联邦和南方联盟的领导人物。“波尔克之家”变成旅游者必经之地，即使是在血腥的那什维尔战争中，这个地方也被视为一个永久中立的地区，而不受战火波及。詹姆斯与萨拉·波尔克在美国扩张的历史上留下了一笔重要的遗产。

12 Death of President Zachary Taylor 扎卡里·泰勒总统之死

扎卡里·泰勒 总统及第一夫人简介

扎卡里·泰勒（Zachary Taylor, 1784.1.24～1850.7.9），第12任美国总统（1849.3.5～1850.7.9），也是美国政治家、军事家。这位戎马生涯40载的将军，长期守卫着边疆阵地，在1846年～1848年的美墨战争中指挥美军作战，成为美国民族英雄。泰勒说话偶尔有点儿口吃，是个粗犷直率、热诚开朗，但又不修边幅的人。1848年代表辉格党的他被选为总统，是19世纪40年代美国统治阶级扩张的热潮把他推到总统候选人的位置，并且他又是以军功赢得竞选胜利而入主白宫的。尽管他在战场上屡屡获胜，但从政却不尽如人意。上任后，面对新州的奴隶制问题，他采取妥协政策，最后由于派系斗争错综复杂，使他政务缠身且非常棘手，在总统任期不到两年时就逝世了。他是继威廉·亨利·哈里森之后，第二位死于任内的美国总统。

马格丽特·麦考尔·史密斯·泰勒（Margaret Mackall Smith Taylor, 1788.9.21～1852.8.18）是第12任美国总统扎卡里·泰勒的妻子。玛格丽特是大陆军一位少校的女儿，身材苗条、端庄秀丽。在家族的熏陶下，她知书达理，善于管理家务，并培养起她毕生所遵从的宗教信仰。他们在肯塔基边区结识，两人一见钟情，21岁的玛格丽特与25岁的泰勒于1810年6月21日在泰勒父亲赠送的农庄里结婚。从此，在丈夫漫长的军旅生涯中，玛格丽特开始了辗转各地的随军生活，直到1841 年才在地方上定居下来。泰勒夫妇生有一子五女，其中四个活到成年。作为第一夫人时，玛格丽特不善社交，很少公开露面，加之体弱多病，只好隐居在白宫的二楼，把白宫女主人的责任交给她的小女儿玛丽•伊丽莎白 •布利斯(Mary Elizabeth Bliss)夫人代劳。

经典原文
Original Text

1 The cause of Zachary Taylor's death has not been fully established. On July 4, 1850, Taylor was known to have consumed copious amounts of iced water, cold milk, green apples, and cherries after attending holiday celebrations and the laying of the cornerstone of the Washington Monument. Within several days, he became severely ill with an unknown digestive ailment. Doctors used popular treatments of the time. He believed he was dying, and at about 10 o'clock in the morning on July 9, Taylor called Margaret to him and asked her not to weep, saying: "I have always done my duty, I am ready to die. My only regret is for the friends I leave behind me." He died within the hour. Contemporary reports listed the cause of death as "bilious diarrhea, or a bilious cholera". Scholars believe it was a kind of severe gastroenteritis.

2 Taylor was interred in *the Public Vault of the Congressional Cemetery*[①] in Washington, D.C. from July 13, 1850 to October 25, 1850. (It was built in 1835 to hold remains of notables until either the grave site could be prepared or transportation arranged to another city.) His body was transported to the Taylor Family plot where his parents are buried, on the old Taylor homestead plantation known as "Springfield" in Louisville, Kentucky.

3 In 1883, the *Commonwealth of Kentucky*[②] placed a

Words & Expressions

copious [ˈkəupiəs] *adj.* 丰富的，很多的，多产的

digestive [daiˈdʒestiv] *adj.* 消化的，助消化的

ailment [ˈeilmənt] *n.* 疾病

bilious [ˈbiliəs] *adj.* 胆汁的，坏脾气的

diarrhea [ˌdaiəˈriə] *n.* 腹泻，痢疾

cholera [ˈkɔlərə] *n.* 霍乱

gastroenteritis [ˌgæstrəue-ntəˈraitis] *n.* 肠胃炎

inter [inˈtəː] *vt.* 埋，葬

remains [riˈmeinz] *n.* 残余

notable [ˈnəutəbl] *n.* 名人

plot [plɔt] *n.* 情节，阴谋，小块土地

initiate [i'niʃieit] *vt.* 开始，创始，发起

mausoleum [ˌmɔːsə'liəm] *n.* 陵墓，阴森森的大厦

limestone ['laimstəun] *n.* 石灰岩

granite ['grænit] *n.* 花岗岩，坚毅，冷酷无情

marble ['mɑːbl] *n.* 大理石，大理石制品

fifty-foot monument in his honor near his grave; it is topped by a life-sized statue of Taylor. By the 1920s, the Taylor family initiated the effort to turn the Taylor burial grounds into a national cemetery. The Commonwealth of Kentucky donated two pieces of land for the project, turning the half-acre Taylor family cemetery into 16 acres (65,000 m^2). On May 6, 1926, the remains of Taylor and his wife (who died in 1852) were moved to the newly constructed Taylor mausoleum nearby. (It was made of limestone with a granite base, with a marble interior.) The cemetery property has been designated as the Zachary Taylor National Cemetery.

背景知识注释
Background Notes

1. the Public Vault of the Congressional Cemetery （美国）国会公墓的公共墓室。

2. Commonwealth of Kentucky 肯塔基联盟，即肯塔基州，是美国中东部的一个州，正式名称为“肯塔基联盟”。其面积104,749平方公里，在全美国排名第37，而人口数在2005年则是4,041,769，全国排名第26位。肯塔基州在美国革命时是弗吉尼亚州的一部分，至1792年脱离弗吉尼亚州，成为美国的第十五个州。肯塔基州以纯种马和威士忌闻名。

中文译文
Suggested Translation

1 扎卡里·泰勒的死因尚未完全确定。1850 年 7 月 4 日，在参加了节日庆祝活动和华盛顿纪念碑基石的奠基之后，泰勒被认为喝了大量的冰水和冷牛奶，并吃了许多青苹果和樱桃等。几天之内，他因患某种未知的消化性疾病而一病不起。医生们对他采取了当时常用的治疗方法。泰勒感觉自己不久于人世，7 月 9 日上午大约 10 点，他将玛格丽特叫到跟前，一边求她不要哭泣，一边说道：“我一直都尽到了我的责任，我可以死得其所了。我唯一的遗憾就是放不下我身后的朋友。”之后不到一个小时他就去世了。现代医学报告将他的死因描述为“胆汁性腹泻”或“急性霍乱”。学者认为这是一种严重的胃肠炎。

2 1850年7月13日至1850年10月25日期间，泰勒被埋葬在华盛顿特区国会公墓的公共墓

室里。(这座公墓建于1835年，旨在存放一些名人的遗骸，直到墓地准备妥当或等待安排运至另一城市。)泰勒的遗体被运到了泰勒家族的土地上，也就是在肯塔基州路易斯维尔市被称为“斯普林菲尔德”的老泰勒宅地种植园，他的父母也被安葬在此。

3 1883年，肯塔基州为了纪念泰勒，在他的坟墓旁树立了一块50英尺高的纪念碑；碑的顶端是一尊真人大小的泰勒雕像。到了1920年代，泰勒家族开始努力将泰勒墓地变成一个国家公墓。肯塔基州为此项目捐赠了两块土地，由此将半英亩的泰勒家族墓地变成16英亩(65,000平方米)。1926年5月6日，泰勒和他妻子(1852年去世)的遗骸被运抵附近新建的泰勒陵墓。(它以石灰岩为主体，以花岗岩为基础，内部装饰有大理石。)墓地产权已经被指定为扎卡里•泰勒国家公墓。

13 Life after Millard Fillmore's Presidency 米勒德·菲尔莫尔总统退休后的生活

米勒德·菲尔莫尔 总统及第一夫人简介

米勒德·菲尔莫尔 (Millard Fillmore, 1800.1.7 ~ 1874.3.8)，第 13 任美国总统（1850 ~ 1853）。菲尔莫尔是在扎卡里·泰勒总统去世后开始他的总统任期的。他任内最著名的事迹是派遣美国东印度舰队前往日本，并由舰队司令马修·培理 (Matthew Calbraith Perry，1794 ~ 1858) 向幕府送出其亲笔国书，促成日本之开国，史称“黑船事件”。他对奴隶制一直采取妥协态度，1850 年妥协案导致了对奴隶制的双轨制，奴隶贸易在哥伦比亚特区和加利福尼亚州被禁止，但与此同时，剩下的蓄奴者的权力却得到了强化。但他也为美国在国际上的地位发挥过重要作用，促进了美国经济的发展。卸任后，他曾再度竞选美国总统，但不幸落败。菲尔莫尔是美国历史上最具争议的总统之一，他位居最差美国总统第十名是因为他未能解决奴隶制危机。

阿碧格尔·鲍尔斯·菲尔莫尔（Abigail Powers Fillmore, 1798.3.13～1853.3.30）是第13任美国总

统米勒德•菲尔莫尔的第一任妻子。两人于1826年2月5日结婚，生有一子一女。1798年鲍尔斯出生在纽约的萨拉托加县的一个浸礼派基督教牧师家庭。她热衷学习，乐于助人，于1853年因肺炎病逝；菲尔莫尔在1856年大选中再次失败后，便把全部身心投入家乡布法罗的公众事业，但已经债台高筑，无力偿还债务。所幸他获得了一位富有的寡妇的爱情，1858年2月10日，在前妻鲍尔斯去世5年之后，菲尔莫尔与卡罗琳•卡迈克尔•麦金托什(Caroline Carmichael McIntosh)(1813～1881)结婚。婚后，卡罗琳为菲尔莫尔还清了债务，使他能在以后的年月里继续从事他热衷的事业。

经典原文
Original Text

1 Millard Fillmore and his family welcomed the escape from Washington after Pierce's election; they had never liked the city. Abigail Fillmore had been so unwell during most of the administration that her daughter, Mary, had been pressed into hostess duty for White House functions. The city, however, took a final, terrible swipe at the family. Abigail Fillmore, compelled to sit outside for hours on Pierce's cold, wet inauguration day, caught pneumonia and died less than a month later. Not long afterward, Fillmore's daughter, Mary, only twenty-two years old, died of cholera. The former President was devastated by the twin calamities, and he searched for something to take his mind off them.

2 Unsurprisingly, Fillmore found solace in politics. Countless former Whigs were now without a party, and some had organized a new one. It had the strange name of the Know-Nothing Party, and its aims were less than savory. Targeting native-born Americans made uneasy by the hordes of immigrants now flocking to the United States, the Know-Nothings advocated immigration restrictions and a waiting period for new citizens to vote. Irish Catholic immigrants, perceived as a threat to the existing labor force, were a prime target. Fillmore refused to be part of the anti-immigrant message dispensed by the party, but the Know-

Words & Expressions

swipe [swaip] *n.* 猛击，尖刻的话

inauguration [inˌɔːgjuˈreiʃən] *n.* 就职，开始，开创

pueumonia [njuːˈməuniə] *n.* 肺炎

cholera [ˈkɔlərə] *n.* 霍乱

devastate [ˈdevəsteit] *vt.* 毁灭，毁坏，使不知所措

calamity [kəˈlæməti] *n.* 灾祸，困苦

solace [ˈsɔləs] *n.* 安慰，慰藉

savory [ˈseivəri] *adj.* 可口的

horde [hɔːd] *n.* 一大群，游牧部落

flock [flɔk] *vi.* 聚集，成群而行

dispense [disˈpens] *vt.* 分配，分发，免除，执行

Nothings made him their presidential candidate in 1856, as did the remnants of the Whig Party. The former President received only 21 percent of the vote, but it prevented another candidate he deeply opposed—John C. Frémont of the new Republican Party—from winning against Democrat James Buchanan.

3 Later, Fillmore would make no more attempts at political office. He retired in *Buffalo*① and married Caroline McIntosh, a wealthy *Albany*② widow, in early 1858. Fillmore was thereafter active in many causes and charities. When the Civil War erupted three years later, Fillmore became a staunch *Unionist*③, helping to organize enlistment and war-financing drives. The last Whig President died of a stroke in March 1874, firmly established as Buffalo's leading citizen. Some, however, never forgot—or forgave—Millard Fillmore's support of the Fugitive Slave Law. After the assassination of Abraham Lincoln in 1865, a mob descended on Fillmore's opulent home and smudged black paint on the building.

remnant [ˈremnənt] *n.* 剩余，部分，幸存者

charity [ˈtʃærəti] *n.* 慈善，施舍，慈善团体，宽容

staunch [stɔːntʃ] *adj.* 坚定的，忠诚的，坚固的

enlistment [inˈlistmənt] *n.* 征募，应征入伍，服兵役期限

mob [mɔb] *n.* 暴徒，民众，乌合之众

descend on 袭击

opulent [ˈɔpjulənt] *adj.* 丰富的，富裕的，大量的

smudge [smʌdʒ] *vt.* 弄脏，涂污，用浓烟熏

背景知识注释
Background Notes

1. Buffalo 布法罗，又译水牛城，美国纽约州西部的一座城市，位于伊利湖东端、尼亚加拉河的源头，是纽约州第二大城市（仅次于纽约市）。对岸为加拿大伊利堡。

2. Albany [ˈɔːbəni] *n.* 奥尔巴尼（美国城市名），是美国纽约州首府。它位于该州东部，哈得孙河西岸，南距纽约 225 公里。市区面积 50.7 平方公里，原为荷兰人建立的贸易站。1797 年成为州府。

3. Unionist （尤指美国南北战争时期的）联邦主义者。

中文译文
Suggested Translation

1 皮尔斯当选总统后，米勒德•菲尔莫尔和他的家人欣喜地离开了华盛顿，他们从来也没有喜欢过这座城市。阿碧格尔•菲尔莫尔在其丈夫执政期间身体一直欠佳，以致她的女儿玛丽在白宫被迫承担起女主人的职责。然而，这座城市最后还是对这个家庭进行了可怕的抨击。阿碧格尔•菲尔莫尔在皮尔斯的就职典礼上不得不在户外坐了数个小时，当时天气寒冷潮湿，事后她患了肺炎，不到一个月就去世了。不久之后，菲尔莫尔年仅22岁的女儿玛丽也死于霍乱。这双重灾难重创了这位前总统，他努力寻找一些能够摆脱此种状态的事情。

2 不出所料，菲尔莫尔在政治中得到了慰藉。无数的前辉格党人现在没有政党归属，另一些则已经组织了一个新党——它有一个奇怪的名字，即一无所知党，其目的也不乏风趣。针对本土美国人因蜂拥而至的移民而深感不安，一无所知党人主张限制移民并且新公民参与投票须有一个等待期。爱尔兰天主教移民被视为是现有劳动力的一大威胁，因此成了一个主要被限制的对象。菲尔莫尔拒绝参与该党反移民消息的发布，但一无所知党人将他推举为1856年的总统候选人——正如残余的辉格党人所做的那样。这位前总统所获得的支持率仅为21%，但这阻止了他极力反对的另一位候选人新共和党的约翰•C•弗里蒙特 (John C. Fremont) 战胜民主党的候选人詹姆斯•布坎南 (Jamés Buchanan)。

3 后来，菲尔莫尔不再试图担任政治职务。他在布法罗市退休，并在1858年初与一位富有的奥尔巴尼寡妇卡罗琳•麦金托什(Caroline McIntosh)成婚。此后，菲尔莫尔在许多活动和慈善机构中表现得非常活跃。当三年后内战爆发时，菲尔莫尔成为一位坚定的联邦主义者，帮助组织征募和战争筹款活动。这位最后的辉格党总统于1874年3月死于中风，奠定了他在布法罗市作为主要市民的地位。然而，有些人对米勒德•菲尔莫尔给予《逃亡奴隶法》的支持刻骨铭心且坚决不原谅。1865年，亚伯拉罕•林肯遇刺身亡后，一群暴徒突袭了菲尔莫尔奢华的家并将整个建筑用黑漆涂得污迹斑斑。

14 The Grieving Franklin Pierce 悲痛的富兰克林·皮尔斯总统

富兰克林·皮尔斯 总统及第一夫人简介

富兰克林·皮尔斯 (Franklin Pierce, 1804.11.23 ~ 1869.10.8)，第 14 任美国总统 (1853 ~ 1857)。皮尔斯是美国民主党总统，而且是第一位出生于 19 世纪的美国总统。在 1852 年民主党全国大会的第 49 轮投票中被提名为“黑马”候选人。他无大的战绩，但却有仕途之运气，在军内供职时间不长即晋升为将军。他不仅年轻时有机会青云直上，而且在总统选举中爆了冷门，被人们称为继詹姆斯 •K• 波尔克之后的又一黑马，创造了自詹姆斯 • 门罗以来从未有的绝对优势。他对外奉行扩张政策，是同情南方政治主张的北方人。由于他对南方的同情不能见容于北部各州，促成了国家的分裂，故任满后便隐退。

珍妮•米恩斯•阿普尔顿•皮尔斯(Jane Means Appleton Pierce, 1806.3.12～1863.12.2)是第14任美国总统富兰克林•皮尔斯的妻子。珍妮是缅因州鲍登大学校长的女儿，是一位腼腆、脆弱而善解人意的姑娘。她大部分时间都是用来参加宗教社会活动和亲朋好友的婚礼以及其他上流社会的活动。1834年两人结婚。1836 年他们的第一个儿子生下来三天就夭折了；1841年第二个儿子出生。因珍妮不赞成她丈夫从政，顺应夫人的要求，1842 年皮尔斯辞去了参议员职位，回家重操律师旧业。

皮尔斯竞选总统时不愿意也不敢跟珍妮直说。结果使妻子不能理解丈夫，造成了更大的误解和思想上的隔阂。特别是他们唯一的儿子死于非命之后，珍妮更是郁郁寡欢、怨天尤人。为此，她既未参加皮尔斯的就职典礼，也未参加白宫的任何活动。这是皮尔斯政治上的悲剧，也是他们家庭和婚姻的不幸。

经典原文 Original Text

1 The year 1853 began full of promise for president-elect Franklin Pierce when, just weeks before the first family was scheduled to move to Washington, tragedy struck. The Pierces' eleven-year-old son, Bennie, died in a train wreck in Andover, Massachusetts. He was caught under a train car and crushed to death while Franklin and Jane Pierce watched helplessly. Jane Pierce was so stricken with grief that she was unable to act as first lady for nearly two years. Jane blamed Franklin for the Pierce family's uprooting from the New Hampshire home and for Bennie's death.

2 Mrs. Pierce believed that their family in general and President Pierce in particular, were being punished by God. Further evidence of the Lord's apparent wrath came with the sudden unexpected death of Pierce's close friend, New Hampshire Senator Charles G. Atherton, an alleged alcoholic who didn't make it to the inauguration.

3 The grieving President turned to the bottle to deaden the pain of Bennie's loss and to deal with his wife's bitterness. Soon critics began to claim that President Pierce was a chronic alcoholic incapable of performing his duties to the nation. But, despite his affection for whiskey and much publicized drinking binges (which included his being slapped with what amounted to a DUI for running over an old woman in the presidential carriage — although it was

Words & Expressions

train wreck 列车失事，失事火车残骸

crush [krʌʃ] *vi.* 挤，被压碎

be stricken with grief 悲痛欲绝

uproot [ʌpˈruːt] *v.* 根除，迫使某人迁离，改变生活方式

wrath [rɔθ] *n.* 愤怒，激怒

alleged [əˈledʒd] *adj.* 所谓的，声称的，被断言的

alcoholic [ˌælkəˈhɔlik] *n.* 酒鬼

deaden [ˈdedən] *vt.* 使减弱，使麻木，隔阻

chronic [ˈkrɔnik] *adj.* 慢性的，长期的，习惯性的

publicize [ˈpʌblisaiz] *vt.* 宣传，公布

binge [bin(d)ʒ] *n.* 狂欢，狂闹，放纵

DUI [ˈdjuːiː] *abbr.* 酒醉驾车（Driving Under the Influence）

carriage [ˈkæridʒ] *n.* 四轮马车，客车厢，运输，运费

never proven), Franklin Pierce managed the affairs of the United States until he left office in 1857. During the final days of his presidency, he was asked about his plan for the future. He replied, "There's nothing left... but to get drunk."

中文译文
Suggested Translation

1 1853年对于总统当选人富兰克林·皮尔斯本是充满希望的，但就在第一家庭准备搬往华盛顿的几周前，悲剧发生了。皮尔斯11岁的儿子，本尼(Bennie)在马萨诸塞州安杜佛镇的一次火车事故中不幸遇难。他被一节车厢压死，皮尔斯夫妇眼睁睁看着却无能为力。这一悲痛事件使珍妮一蹶不振，以至于她在近两年的时间内难以履行第一夫人的职责。她也因为皮尔斯家背井离乡的生活以及本尼的意外死亡而常责备富兰克林。

2 皮尔斯夫人坚信他们全家——尤其是皮尔斯总统——正在被上帝惩罚。另一件可以证明上帝显然在发怒的事情是皮尔斯最亲近的朋友，新罕布什尔州议员查尔斯·G·艾瑟顿，突然意外死亡。死亡原因据称是因为饮酒过多，但是在就职典礼上他根本没有喝酒。

3 悲痛的总统开始通过酗酒的方式来缓解本尼去世所带来的痛苦以及妻子的怨恨所带来的影响。很快就有人批评皮尔斯总统是一个长期酗酒的酒徒，不能担当起处理国家事务的职责。但是，尽管皮尔斯嗜好威士忌，以及传得沸沸扬扬的其无节制狂饮的行为（其中包括他被斥责因酒后驾车而使总统马车碾过一位老妇人，虽然没有被证实），但直到1857年他离开白宫之前，他依旧处理了美国所存在的一些问题。在他任期的最后阶段，当被问及以后的打算时，他说："除了饮酒已经没有任何东西值得留恋了。"

15 James Buchanan's Final Struggle 詹姆斯·布坎南总统最后的斗争

詹姆斯·布坎南 总统及第一夫人简介

詹姆斯•布坎南 (James Buchanan, 1791.4.23～1868.6.1)，第15任美国总统(1857～1861)，并担任过美国第17任国务卿。詹姆士•布坎南生于宾夕法尼亚州一个富有的家庭，当过律师，属杰克逊一派的民主党人，曾任众议员和参议员多年，两度出使国外。布坎南是唯一一位没有结过婚的总统。出任总统时，正值美国处于历史上的一个重大关头。当时，南北双方在奴隶制问题上的斗争愈演愈烈。任内，许多对内对外计划均因国内奴隶制问题的矛盾尖锐化而未得到实现。他尽管为避免南北分裂做过不少努力，但还是无力扭转局势。他卸任后，内战爆发，由此他受到很多指责。

詹姆斯•布坎南终生未婚，在未婚妻安•科尔曼去世之前，布坎南本欲弃政归隐，与妻子过平凡、幸福的生活。但未婚妻的去世，感情上的重大打击，使他改变了主意——立志从政，激流勇进，与政治结为终身伴侣。担任总统后，白宫缺少女主人，布坎南将自己的侄女哈丽雅特•莱恩(Harriet Lane)接入白宫负责日常事务，在其任期内行使“第一夫人”的职责(1857～1861)。哈丽雅特既是优雅的主人，又负责对他的一切安排。

经典原文
Original Text

Words & Expressions

credence [ˈkriːdəns] *n.* 信任，凭证，祭器台
ridiculous [riˈdikjuləs] *adj.* 可笑的，荒谬的
truce [truːs] *n.* 休战；停止争辩
overrule [ˌəuvəˈruːl] *vt.* 否决，统治，对…施加影响
veto [ˈviːtəu] *v.* 否决；禁止
reinforce [ˌriːinˈfɔːs] *vt.* 加强，加固，强化，补充
adverse [ˈædvəːs] *adj.* 不利的，相反的，敌对的
bond [bɔnd] *n.* 债券
plot [plɔt] *vi.* 密谋，策划，绘制
deface [diˈfeis] *vt.* 损伤外观，丑化
vigorously [ˈvigərəsli] *adv.* 精

1 Alone among American former presidents, Buchanan was denied a pleasant and honorable retirement. His well-known southern sympathies gave credence to ridiculous Republican charges that he had somehow been responsible for the fall of *Fort Sumter*① and for the war itself. Stores exhibited banknotes picturing a red-eyed Buchanan with a rope around his neck and the word *Judas*② written on his forehead. Lincoln's war message of 4 July drew heavily from an inaccurate report by General *Scott*③ and unfairly damaged Buchanan's reputation still further. A Senate resolution to condemn Buchanan failed but received wide publicity. Newspapers charged that he had failed to prevent secession and war by not strengthening the fort earlier, had negotiated truces with the enemy, had overruled General Scott by sending the Star of the West instead of the Brooklyn, had vetoed Scott's proposals to reinforce Sumter, had scattered the fleet around the world, and had tried to arm the South. Buchanan's most recent former cabinet officers could have come to his rescue with true accounts, but five of them had accepted positions with Lincoln, the others were frightened by adverse public opinion, and none would say a word in his defense. On successive days, newspapers announced that he was in England selling Confederate bonds and that he was in Pennsylvania plotting with spies. His portrait was removed from the *Capitol rotunda*④ to keep it from being defaced, and he was even accused of stealing pictures from the White House and keeping the gifts brought by a Japanese delegation.

2 At first, the attacks made him violently ill, but he soon

recovered and defended himself vigorously. He demolished the charges of Scott in an exchange of public letters and finished his memoirs in 1866. The book refuted the charges of malfeasance, demonstrated the hypocrisy of his accusers, and restored his peace of mind. It also blamed the Civil War primarily on northern radicalism and clearly revealed the greatest weakness of his presidency—his thorough emotional identification with the South and his inability to understand and deal with northern public opinion on the issues that had separated the sections. He died on 1 June 1868 with no regrets and still certain that history would vindicate his memory.

神旺盛地，活泼

demolish [diˈmɔliʃ] *vt.* 拆除，毁坏，推翻，驳倒

refute [riˈfjuːt] *vt.* 反驳

malfeasance [mælˈfiːz(ə)ns] *n.* 渎职，违法行为，不正当

demonstrate [ˈdemənstreit] *vt.* 证明，展示，论证

hypocrisy [hiˈpɔkrisi] *n.* 虚伪，伪善

vindicate [ˈvindikeit] *vt.* 维护，证明…无辜，证明…正确

背景知识注释
Background Notes

1. Fort Sumter　萨姆特要塞。1861年4月12日，南部联盟军队炮击并于14日占领了联邦军的萨姆特要塞，挑起了内战(1861～1865)，这是南部联盟从联邦那里夺取的第一个海港要塞。
2. Judas　犹大，《圣经》人物，耶稣十二门徒之一，又称“加略人犹大”。据《新约》载，犹大生于加略，皈依耶稣后为其掌管钱财。后为30块银元将耶稣出卖。耶稣被钉死后，犹大因悔恨而自杀。以后犹大成了叛变者的代名词。
3. Scott　即Winfield Scott 温菲尔德•斯科特(1786～1866年)，美国陆军中将，美墨战争名将，美国历史上任期最长的军队统帅。指挥美军击败墨西哥，为美国夺得大片领土；并在内战初期制定了击溃南方的战略计划。
4. Capitol rotunda　国会大厦圆形大厅。

中文译文
Suggested Translation

1 在美国前总统中，布坎南可谓是独树一帜，他的退休生活并不愉快和光彩。他同情南部已是众人皆知，以至于使人轻信了共和党人的荒谬指责：无论如何，他都要对萨姆特堡的

沦陷以及战争本身负责。商店展出的钞票勾勒出了一幅红眼的布坎南的图像，脖子上套着绳索，额头上写着“犹大”这个词。林肯许多有关7月4日战争的消息都是从斯科特将军的一个不准确的报告中来的，不公平地进一步破坏了布坎南的声誉。参议院谴责布坎南的决议虽然未通过，但却得到了广泛的宣传。报纸指责他由于未能事先加固要塞，从而未能阻止分裂和战争；指责他曾与敌人谈判达成和解；指责他施压斯科特将军派遣“西部之星号”船，而不是“布鲁克林号”船；指责他曾否决了斯科特提出巩固萨姆特要塞的提议；指责他将舰队分散于世界各地，并曾试图武装南部。布坎南最亲近的前内阁官员可能已经开始以真实的记录来支援他，但是他们其中五位已接受了林肯政府的职位，其余的也被负面的公众舆论所吓倒，谁也不愿开口为他辩护。一连数天，报纸宣布：他在英格兰兜售南部联盟的债券；他在宾夕法尼亚州与间谍密谋。他的肖像被从国会大厦圆形大厅取下，以防外观损伤。他甚至被指控从白宫偷窃画像并保留了一个日本代表团所带来的礼物。

2 起初，这些攻击使他难受至极，但他很快就恢复过来，积极为自己辩护。他与公众交换信件，推翻了斯科特的指控，并于1866年完成了他的回忆录，该书批驳了对他渎职的指控，展示了那些指控者的虚伪，恢复了他内心的宁静。它还将内战的起因主要归咎于北方激进主义，并昭示了他总统任期的最大弱点——他与南方具有彻底的情感认同，他无法理解和处理北部公众对地区分离问题的看法。詹姆斯•布坎南于1868年6月1日去世，无怨无悔并始终坚信他将彪炳千秋。

16 Abraham Lincoln's Sense of Humor 幽默的亚伯拉罕·林肯

亚伯拉罕·林肯 总统及第一夫人简介

亚伯拉罕•林肯 (Abraham Lincoln, 1809.2.12～1865.4.15)，第16任美国总统(1861～1865)，美国政治家，也是首位共和党籍总统。在其总统任内，美国爆发了内战，史称“南北战争”。林肯击败了南方分离势力，发布了《解放奴隶宣言》(*Emancipation Proclamation*)，废除了奴隶制度，维护了国家的统一。但就在内战结束后不久，林肯不幸遇刺身亡。他是第一位遭到刺杀的美国总统，更是一位出身贫寒的伟大总统。在美国于2005年举办的在线票选活动《最伟大的美国人》中，林肯被选为美国历史上第二位最伟大的人物。

玛丽•托德•林肯(Mary Todd Lincoln, 1818.12.13～1882.7.16)是第16任美国总统亚伯拉罕•林肯的妻子，出生于肯塔基州莱克星敦市。其父是一位银行家，其母出生名门望族。女子时期，玛丽接受了良好的教育。1841年与林肯结婚，育有四个儿子。由于出身于美国南方，在内战中她的处境非常艰难。作为女主人，她优雅的表现最初获得称赞，但后来因购买衣服及白宫的家具铺张浪费而被批。她亲眼目睹了1865年林肯总统被枪杀，这已超出其所能承受之极限。她在第三个儿子死后精神崩溃。她于1882年去世，并安葬于斯普林菲尔德市橡树林公墓，林肯的墓旁。

经典原文
Original Text

Words & Expressions

business card 名片，商务名片

swap [swɔp] *vt.* 与…交换，以…作交换

dispense [dis'pens] *vt.* 执行，分配，分发，免除

mosquito [mə'skiːtəu] *n.* 蚊子

break the ice 破冰，打破沉默，打破僵局

1 Lincoln is best known for his policies on abolishing slavery and his belief in self-government; he took his job as president very seriously. About the night he knew he'd won the election he later said, "I went home, but not to get much sleep, for I then felt as I never had before, the responsibility that was upon me."

2 Lincoln had another side to his personality; he had a good sense of humor and liked to make jokes. Here you can see Lincoln's "business card," a joke that the opposing Democratic party played on him during the 1864 presidential election. The card says that Lincoln will be returning to *Springfield* [①], Illinois, to his law practice, where he will be ready to "swap horses, dispense law, make jokes, split rails, and perform other matters." As it turned out, Lincoln and the Republicans had the last laugh on this joke because he won reelection as president in 1864. What other things do you think Lincoln joked about?

3 Lincoln liked to tell tales about his experiences. After his time as a soldier in ***the Black Hawk War*** [②], Lincoln joked that he had seen no "live, fighting Indians" during the war but had "a good many bloody struggles with the mosquitoes." He knew that laughing with visitors helped break the ice and that he could tell a funny story to avoid a reporter's difficult question. His sense of humor was well-known. Here are the words to a song that was inspired by Lincoln, called "Hey! Uncle Abe, are you joking yet?" Keep in mind that it was written by members of the political party that opposed Lincoln's reelection.

背景知识注释
Background Notes

1. Springfield　斯普林菲尔德，美国伊利诺伊州首府。
2. the Black Hawk War　黑鹰战争。随着印第安人与开拓西部的新移民之间错综复杂的争斗，在伊利诺以北地区，从1832年开始就爆发了“黑鹰战争”。印第安酋长“黑鹰”英勇机智，神出鬼没地打击美军，造成美军伤亡惨重。最终“黑鹰”战败被俘，但他却成了美国的英雄人物。一种先进的武装直升机就以“黑鹰”的名字命名。他的战术与毛泽东的游击战一并列入西点军校的必修课。

中文译文
Suggested Translation

1 林肯最为外人所知的是他的废奴政策及对自治的信念。他严肃地看待他的总统一职。在得知他当选总统的当天夜晚，他说：“我回到家，但却无法安然入睡，因为我感受到前所未有的责任正压在肩头。”

2 林肯的个性中也有不为人所知的一面——他幽默感十足而且喜欢开玩笑。此处有一张林肯本人的“名片”(business card)，上面就印有源自于1864年的总统选举对手民主党对他开的玩笑。名片上说林肯将会回到伊利诺伊州的斯普林菲尔德市(Springfield)，继续他的律师职业，他总是乐于“交换马匹、操律师业、开开玩笑、劈劈横木及完成其他的工作”。结果，真正笑出来的人是林肯及其共和党人，因为他们赢得了1864年的总统连任。您猜猜林肯还对哪些事情开过玩笑呢？

3 林肯喜欢谈论他的生活经历。林肯退出“黑鹰”战争结束军人的身份后，总是开玩笑说：战争期间，他从未见过任何“活生生的印第安士兵”，但倒是“跟蚊子有过不少的血战。”他知道这个笑话会打破他与访客之间的僵局，而且他可以利用有趣的故事来回避记者的刁难提问。他的幽默感遐迩闻名，以下的歌词灵感就是源自于林肯，歌名为“嘿！亚伯大叔，您开玩笑了没？”(Hey! Uncle Abe, are you joking yet?) 请注意，这是林肯竞选连任总统时，他的对手政党成员所写的歌词！

17 President Andrew Johnson Impeached
安德鲁·约翰逊总统遭弹劾

安德鲁·约翰逊 总统及第一夫人简介

安德鲁·约翰逊 (Andrew Johnson, 1808.12.29～1875.7.31)，第17任美国总统(1865～1869)。幼时家境贫寒，当过徒工，后来做过裁缝。1857 年当选为国会参议员，是南北战争时期参议院里受到北方欢迎和林肯总统信任的唯一的南方人。1864年大选时当选为美国16任副总统。在亚伯拉罕·林肯遇刺身亡后，继任为总统。他在南方重建问题上采取妥协立场(他曾两次担任田纳西州州长)，与国会的共和党议员意见不合，这使他成为美国历史上首位被提出弹劾议案的总统(1868年)，但最终在参议院以一票之微避过被罢免的命运。尽管如此，他任期内依然有一定政绩，其中包括《美国宪法》第14条修正案的通过和阿拉斯加的收购。

伊莱扎·麦卡德尔·约翰逊(Eliza McCardle Johnson, 1810.10.4～1876.1.15)是第17任美国总统安德鲁·约翰逊的妻子。1827年5月17日，18岁的约翰逊在田纳西州的格林维尔迎娶了16岁的伊莱扎·麦卡德尔。他是美国总统中结婚最早的一位，婚后，生有三子两女。约翰逊没有受过正规教育，但是却野心勃勃，他的妻子发现丈夫对政治很感兴趣，傍晚，就教他读书写字，并帮助他阅读有关政治情况和政治事务的报道以及著名人物的重要演说，鼓励他参加政治辩论、发表演说。在妻子的鼎力支持下，约翰逊开始积极投入社会活动，他的政治生涯就是从格林维尔开始的。

经典原文
Original Text

1 The U.S. House of Representatives votes 11 articles of impeachment against President Andrew Johnson, nine of which cite Johnson's removal of Secretary of War Edwin M. Stanton, a violation of the *Tenure of Office Act*①. The House vote made President Johnson the first president to be impeached in U.S. history.

2 At the outbreak of the Civil War in 1861, Andrew Johnson, a senator from Tennessee, was the only U.S. senator from a seceding state who remained loyal to the Union. In 1862, President Abraham Lincoln appointed him military governor of Tennessee, and in 1864 he was elected vice president of the United States. Sworn in as president after Lincoln's assassination in April 1865, President Johnson enacted a lenient *Reconstruction*② policy for the defeated South, including almost total amnesty to *ex-Confederates*③, a program of rapid restoration of U.S.-state status for the seceded states, and the approval of new, local Southern governments, which were able to legislate "Black Codes" that preserved the system of slavery in all but its name.

3 The Republican-dominated Congress greatly opposed Johnson's Reconstruction program and in March 1867 passed the *Tenure of Office Act* over the president's veto. The bill prohibited the president from removing officials confirmed by the Senate without senatorial approval and was designed to shield members of Johnson's Cabinet like Secretary of War Edwin M. Stanton, who had been a

Words & Expressions

impeachment [imˈpiːtʃmənt] *n.* 弹劾，控告，怀疑，指责

assassination [əˌsæsiˈneiʃən] *n.* 暗杀，行刺

lenient [ˈliːnjənt] *adj.* 宽大的，仁慈的

amnesty [ˈæmnisti] *n.* 大赦，特赦

legislate [ˈledʒisleit] *vt.* 用立法规定，通过立法

shield [ʃiːld] *vt.* 遮蔽，避开，保护

leading Republican radical in the Lincoln administration. In the fall of 1867, President Johnson attempted to test the constitutionality of the act by replacing Stanton with General Ulysses S. Grant. However, *the U.S. Supreme Court*④ refused to rule on the case, and Grant turned the office back to Stanton after the Senate passed a measure in protest of the dismissal.

4 On February 21, 1868, Johnson decided to rid himself of Stanton once and for all and appointed General Lorenzo Thomas, an individual far less favorable to the Congress than Grant, as secretary of war. Stanton refused to yield, barricading himself in his office, and the House of Representatives, which had already discussed impeachment after Johnson's first dismissal of Stanton, initiated formal impeachment proceedings against the president. On February 24, Johnson was impeached, and on March 13 his impeachment trial began in the Senate under the direction of U.S. Supreme Court *Chief Justice*⑤ Salmon P. Chase. The trial ended on May 26 with Johnson's opponents narrowly failing to achieve the two-thirds majority necessary to convict him.

constitutionality [ˌkɔnstiˌtjuːʃəˈnæliti] *n.* 符合宪法，立宪

rid oneself of 摆脱，戒除，使自己免除…

once and for all 一劳永逸地，彻底地，最后一次

barricade [ˌbæriˈkeid] *vt.* 设路障，阻碍

initiate [iˈniʃieit] *vt.* 开始，创始，发起

proceeding [prəˈsiːdiŋ] *n.* 进行，程序，诉讼，事项

convict [kənˈvikt] *vt.* 证明…有罪，宣告…有罪

背景知识注释
Background Notes

1. *Tenure of Office Act* 《任职期限法》，1867 年 3 月 2 日由美国国会通过，禁止总统在没有得到参议院同意的情况之下，开除任何政府官员，总统自己的内阁成员也包括在内。

2. Reconstruction 重建纲领，重建时期。它是美国内战结束后对南部社会政治、经济和社会生活的改造与重建时期的通称。其历史任务是用政治和立法手段巩固和扩大内战成果，在南部各叛乱州重新建立忠于联邦的州政权，恢复南部各州同联邦的正常关系，重建并巩固联邦的统一。林肯早在1863年12月 8日就在《大赦与重建宣言》中提出宽大和解的重建纲领，并于1864年春到1865年春之间，在路易斯安那、弗吉尼亚、阿肯色和田纳西4个州开始付诸实施。

3. ex-Confederates （美国内战时期）前支持南部联盟的人。

4. the U.S. Supreme Court 美国最高法院。

5. Chief Justice （美国）首席法官；法院院长；审判长。

中文译文
Suggested Translation

1 美国众议院就针对安德鲁•约翰逊总统的11项弹劾指控进行投票，其中9项都提出约翰逊罢免战争部长埃德温•M•斯坦顿 (Edwin M. Stanton) 违反了《任职期限法》。众议院的投票使约翰逊总统成为美国历史上第一位被提出弹劾的总统。

2 1861年内战爆发时，来自田纳西州的参议员安德鲁•约翰逊是唯一一位来自脱离联邦的州的美国参议员。他坚持效忠于联邦。1862年，亚伯拉罕•林肯总统任命他为田纳西州的军事总督。1864年，他当选为美国副总统。1865年4月，林肯总统遇刺后他宣誓就任美国总统。约翰逊总统为战败的南部颁布了一项宽大的重建纲领，包括几乎完全赦免先前支持南部联盟的人、一个为脱离联邦的各州快速恢复美国州地位的计划，批准当地的新南方政府有权通过“黑人法典”的立法，以保存除其称呼之外的整个奴隶制。

3 由共和党主导的国会强烈反对约翰逊的南方重建纲领，并于1867年3月通过了《任职期限法》推翻了总统的否决。该法案禁止总统未经参议院批准免除由参议院核准的官员的职务，旨在保护约翰逊的内阁成员，诸如战争部长埃德温•M•斯坦顿，他在林肯政府中曾是一位主要的共和党激进派。1867年秋，约翰逊总统试图通过用尤利塞斯•格兰特(Ulysses S. Grant)将军替换斯坦顿来测试该法案的合法性。然而，美国最高法院拒绝就此案进行裁决，在参议院通过了一项措施以抗议解职行为后，格兰特只得将该职位交还给斯坦顿。

4 1868年2月21日，约翰逊决定要一劳永逸地摆脱斯坦顿，任命了洛伦佐•托马斯(Lorenzo Thomas)将军作为战争部长，托马斯比起格兰特更不讨国会喜欢。斯坦顿拒绝服从，将自己关在办公室里。在约翰逊第一次罢免斯坦顿的职务后，众议院就讨论了对总统弹劾的事宜，这次众议院发起了正式弹劾总统的程序。2月24日，约翰逊被弹劾了；3月13日，对他的弹劾审讯在美国最高法院首席大法官赛蒙•P•蔡斯(Salmon P. Chase)的指导下于参议院进行。5月26日庭审结束，约翰逊的对手勉强未能达到将他定罪所必要的三分之二多数票。

18 Ulysses Simpson Grant, the War Hero
战争英雄尤利塞斯·辛普森·格兰特

尤里西斯·辛普森·格兰特 总统及第一夫人简介

尤里西斯•辛普森•格兰特 (Ulysses Simpson Grant, 1822.4.27～1885.7.13)，第18任美国总统(1869～1877)，也是美国军事家和陆军上将。他是美国历史上第一位从西点军校毕业的总统。在美国南北战争后期任联邦军总司令，1865年4月2日率部攻占南部联盟“首都”里士满，迫使南军于4月9日在阿波马托克斯投降。但能征惯战并不等于善于理政，格兰特的平平政绩与他的赫赫战功形成鲜明对照。特别是在第二次总统任期内，他对南方奴隶主的妥协让步和对贪污腐化的属员姑息纵容，这引起了选民的普遍不满。格兰特卸职后曾周游世界，并想在政治上东山再起，但未能如愿。他晚年经商失败，抑郁病逝。他著有《U•S•格兰特的个人回忆录》。

朱莉亚•登特•格兰特(Julia Dent Grant, 1826.1. 26～1902.12.14)是第18任美国总统尤里西斯•辛普森•格兰特的妻子。朱莉亚是格兰特在西点军校一位同学的妹妹， 1848 年8 月格兰特在家乡圣路易斯迎娶朱莉亚。婚后朱莉亚随军生活，生有三子一女，她用温柔来支持丈夫上战场。墨西哥战争结束后，格兰特随部队回国，1854年8月格兰特辞去军职后与家人团聚。南北战争爆发后，希望丈夫成名的朱莉亚认为格兰特应回到曾经为他带来光荣的军队中去，并得到了他的同意。格兰特在美国南北战争中屡建奇功。朱莉亚是第一位写回忆录的美国第一夫人，但她的回忆录直到1975年才出版，而她于1902年就去世了，享年76岁。

经典原文 Original Text

1 One of the most honored and respected military leaders in U.S. history never even wanted a military career. Despite that, he became a general and served two terms as president of the United States. Ulysses Simpson Grant, born on April 27, 1822, in Point Pleasant, Ohio, wrote, "A military life had no charms for me, and I had not the faintest idea of staying in the army even if I should be graduated, which I did not expect." However, Grant did graduate from *the U.S. Military Academy at West Point*① in 1843 and later began leading soldiers in battle.

2 The quiet, unassuming, and keenly intelligent Grant suddenly found himself on the battlefields of the Mexican War (1846 — 1848), a conflict he personally opposed but fought with great bravery. (During *the Mexican War*②, the U.S. fought its neighbor to the south over disputed Texan land.) After the war, he returned home to wed his longtime fiancée, Julia Dent, but the couple only had four years together before Grant was transferred. Even the promotion did not relieve Grant's longing for his family and boredom with army routine. The 32-year-old captain resigned his commission in 1854.

3 After failed business ventures, Grant returned to the army in 1861. Within months, he was promoted to brigadier general and placed in charge of 20,000 Union troops, which he led to many victories during the Civil War. Grant commanded larger and larger armies as the war

Words & Expressions

faint [ˈfeint] *adj.* 模糊的，头晕的，虚弱的，衰弱的

unassuming [ˌʌnəˈsjuːmiŋ] *adj.* 谦逊的，不装腔作势的，不出风头的

keenly [ˈkiːnli] *adv.* 敏锐地，强烈地，锐利地

fiancée [ˈfiːɑːnsei] *n.* 未婚妻

transfer [trænsˈfəː] *vi.* 转让，调任，转移，转学

relieve [riˈliːv] *vt.* 解除，减轻，解围，使放心

venture [ˈventʃə] *n.* 企业，风险，冒险

went on and, by 1864, he commanded the whole U.S. army as general-in-chief. Just as he had drifted into the military, Grant drifted into politics. He easily won the presidential elections of 1868 and 1872. In 1884, the war hero, diagnosed with cancer, managed to write one of the finest military autobiographies ever written. It was published by his friend, *Mark Twain*③. Ask your family if they have ever read the memoirs of Ulysses Simpson Grant.

autobiography [ˌɔːtəubaiˈɔgrəfi] *n.* 自传，自传文学

背景知识注释
Background Notes

1. the U.S. Military Academy at West Point 美国西点军校，是美国第一所军事学校，创建于1802年3月16日，从该军事学校毕业的学生将获得理学学士，毕业后的军衔是陆军少尉。毕业生必须在军队中至少服役5年和3年的后备役。西点军校的校训是“责任、荣誉、国家”，它是美国历史最悠久的军事学院之一。它曾与英国桑赫斯特皇家军事学院、俄罗斯伏龙芝军事学院以及法国圣西尔军事专科学校并称世界“四大军校”。
2. the Mexican War 墨西哥战争，1846年～1848年墨西哥抗击美国入侵的战争，亦称美墨战争。美国扩张主义者力图侵占墨西哥北部领土(从东至西包括得克萨斯、新墨西哥和加利福尼亚)，逐步建立美洲霸权。1835年美国策动得克萨斯美籍种植园主叛乱，1836年建立美国傀儡政权“孤星国”，1845年美政府正式将得克萨斯并入美国。同年美国还策动加利福尼亚美籍移民举行暴乱。1846年春，美军进一步侵入墨西哥境内，迫使墨方起而应战，然后把战争责任加诸于对方，同年5月13日正式对墨西哥宣战。墨西哥进行的是正义战争，但缺乏强有力的中央政府的领导，中央和地方统治集团的某些人进行叛卖活动，加上军事上采取消极防御战略，不支持人民群众的武装斗争，因而招致失败，墨西哥丧失北部半壁河山。
3. Mark Twain 马克·吐温，(1835.11.30～1910.4.21)，原名塞姆·朗赫恩·克列门斯(Samuel Langhorne Clemens)，是美国幽默大师、小说家、作家和著名演说家，是19世纪后期美国现实主义文学的杰出代表，他以其幽默和机智而闻名于世。40年的创作生涯中，他写出了10多部长篇小说、几十部短篇小说及其他体裁的大量作品，其中著名的有短篇小说《竞选州长》、《哥尔斯密的朋友再度出洋》和《百万英镑》等，长篇小说《镀金时代》、《汤姆·索亚历险记》、《王子与贫儿》等。《哈克贝利·费恩历险记》是他最优秀的作品，曾被美国小说家海明威誉为是“第一部”真正的“美国文学”。

中文译文
Suggested Translation

1 虽然身为美国历史上获得最多荣耀也最受人尊敬的军事领袖之一，他却从未想过要把军旅生涯作为终生职业；尽管如此，他还是成了一名将军，并且还是两届美国总统。尤利赛斯·格兰特 1822 年 4 月 27 日出生在俄亥俄州的快乐镇 (Point Pleasant) 。他曾写道："军旅生涯对我一点吸引力也没有。就算是我毕业了，也一点都没有要永远留在军队里的想法。" 可是，格兰特在 1843 年真的从西点军校 (West Point) 毕业了，后来还在战场上带兵作战。

2 格兰特是一个缄默、谦卑、热心且聪慧的人，他投入到了墨西哥的战争中 (Mexican War, 1846～1848) ，他个人虽然反对这场战争，但是他在战场上却表现出了无比的勇气。 (在墨西哥战争中，美国为了得到得克萨斯有争议的领土，不惜与其南部的邻国发生冲突。) 战后，格兰特回到家乡迎娶等待他许久的未婚妻朱莉亚•登特(Julia Dent) 。然而他们只一起相处了四年，就因为格兰特的军事移防而必须分隔两地。虽然得到晋升，但是却无法抚平格兰特对家人的思念或者消减他对军队生活的厌烦。于是这个年仅32岁的上尉在1854年提出了辞呈。

3 不过，当格兰特经商失败后，他在1861年又回到了军队。几个月内，他就被晋升为准将，并领导一支两万人的美国军队，在内战 (Civil War) 期间打了许多胜仗。战争一直持续着，而格兰特所率领的军队人数也越来越多，到了1864年，格兰特成为统领全国军队的总指挥官。如同他进入军队一样，格兰特后来也进入了政坛。他轻易地赢得了1868年与1872年的总统大选。到了1884年，这位战争英雄被诊断得了癌症。他开始着手撰写有史以来最好的军人自传。他的自传后来由他的朋友马克•吐温 (Mark Twain) 出版。你可以问问你的家人，看他们有没有读过格兰特的自传。

19 Rutherford Birchard Hayes' Firsts 拉瑟福德·伯查德·海斯总统的数个“第一”经历

拉瑟福德·伯查德·海斯 总统及第一夫人简介

拉瑟福德·伯查德·海斯 (Rutherford Birchard Hayes, 1822.10.4 ～ 1893.1.17)，第19任美国总统（1877 ～ 1881），生于俄亥俄州。南北战争时期，因军功屡次晋升，直至志愿军少将。战后开始政治生涯。两度当选国会议员，三度出任俄亥俄州州长，以“为人正直和办事有效率”著称。1876年大选中，因发生了美国历史上最大一次选票计算纠纷，海斯直至总统就职日前两天才被宣布为合法总统。海斯就任总统后，努力改善内战后国内状况，取得了一些成就。他保证黑人在南方的权利，在打破“政党分肥”、实行文官制方面做了一些有益工作，开了文官公开考试、择优录取之先河。海斯任期内，美国科技有了飞速发展；在外交方面也有些成就，值得一提的是，他采取了对华友好的政策。海斯是第一个接见中国常驻使节的总统。

露西·韦尔·韦伯·海斯(Lucy Ware Webb Hayes, 1831.8.28～1889.6.25)是第19任美国总统拉瑟福德·伯查德·海斯的妻子。他们于1852年结婚，生有七子一女。露西这位美丽的第一夫人于1877年随丈夫进入白宫,很快便以出色的女主人和丈夫的政治伙伴的形象出现在公众面前。由于露西喜欢孩子、小动物和音乐，没有种族偏见，白宫很快便成了一个充满趣味、积极向上的世界。作为第一位拥有大学学历的第一夫人，露西有着强烈的平等意识，其政治观念较海斯总统进步得多。露西改变了海斯的观点，她甚至最终说服他站在那些逃亡奴隶的立场上，为他们说话，这在当时已是十分难得。不仅如此，露西还对妇女选举权十分感兴趣，并呼吁改善妇女的生活环境。为了赞美和接近大自然，露西还与海斯总统一起广泛游历了整个国家，期间被新闻界称之为“国家的第一夫人”，据说这是“第一夫人”这一称呼被首次使用。尽管只在白宫停留了四年，但露西对第一夫人们的影响是深远的。1889年6月25日，全美各地降半旗纪念去世的“美国妇女偶像”——露西•韦尔•韦伯•海斯。

经典原文 Original Text

1 On the night of the 1876 presidential election, Republican candidate Rutherford Birchard Hayes went to bed early. He assumed that he had lost the election to his opponent, Democrat Samuel J. Tilden. Tilden did win the *popular vote*① that night, but the Republicans challenged the validity of the *electoral votes*② from three states. (Under the *Electoral College*③, each state chooses electors to vote for the president.) A candidate must win the electoral vote to become President.

2 Congress appointed a special *Electoral Commission*④ to make a decision on the matter. The commission was made up of five senators, five members of the House of Representatives, and five Supreme Court justices. In the end, the commission determined that Hayes was elected president by a margin of one electoral vote. Because of the tension surrounding his election, Hayes's first official duty was done in secret.

3 Hayes' first duty was to take the oath of office, which he did secretly in the *Red Room*⑤ of the White House, becoming the first president to be sworn in there.

4 Rutherford Birchard Hayes was born on October 4, 1822. The Civil War had been over for 12 years by the time

Words & Expressions

validity [vəˈlidəti] *n.* 有效性，正确，正确性

electoral [iˈlektərəl] *adj.* 选举的，选举人的

senators [ˈsenətə] *n.* 参议员

margin [ˈmɑːdʒin] *n.* 边缘，余裕，页边的空白

Hayes became president in 1877. Once in office, Hayes withdrew all remaining federal troops from the South and designated funds for improvements in the war-torn South. Surprising many, President Hayes also signed the bill that allowed women attorneys to appear for the first time before the U.S. Supreme Court. At least two other "firsts" occurred at the White House while Hayes was president.

designate [ˈdezigneit] *vt.* 指定，指派，标出，把…定名为

attorney [əˈtə:ni] *n.* 律师，代理人

5 Hayes was the first president to host the "*Easter Egg Roll*⑥" for children on the White House lawn. The original site was on the grounds of the United States Capitol. Congress ended the tradition after a particularly active "Easter Egg Roll" in 1876. At the request of several children, President Hayes brought the event to the White House in 1878.

6 In 1879, the first telephone was installed in the White House. President Hayes did not use it very often, however, because there were not many other telephones in Washington.

7 Hayes spent his retirement working toward prison reform and creating educational opportunities for Southern black youth. He died in 1893 at his home in Fremont, Ohio.

背景知识注释
Background Notes

1. popular vote　普选（票）；直接投票，美国总统选举先由党派内部选举确定其总统候选人，然后由每个州的选民分别进行——普选 (popular vote)，直接选出总统选举团 (electoral college)，并将普选票投给支持的总统候选人。然后，在每个州普选获胜的候选人将在之后正式的总统大选中获得该州的全部选票（每个州的选票数量等于是该州众议员和参议员的人数）。而正式的总统大选只是一个仪式，由总统选举团根据普选的结果进行——总统选举团投票 (electoral vote)，也就是说大选结果在普选的统计阶段已经知道。但是值得注意的是获得普选票数多的获选人不一定赢得的总统选举团票数多（即不一定成为总统）。如 A 州的普选结果是 X 党：600，Y 党：

601，该州的总统选举团票数是6；B州的普选结果是X党：700，Y党：701，该州的总统选举团票数是7；C州的普选结果是X党：450，Y党：400，该州的总统选举团票数是4；所以普选的结果是X党1750，Y党1702，而总统选举团投票结果是X党4，Y党13，最终决定总统人选的是总统选举团投票的结果。换言之，总统选举是选民的间接选举结果，总统选举团是选民的直接选举结果。

2. electoral vote　选举人票。

3. Electoral College　总统选举团(由美国各州选举人选出的538名选举人组成的选举团履行选举总统和副总统职责)。

4. Electoral Commission　选举委员会。

5. Red Room　红厅。美国白宫一层主要有五大房间，由西至东依序是：国宴厅、红厅、蓝厅、绿厅和东厅。其中，红厅是第一夫人们最喜爱的房间，多用于总统夫人招待来宾，该室仍按照早期形式布置，摆设在大理石壁炉上的一座法式音乐钟，是法国总统1952年赠送的。

6. Easter Egg Roll　复活节滚彩蛋比赛，复活节滚彩蛋是一项在复活节举行的传统活动。在美国，复活节滚彩蛋是一项一年一度的大事，每年复活节都在白宫的草坪上为儿童及其父母举行。这个活动在不同国家有不同的形式，通常用煮熟和装饰过的鸡蛋。

中文译文
Suggested Translation

1 在1876年总统选举的那一晚，共和党候选人拉瑟福德•伯查德•海斯很早就上床睡觉了。他觉得他输给了对手，也就是民主党的萨慕尔•提登 (Samuel J. Tilden)。那晚，提登的确赢得普选胜利，但是共和党却质疑有三个州的选举人票无效。(根据选举人团的规定，每一个州选择自己的选举人来投票选举总统，总统候选人必须赢得选举人票才能成为总统。)

2 国会因此指派一个特别“选举委员会”，针对这项争议做出裁决。委员会的成员包括5位参议员、5位众议员以及5位最高法院法官。最后，委员会决议海斯以多出一张选举人票的优势赢得了总统大选。因为选举期间的紧张气氛，海斯的第一项官方任务是秘密完成的。

3 海斯的第一项任务就是宣誓就职，他在白宫的“红厅” (Red Room) 里秘密完成了这项工作，成为在此宣誓就职的第一位总统。

4 拉瑟福德•伯查德•海斯生于1822年10月4日。到海斯于1877年就任总统时，内战已经结束达12年之久。在任内，海斯下令将驻扎在南方各州的联邦军队全部撤除，并且拨款协助重建因战火受创的南方各州。让人惊讶的是，海斯总统还签署了法案，首次允许女性律师在美国最高法院前出庭。海斯总统在位时，白宫至少还发生了另外两个“第一次”的经历。

5 海斯是第一位在白宫草坪上举办儿童“复活节滚彩蛋比赛”(Easter Egg Roll) 的总统。最初的举办场地是在美国国会大厦的草坪上。因为1876年的比赛过于激烈，国会于是停止了这项传统活动。在一些孩子们的要求下，海斯总统在1878年于白宫举办了这项赛事。

6 白宫在1879年安装了第一部电话机。然而，海斯总统并没有经常使用电话，因为华盛顿当地并没有太多人拥有电话。

7 海斯退休之后致力于监狱改革和为南方黑人青年创造更多教育机会。他于1893年在俄亥俄州佛瑞蒙 (Fremont) 的家中去世。

20 Assassination of James Abram Garfield 詹姆斯·艾伯拉姆·加菲尔德总统惨遭暗杀

詹姆斯·艾伯拉姆·加菲尔德 总统及第一夫人简介

詹姆斯•艾伯拉姆•加菲尔德 (James Abram Garfield, 1831.11.19～1881.9.19)，第20任美国总统(1881～1881)，美国政治家、数学家，共和党人，生于俄亥俄州。南北战争期间加入北方军队，与南方奴隶制军队作战，拥有少将军衔。他担任过基督会的长老，是美国首位具有神职人员身份的总统。他的任期正处于从政党分肥制到文官制的过渡时期，他在上任半年后被一名谋官未成者暗杀而死，成为继林肯之后第二位被暗杀的美国总统。他也是美国历史上唯一一位数学家出身的总统，在数学方面的贡献主要是在勾股定理的证明方面。

卢克丽霞·鲁道夫·加菲尔德 (Lucretia Rudolph Garfield, 1832.4.19 ～ 1918.3.14) 是第 20 任美国总统詹姆斯·艾伯拉姆·加菲尔德的妻子。卢克丽霞是一位农场主的女儿，与加菲尔德同龄。两人是中学同学，中学毕业后加菲尔德继续上大学，卢克丽霞去教书。加菲尔德本来打算一毕业就结婚，后来觉得应该多挣点钱再结婚，于是两人于 1858 年 11 月 11 日结婚，共生有五子二女。成为第一夫人后，卢克丽霞很想大有可为一番，可是她很快就患上了疟疾，在海滨养病时她得知总统遇刺，就赶紧坐火车回来，中途还差点出了车祸。加菲尔德和死神搏斗了将近三个月，全美人民也一直关心他的生死。在他去世后，美国人为卢克丽霞募捐了35万美元，这足够她安度晚年。她守寡36年，于1918年去世。

经典原文
Original Text

Words & Expressions

be scheduled to 预定，预期，计划做

alma mater [ˈælməˈmaːtə] (拉丁语)母校，校歌

bodyguard [ˈbɔdigaːd] *n.* 保镖

at point-blank range 以近距离平射射程，近距离地

fling [fliŋ] *vt.* 掷，抛，嘲笑，使陷入，猛动

graze [greiz] *vt.* 放牧，擦伤

lumbar vertebra 腰椎

spinal cord 脊髓

pancreas [ˈpænkriəs] *n.* 胰腺

pistol [ˈpistl] *n.* 手枪

cab [kæb] *n.* 驾驶室，出租马车，出租汽车

apprehend [ˌæpriˈhend] *vt.* 理解，逮捕，忧虑

1 Garfield was scheduled to leave Washington on July 2, 1881 for his summer vacation. On that day, *Guiteau*[①] lay in wait for the President at the Baltimore and Potomac Railroad station, on the southwest corner of present day Sixth Street and Constitution Avenue NW, Washington, D.C..

2 President Garfield came to the Sixth Street Station on his way to his alma mater, *Williams College*[②], where he was scheduled to deliver a speech. Garfield was accompanied by two of his sons, James and Harry, and Secretary of State Blaine. Secretary of War Robert Todd Lincoln waited at the station to see the President off. Garfield had no bodyguard or security detail; with the exception of Abraham Lincoln during the Civil War, early U.S. presidents never used any guards.

3 As President Garfield entered the waiting room of the station Guiteau stepped forward and pulled the trigger from behind at point-blank range. "My God, what is that?" Garfield cried out, flinging up his arms. Guiteau fired again and Garfield collapsed. One bullet grazed Garfield's shoulder; the other hit him in the back, passing the first lumbar vertebra but missing the spinal cord before coming to rest behind his pancreas.

4 Guiteau put his pistol back in his pocket and turned to leave the station for the cab he had waiting outside, but he was apprehended before he could leave by policeman Patrick Kearney, who was so excited at having arrested

the man who shot the president that he neglected to take Guiteau's gun from him until after their arrival at the police station. The rapidly gathering crowd screamed "Lynch him!" but Kearney took Guiteau to the police station a few blocks away. As he surrendered to authorities, Guiteau uttered the exulting words, repeated everywhere: "I am a stalwart of the Stalwarts! I did it and I want to be arrested! *Arthur*[3] is President now!" This statement briefly led to unfounded suspicions that Arthur or his supporters had put Guiteau up to the crime. The Stalwarts were a Republican faction loyal to ex-President Grant; they strongly opposed Garfield's *Half-Breeds*[4]. Like many Vice Presidents, Arthur was chosen for political advantage, to placate his faction, rather than for skills or loyalty to his running-mate. Guiteau, in his delusion, had convinced himself that he was striking a blow to unite the two factions of the Republican Party.

lynch [lintʃ] *vt.* 处以私刑，以私刑处死

utter [ˈʌtə] *v.* 说；出版；发出声音

exult [igˈzʌlt] *vi.* 狂喜，欢欣鼓舞，非常高兴

stalwart [ˈstɔːlwət] *n.* 坚定分子，忠实拥护者

placate [pləˈkeit] *vt.* 抚慰，怀柔，使和解

running-mate 竞选伙伴

delusion [diˈluːʒən] *n.* 迷惑，欺骗，错觉，幻想

背景知识注释
Background Notes

1. Guiteau　即Charles Guiteau 查尔斯•吉托，是一位谋官未成、有长久心智疾病病史的律师，他在1881年7月2日朝加菲尔德总统的背部开枪，他认为是上帝叫他射杀总统的。他痴迷于一个想法：如果他杀了加菲尔德，共和党就会重新团结起来，感恩的共和党人将会因为他的功劳而奖励他一个行政职务！

2. Williams College　威廉姆斯学院，创建于1793年，位于马萨诸塞州的西北角，与波士顿和纽约在地理上呈三角关系，其中距波士顿135英里，距纽约165英里。威廉姆斯学院是美国最有名的文理学院之一，一直被《美国新闻与世界报道》评为最佳文理学院的前三名，学术声望排名连年位于全美文理学院第一。

3. Arthur　亚瑟，这里指的是第21任美国总统切斯特•艾伦•阿瑟(Chester Alan Arthur)。

4. half-breed　混血儿，混合派，这里指的是19世纪末期美国共和党中的一个派系。混合派为温和派，赞成行政部门改革，其代表人是缅因州参议员詹姆斯•G•布莱恩(James G. Blaine)，他们与共和党的另一个派系——中坚派(the Stalwarts) ——相对立，中坚派为保守派。

中文译文
Suggested Translation

1 加菲尔德总统原定于1881年7月2日离开华盛顿去度暑假。那天，刺客吉托 (Guiteau) 躺在巴尔的摩波拖马可火车站等候着总统，该火车站在今天华盛顿特区的第六街与西北宪法大街交界处的西南角。

2 加菲尔德总统来到第六街车站，正准备前往他的母校——威廉姆斯学院，他原定在那里发表演讲。陪同加菲尔德前往的还有他的两个儿子——詹姆斯和哈利(James and Harry)，以及国务卿布莱恩(Blaine)。战争部长罗伯特•托德•林肯(Robert Todd Lincoln)在车站等着给总统送行。加菲尔德未带保镖，也未布置安全细节；除了内战期间的亚伯拉罕•林肯之外，早期的美国总统从未使用过任何警卫。

3 当加菲尔德总统进入车站的候车室时，吉托走上前去，对着总统的背后近距离地扣动了扳机。“我的天啊，这是怎么回事?”加菲尔德喊道，他猛地举起了双臂。吉托再次扣动扳机，加菲尔德倒了下去。一颗子弹擦过加菲尔德的肩膀，一颗击中了他的背部，穿过了第一腰椎，但未伤着脊髓，停在了胰腺跟前。

4 吉托将手枪放回口袋，然后转身离开车站，走向一直在外面等候他的出租马车，但他还未来得及离开就被警察帕特里克·科尔尼 (Patrick Kearney) 给逮住了。科尔尼抓住了开枪射杀总统的刺客后非常激动，以至于直到抵达警察局后他才想到要收缴吉托的枪。迅速聚拢过来的人群大声喊道：“处死他！”但科尔尼把吉托带到了数个街区之外的警察局。当吉托向当局投降时，他异常兴奋地重复着一句话：“我是一个坚定的中坚派！我做到了，你们逮捕我吧！现在亚瑟 (Arthur) 是总统了！”这一声明直接导致了人们毫无根据地怀疑亚瑟或他的支持者们指使吉托犯下如此罪行。中坚分子是指共和党内部忠于前总统格兰特的一个派别；他们强烈反对加菲尔德的混合派。正如许多副总统一样，由于政治上的优势而不是具有技巧或忠诚于他的竞选伙伴，亚瑟被选为总统以安抚他的党派。吉托在幻觉中说服了自己：他之所以进行谋杀就是想要使共和党中的两派能携起手来。

21 The Trajectory of Chester Alan Arthur's Life
切斯特·艾伦·亚瑟总统的人生轨迹

切斯特·艾伦·亚瑟 总统及第一夫人简介

切斯特·艾伦·亚瑟 (Chester Alan Arthur, 1829.10.5 ~ 1886.11.18)，第 21 任美国总统 (1881 ~ 1885)。他是威廉·阿瑟和马尔维娜·斯通·阿瑟的八个孩子中的第五个，原为詹姆斯·加菲尔德的副总统。1881 年 7 月 2 日总统詹姆斯·加菲尔德遇刺，于 9 月 19 日离世后，他随即接任为总统。亚瑟就职后采取了超党派的态度，他签署了《排华法案》和《文官改革法》，前者令他饱受争议，后者则令他备受赞誉。亚瑟还十分重视海军建设，使海军有了较大的发展。他执政三年多，推行了一些"开明"政策，如废除了"分赃制度"，实施量才录用的文官制度，签署反对一夫多妻法案，但他在党内威望不高，未能再次被提名为总统候选人。阿瑟任满后重操律师业务，但百病缠身，不到一年便在纽约去世。

埃伦·刘易斯·赫恩登·亚瑟 (Ellen Lewis Herndon Arthur, 1837.8.30 ~ 1880.1.12) 是第 21 任美国总统切斯特·艾伦·亚瑟的妻子。两人于 1859 年 10 月 25 日结婚，生有两子一女。亚瑟接任总统时，妻子埃伦已于一年半前就去世了。他和埃伦是通过朋友介绍认识的，结婚的时候他 30 岁，埃伦22岁。埃伦是弗吉尼亚人，在内战中私下倾向南方。她是一位很出色的歌唱家，经常在纽约的俱乐部里演唱。她一直担心亚瑟的健康，但她自己却先去世了，时年仅42岁。妻子去世后，亚瑟发誓不再婚，下令每天在白宫里妻子的画像前摆放鲜花。由于子女还未成年，"第一夫人"的职责就由他小妹玛丽担当。玛丽自己也有家有孩子，因此只在冬季来履行职责，尽管如此，她还是把白宫管理得井井有条。

经典原文 Original Text

1 Chester Alan Arthur was born in 1829 in Fairfield, Vermont. He was the oldest son of William Arthur, an Irish minister and schoolteacher. His mother's name was Malvina Stone Arthur. They lived in several towns before moving to Saratoga County, New York in 1848. He studied law and taught in a local school.

2 In 1852 he was appointed principal of the school. He then moved to New York City to work in the office of *Erastus Dean Culver* ①. In 1854 he passed the bar exam and got his license to study law. He quickly gained the reputation for supporting blacks, and in 1855 he won a case that granted blacks to ride any streetcar in New York City. Finally in 1856 he opened his own law firm.

3 He was a young attorney and a well mannered man. He would always got to the best tailors in town and he would always ware the latest fashions. He soon fell in love with Ellen Lewis Herndon, and in 1859 they were married. In 1868 he was an aide to the republican senator Rascal Cocking. They also supported General Ulysses Simpson Grant as the republican candidate for president. He became the collector of customs and controlled a customhouse of New York. In 1877 he was forced to resign from the customhouse because of a scandal. Even though he was forced to resign he still studied law in New York City.

Words & Expressions

the bar exam 律师资格考试

grant [grɑ:nt] *vt.* 授予，允许，承认

streetcar ['stri:tkɑ:] *n.* 有轨电车

law firm 法律事务所

attorney [ə'tə:ni] *n.* 代理人；律师

ware [weə] *vt.* 留心，小心

collector of customs 海关征税员

customhouse ['kʌstəmhaus] *n.* 海关

scandal ['skændl] *n.* 丑闻；流言蜚语

4 In the election of 1880 republican senator James Abram Garfield became president. Arthur was chosen as his Vice-president, but during the campaigns the Democrats would attack him with foolish things that he did in the past like the customhouse scandal. However, Garfield and Arthur won the elections, and on March 4, 1881 he was sworn in as Vice-president of the United States. Not all was well for Garfield and Arthur. On July 2, 1881, Garfield was assassinated by Charles J. Guiteau, who was a disappointed office-seeker because he lost his job when Garfield became president. Garfield died 11 weeks later on September 19, 1881, and on the following morning Arthur took oath of office at his house in New York City.

5 The people didn't believe that he would become a good president, but he sure showed them. He positioned himself between the Republicans and Democrats, and his qualifications for presidency were excellent. As a lawyer he was well experienced with the constitutional law. His skills lead him to become a good president. In 1883 congress passed the *Pedleton Act* ②. This act created the Civil Service Commission. It required competitive tests for some federal jobs, and prohibited political tests for officeholders. Although this act was important it only applied to about 14,000 of the 131,000 federal employees. Arthur demonstrated his support for the act by choosing Dorman B. Eaton as chairman of the Civil Service Commission.

6 In 1884 Arthur lost more political support by vetoing a *Rivers and Harbors Act* ③. He was more successful in his dealings with congress when he requested money to strengthen the U.S. navy. This made congress authorize the construction of three steel cruisers and a dispatch boat.

office-seeker 追求权力者，谋官者

take oath 宣誓

position *vt.* 安置，把…放在适当位置 *n.* 位置，方位，职位

officeholder [ˈɔfisˌhəuldə] *n.* 公务员，官员，办公人员

veto [ˈviːtəu] *v.* 否决；不同意；禁止

navy [ˈneivi] *n.* 海军

cruiser [ˈkruːzə] *n.* 巡洋舰，巡航飞机，警察巡逻车

dispatch boat 通信快船，邮件（或公文）快艇

When Arthur left office congress agreed to build four more vessels. Before leaving office he tried one more time to run for president, but he lost to *Grover Cleveland* ④. After turning the White House over to Cleveland on March 4, 1885, he resumed practicing law in New York. In 1886 he got ill and died of cerebral hemorrhage. This was the biggest secret of his life and he never told anyone.

resume [ri'zju:m] *vt.* 重新开始，重新获得 *n.* 简历

cerebral hemorrhage 脑出血，脑溢血

背景知识注释
Background Notes

1. Erastus Dean Culver　伊拉斯塔斯•D•卡尔弗(1803～1889)，来自纽约的国会众议员，1826年毕业于佛蒙特大学；他研习法律，1831年进入律师界并开始经营律师行；1838年至1840年成为州议会成员；1845年3月至1847年3月他作为辉格党人当选为第29届国会议员；1854年至1861年成为纽约布鲁克林城市法院法官；1862年至1866年他被林肯总统任命为美国驻委内瑞拉公使。
2. *Pendleton Act*　《彭德尔顿法》，1883年由美国国会通过，确立了一套以功绩制为核心的文官选拔和奖惩机制，旨在调节和完善美国的文官制度。该法案彻底改革了美国的文官体制，打破了政治机器垄断职位任命权的局面，奠定了以“功绩原则”为国家人事行政制度选才的基石，杜绝了美国政坛长期以来的“政治分赃”现象。在21世纪的美国政界，依然有这个法案的痕迹。
3. *Rivers and Harbors Act*　《河流与港口法》，1882年通过，这项法案耗资9,000万美元用于全国的道路、桥梁、河道的建设。亚瑟总统认为许多项目是不必要的，因此否决了这项法案，但国会再次通过了这项法案，使之成为法律。
4. Grover Cleveland　即Stephen Grover Cleveland 斯蒂芬•格罗弗•克利夫兰(1837～1908)，美国政治家，第22和24任美国总统，是唯一分开任两届的总统，也是内战后第一位当选总统的民主党人。

中文译文
Suggested Translation

1 切斯特•艾伦•亚瑟于1829年出生在佛蒙特州的费尔菲尔德。他是爱尔兰裔牧师兼教师威廉•亚瑟(William Arthur)的长子，他母亲名叫玛尔维娜•S•亚瑟(Malvina Stone Arthur)。1848年搬到纽约的萨拉托加县之前，他们一家在数个城镇生活过。他在当地一所学校学习法律并留校教书。

2 1852年，他被任命为该校的校长。随后他搬到纽约市在伊拉斯塔斯•D•卡尔弗的办公室工作。1854年,他通过律师资格考试，获得了研习法律的许可证。他支持黑人的声誉很快就不胫而走，1855年他赢了一个案子，该案判决准许黑人乘坐纽约市的任何有轨电车。1856年，他终于开办了自己的律师事务所。

3 他既是一位年轻的律师也是一个温文尔雅的人。他总是光临城里最好的裁缝店,他总是留意最新潮的时装。他很快就爱上了埃伦•刘易斯•赫恩登(Ellen Lewis Herndon)，并于1859年与其完婚。1868年，他成为共和党参议员拉斯卡尔•卡卿(Rascal Cocking)的助手。他们还支持尤利塞斯•格兰特将军作为共和党的总统候选人。他成了海关征税官并监控整个纽约海关。1877年，由于发生丑闻案他被迫辞去在海关的职务。尽管如此，他在纽约市仍然坚持研习法律。

4 在1880年的大选中，共和党参议员詹姆斯•艾伯拉姆•加菲尔德成了总统。亚瑟被选为副总统，但在竞选过程中，民主党总是借用过去他过去的诸如海关丑闻等愚蠢事情来攻击他。然而，加菲尔德和亚瑟还是赢得了选举，1881年3月4日亚瑟宣誓就任美国副总统。但是，并不是所有的人都对加菲尔德和亚瑟有好感。1881年7月2日，加菲尔德被查尔斯•J•吉托枪杀。加菲尔德成为总统时，吉托已失业在家，再加上谋官未成，因此心怀不满。11周后，即1881年9月19日，加菲尔德离开了人世，第二天上午亚瑟就在纽约市的家中宣誓就职。

5 人们都不相信亚瑟会成为一位好总统，但他肯定地向他们展示了他的能力。他摆正自己的位子，在共和党和民主党之间求得平衡，他具有担任总统的优秀资历。作为一位律师，他谙熟涉及宪法的法律。他的才能使他成了一位好总统。1883年，国会通过了《彭德尔顿法案》。这个法案创建了公务员委员会。它要求对一些联邦工作进行竞争测试，对公职人员禁止政治测试。虽然该法案很重要，但这只适用于131,000联邦雇员当中的大约14,000。亚瑟通过选择多尔曼•B•伊顿 (Dorman B. Eaton) 担任公务员委员会主席来表明了他对该法案的支持。

6 1884年亚瑟因为否决了《河流与港口法》而失去了更多的政治支持。他与国会打交道，要求资金来加强美国海军——这方面他做得更成功。这使得国会授权建造三艘钢铁造的巡洋舰和一艘通信快船。当亚瑟离任时，国会同意再建造四艘船。在卸任前，他试着再一次竞选总统，但他输给了格罗弗•克利夫兰(Grover Cleveland)。1885年3月4日在将白宫交给克利夫兰之后，亚瑟继续在纽约执业当律师。1886年，他病倒了并死于脑出血。这是他生命中最大的秘密，他从未告诉任何人。

22 Stephen Grover Cleveland's Qualities
斯蒂芬·格罗弗·克利夫兰总统的高尚品德

斯蒂芬·格罗弗·克利夫兰 总统及第一夫人简介

斯蒂芬•格罗弗•克利夫兰(Stephen Grover Cleveland, 1837.3.18～1908.6.24)，第22和24任美国总统，是美国历史上唯一一位担任了两个非连续任期的总统，也是唯一一位在白宫里结婚的总统。他任期内面临着机构改革、关税纷争、工人罢工等难题。他推行了文官制度改革，免去了近10万共和党人的官职并换上了民主党人；他勒令铁路公司退出了近8千英亩非法占用的土地；他力图维持和制订有利于民主党利益的低关税政策。对外，他实行孤立主义。

弗朗西斯•福尔索姆•克利夫兰(Frances Folsom Cleveland, 1864.7.21～1947.10.29)，格罗弗•克利夫兰总统的妻子。1886年克利夫兰与比他小27岁的弗朗西斯在白宫结婚。婚后他们育有两子三女。有趣的是第一夫人由总统抚养长大，是历史上最年轻的第一夫人。虽然很年轻，但当时她和克利夫兰相识已经有21年了。克利夫兰第一次认识未来的妻子时(1864)，对方只有1岁。1875年弗朗西斯•福尔索姆的父亲去世时托付克利夫兰管理财产并照顾弗朗西斯•福尔索姆，当时弗朗西斯只有11岁。新的总统夫人年轻貌美，很受欢迎，为白宫带来了年轻的活力。但克利夫兰认为第一夫人不应该插手政治，所以弗朗西斯也没有太大的作为。1908年克利夫兰去世。5年后弗朗西斯再婚，她嫁给了普林斯顿的一位考古学教授，成为第一位再婚的总统夫人。她于1947年去世，享年83岁。

经典原文
Original Text

1 Stephen Grover Cleveland was the 22nd and 24th President of the United States. Cleveland is the only president to serve two non-consecutive terms (1885 — 1889 and 1893 — 1897) and therefore is the only individual to be counted twice in the numbering of the presidents. He was the winner of the popular vote for president three times — in 1884, 1888, and 1892 — and was the only Democrat elected to the presidency in the era of Republican political domination that lasted from 1860 to 1912.

2 Cleveland was the leader of the pro-business *Bourbon*① Democrats who opposed high tariffs, *free silver* ②, inflation, imperialism and subsidies to business, farmers or veterans. His battles for political reform and fiscal conservatism made him an icon for American conservatives. Cleveland won praise for his honesty, independence, integrity, and commitment to the principles of classical liberalism. As a reformer he worked indefatigably against political corruption, patronage, and bossism. His second term coincided with the *Panic of 1893*③, a severe national depression that Cleveland was unable to reverse. It ruined his Democratic party, opening the way for Republican landslides in 1894 and 1896, and for the agrarian and *silverite*④ seizure of his Democratic Party in 1896. The result was a political realignment that ended *the Third Party System*⑤ and launched *the Fourth Party System*⑥ and *the Progressive Era*⑦.

Words & Expressions

non-consecutive [ˌnɔnkən'sekjutiv] *adj.* 不连贯的

domination [ˌdɔmi'neiʃən] *n.* 控制，支配

pro-business *adj.* 亲企业的，亲商业的，利商的

fiscal ['fiskəl] *adj.* 会计的，财政的，国库的

icon ['aikɔn] *n.* 图标，偶像，肖像，画像

integrity [in'tegriti] *n.* 完整，正直，诚实，廉正

commitment [kə'mitmənt] *n.* 保证，委托，承担义务，献身

indefatigably [ˌindi'fætigəbli] *adj.* 不厌倦地，不屈不挠地

patronage ['pætrənidʒ] *n.* 赞助，光顾，任免权

bossism ['bɔsiz(ə)m] *n.* 领袖的政党控制，头领的支配

coincide with 符合

landslide ['lændslaid] *n.* 山崩

agrarian [ə'greəriən] *adj.* 土地的，耕地的，有关土地的

realignment [ˌriə'lainmənt] *n.* 重新排列，重新组合，改组

gold standard （金融）金本位，金本位制
alienate [ˈeiljəneit] *vt.* 使疏远，离间，让与
overwhelm [ˌəuvəˈhwelm] *vt.* 压倒，淹没，受打击
endowment [inˈdaumənt] *n.* 捐赠，捐款，天资，才能

3 Cleveland took strong positions and in turn took heavy criticism. His intervention in the *Pullman Strike of 1894*⑧ to keep the railroads moving angered labor unions nationwide and angered the party in Illinois; his support of the gold standard and opposition to free silver alienated the agrarian wing of the Democratic Party. Furthermore, critics complained that he had little imagination and seemed overwhelmed by the nation's economic disasters —depressions and strikes — in his second term. Even so, his reputation for honesty and good character survived the troubles of his second term. Biographer Allan Nevins wrote, "in Grover Cleveland the greatness lies in typical rather than unusual qualities. He had no endowments that thousands of men do not have. He possessed honesty, courage, firmness, independence, and common sense. But he possessed them to a degree other men do not."

背景知识注释 Background Notes

1. Bourbon [ˈbuəb(ə)n] *n.* (法国的)波旁皇族；政治上的极端保守分子。
2. free silver （美）银币的自由铸造；复本位制。
3. Panic of 1893 美国“1893年大恐慌”，自1893年开始美国经济就陷入衰退，数以千计的工商企业、银行关门，铁路倒闭，数百万人失业，外国投资者从美国撤资，而国内那些有钱人也对投资很担心。由此引发的社会动荡和“美国进步时代”的到来，削弱了民主党总统格罗夫•克里夫兰的执政基础。此后的16年，白宫便一直被共和党控制。
4. silverite [ˈsilvərait]（美）金银复本位制论者；主张自由铸造银币者。在19世纪的90年代，美国人因为该国的货币政策而分成两派，是支持现行的金本位货币政策还是支持以黄金和白银为共同支撑的货币政策这个问题自然也就成了1896年美国总统大选中的一个主要话题。

   许多美国人希望保持金本位货币政策，他们认为：美国应该实行以黄金为唯一支撑的货币政策，金本位货币政策能够使美元保持一个高币值，这些人被称为“金币政策者(gold bugs)”，他们中绝大多数是工商界人士、银行家和投资者。其他美国人则希望美国实行以金银为共同支

撑的货币政策，他们认为现在的美元币值太高了，他们说，高币值的美元意味着农产品价格只能维持低水平，而以白银为货币的支撑，就可以使美元币值下降。这些人被称之为“银币政策者(silverites)”，他们中绝大多数是农民、工人和小生产者。

有关“金银”之争显得特别重要，因为自1893年开始美国经济就陷入衰退，许多人认为如果政府的货币政策回归到以黄金和白银作为货币的共同支撑的话，美国的经济衰退就会结束。然而，格罗弗•克利夫兰总统则不这么认为，而且他还反对任何旨在动摇金本位的立法建议。

5. the Third Party System 第三次政党制。当代美国政治学者认为，美国的两党制迄今经历了五次政党制度(目前仍处于第五次政党制时期)。第一次政党制是建国初期联邦党与共和党对立的政党制。第二次政党制是19世纪20年代末到40年代初辉格党与民主党对峙时期。第三、四、五次政党制均为民主党与共和党对立，不同在于多数选民的党派倾向发生了变化，从而造成两党力量对比的重大变更。第四次政党制也被称为“美国进步时代”。
6. the Fourth Party System 第四次政党制。
7. the Progressive Era 美国进步时代。
8. Pullman Strike of 1894 普尔曼大罢工。1894年，芝加哥世博会期间，在金融危机的持续影响下，普尔曼豪华汽车公司将工人的工资削减25%，当地铁路工会会员发起罢工，董事长乔治•普尔曼在全国铁路经理联合会的支持下，拒不接受仲裁。在铁路工会的领导下，全美27个州发起了数十万人的同情式罢工。7月1日，芝加哥近郊的蓝岛车站发生数千人的骚乱，局势失控。当日，克利夫兰总统违宪地向芝加哥派兵前往镇压暴乱。7月4日，美国独立纪念日，美国军队到达芝加哥平暴。经过数天的激战，美国铁路工人联合会主席德布兹被捕，失去领袖的工会逐渐被镇压，20日，克利夫兰召回了军队。这是内战结束以来，美国政府第一次派兵对本国公民采取行动。

中文译文
Suggested Translation

1 斯蒂芬•格罗弗•克利夫兰是第22任和第24任美国总统。克利夫兰是唯一分开任两届的总统 (1885～1889和1893～1897)，因此也是唯一一位总统的编号被统计两次的人。他曾三次赢得过总统选举的普选票——1884年、1888年和1892年——在共和党政治占主导地位的时代(1860～1912)，他是唯一一位当选为总统的民主党人。

2 克利夫兰是位亲商又极端保守的民主党人领袖，他反对高关税、银币自由铸造(复本位制)、通货膨胀、帝国主义，而且还反对给商业、农民及内战老兵发放补贴。他为政治改革和财政保守主义而战使得他成为美国保守派的化身。克利夫兰由于诚实、独立、正直和奉行古典自由主义的原则而赢得了赞誉。作为一个改革者，他不屈不挠地与政治腐败、政党分赃和专制进行抗争。他的第二任期时间恰好遭遇“1893年大恐慌”，这是克利夫兰无法逆转的一次严重的国家经济大萧条，它动摇了民主党的执政基础，从而为共和党在1894年和1896年竞选大获全胜，并为土地派和复本位制在1896年占据民主党的地位奠定了基石。结果是政治的重组结束了第三次政党制，并推动了第四次政党制及“美国进步时代”的到来。

3 克利夫兰采取了强硬立场，并因此遭到了严厉的批评。他对 1894“普尔曼罢工”的干预使得全国的铁路工会群情激愤，并激怒了伊利诺伊州的民主党；他支持金本位制，反对复本位制致使他疏远了民主党的土地派。此外，批评者抱怨说克利夫兰缺乏想象力，而且似乎被他第二任期内国家所遭遇的经济灾难——萧条和罢工——所压垮。即便如此，他所具有的诚实和良好品格的声誉超越了他第二任期内所经历的困难。传记作家艾伦·内文斯 (Allan Nevins) 写道：“在格罗弗·克利夫兰身上，伟大之处在于典型的而不是特殊的品德。他和成千上万的人们一样并没有天赋才能。他拥有的只是诚实、勇敢、坚定、独立和常识。然而，他拥有这些品质的程度并非他人所能企及。”

23 President Benjamin Harrison on U.S. Postage stamps 美国邮票上的本杰明·哈里森总统

本杰明·哈里森 总统及第一夫人简介

本杰明•哈里森(Benjamin Harrison, 1833.8.20～1901.3.13)，第23任美国总统(1889～1893)。其曾祖父本杰明•哈里森五世(Benjamin Harrison V)为《美国独立宣言》签署人之一；其祖父为威廉•亨利•哈里森(William Henry Harrison)，是第9任美国总统。本杰明•哈里森受过良好的教育，毕业于迈阿密大学，毕业后操律师业。南北战争期间他曾参加联邦军，获准将衔。1881年，他成为参议员。1888年，他被共和党提名为总统候选人并在竞选中获胜。他上台时，美国工业化臻于完成，经济结构发生了历史性变革。哈里森顺应潮流，制定了旨在稳定局势、防止社会动荡的《谢尔曼反托拉斯法》。对外，哈里森积极扩大美国的影响，组织召开了第一届泛美会议，成立泛美联盟。哈里森政府还与许多国家签订了贸易互惠协定。

卡罗琳·拉维尼娅·斯科特·哈里森 (Caroline Lavinia Scott Harrison, 1832.10.1 ~ 1892.10.5) 是第 23 任美国总统的第一个夫人，与总统育有一儿一女。作为第一夫人时，她曾设法让国会拨款

35,000美元修葺白宫。1889年她第一次在白宫设置了圣诞树。她是“美国革命女儿会”的第一任主席。在哈里森争取连任总统竞选时，她正患肺病。1892年10月25日，她在总统大选前两周逝世。1896年4月6日，卸任后的哈里森在62岁时与37岁的寡妇玛里丽·斯科特·洛德·迪米克(她是卡罗琳的侄女，曾在白宫当第一夫人的助理。)结婚。

经典原文
Original Text

Words & Expressions

deceased [di'si:st] *adj.* 已死的，已故的，死去了的，死亡的

definitive stamps 普通邮票

commemorative stamps 纪念邮票

revenue ['revənu:] *n.*税收，收入，税务局

1 For more than 160 years, the one subject that has appeared most frequently on the face of U.S. postage stamps is that of American presidents. When the U.S. Post Office released its first two postage stamps in 1847, George Washington and Benjamin Franklin were the subjects depicted upon them. These two stamps set the precedent (images of deceased statesmen) that U.S. designs for definitive stamps would follow for many generations.

2 Benjamin Harrison (August 20, 1833 — March 13, 1901) was the 23rd President of the United States, serving one term from 1889 to 1893. Harrison was born in *North Bend* ①, Ohio, and at the age of 21 moved to *Indianapolis* ②, Indiana, where he became involved with Indiana state politics. During the *American Civil War* ③ Harrison served as a *Brigadier General* ④ in the *Army of the Cumberland* ⑤.

3 Under Benjamin Harrison and his *Postmaster General* ⑥ *John Wanamaker* ⑦ the nation's first commemorative stamps were made available and were first issued at the *World Columbian Exposition* ⑧ in Chicago, Illinois, in 1893. Wanamaker originally introduced the idea of issuing the nation's first commemorative stamp to Harrison, the Congress and the U.S. Post Office. Contrary to the general opinion of Congress at the time Wanamaker predicted that commemorative stamps would generate needed revenue for the country. Shortly thereafter the nation's first

commemorative stamps were issued in conjunction with the World Columbian Exposition, both of which were in commemoration of the 400th anniversary of Columbus' discovery of America. To demonstrate his confidence in the new commemorative stamp issues Wanamaker purchased $10,000 worth of stamps with his own money. Harrison was also present at the World Columbian Exposition and ceremony and delivered a speech where he said. "In the name of the Government and of the people of the United States, I do hereby invite all the nations of the earth to take part in the commemoration of an event that is pre-eminent in human history, and of lasting interest to mankind." The exposition lasted several months and by the time it was over more than $40 million dollars had been generated in commemorative postage stamp sales alone. From that point onward *the U.S. Post Office*⑨ would issue commemorative postage on a regular basis. Harrison appears on four regular issues and on two commemorative issues.

4 The 1902 13-cent postage stamp was the 1st issue to honor Benjamin Harrison, issued on November 18, 1902, less than two years after his death. It was the first 13-cent stamp issued by the U.S. Post Office, and the first of 14 stamps to be released to the public in the 1902 — 1903 series. The stamp was designed by *R.O. Smith*⑩ from a photograph supplied by Mrs. Harrison. The image was engraved by *Marcus W. Baldwin*⑪.

5 The 1926 issue of Harrison was engraved by *Clair Aubrey Houston*⑫ who based the image design on the same photograph of Harrison that was used to model the 1902 stamp.

6 The 24-cent 1938 issue of Harrison image was

commemoration [kəˌmeməˈreiʃn] *n.* 纪念，纪念物，庆典

engrave [inˈgreiv] *v.* 雕刻，刻上，铭记

inspired by a bust by *Adolph A. Weinman* ⑬, on view at the *John Herron Art Institute* ⑭.

7 Harrison's image on the 12-cent 1959 issue was taken from a photograph taken by *Charles Parker* ⑮.

8 The 22-cent Harrison commemorative stamp was issued on May 22 of 1986 as part of a series of stamps honoring U.S. Presidents, first issued during *AMERIPEX'86* ⑯, the international philatelic show held in *Rosemont* ⑰, Illinois. Artist *Jerry Dadds* ⑱ of *Baltimore* ⑲, Maryland, designed the four sheets containing thirty-six stamps. Dadds also executed the designs in the woodcut style. There is only one commemorative stamp that honors Harrison.

9 In 2003 the U.S. Post Office issued a 37-cent *Old Glory* ⑳ commemorative stamp on April 3, 2003, at *the Mega Stamp Show* ㉑ in New York, New York. The stamp was designed by *Richard Sheaff* ㉒. The stamp depicts a 1888 presidential campaign badge with a photograph of Benjamin Harrison at its center.

bust [bʌst] *n.* 半身雕塑像

on view 展览，陈列着

philatelic [ˌfiləˈtelik] *adj.* 集邮的

depict [diˈpikt] *vt.* 描绘，描述

badge [bædʒ] *n.* 徽章，像章，奖章

背景知识注释
Background Notes

1. North Bend 北本德，美国俄亥俄州西南部汉密尔顿县俄亥俄河沿岸的一个村庄，县治是辛辛那堤，成立于1790年，县名是为纪念首任财政部长亚历山大•汉密尔顿。
2. Indianapolis　印第安纳波利斯，美国印第安纳州最大城市和首府，美国第二大的州首府，仅次于亚利桑那州的菲尼克斯。
3. American Civil War　美国南北战争，美国历史上最大规模的内战，参战双方为北方的美利坚合众国（简称联邦）和南方的美利坚联盟国（简称邦联）。它造成约 750,000 名士兵死亡，平民伤亡人数不详。这场战争的起因为美国南部十一州以亚伯拉罕 • 林肯于 1861 年就任总统为由而陆续退出联邦，另成立以杰斐逊 • 戴维斯为“总统”的政府，并驱逐驻扎南方的联邦军，而林肯下令攻打“叛乱”州。此战不但改变了当时美国的政治经济情势，导致奴隶制度在美国南方最终被废除，也对日后美国的民间社会产生巨大的影响。

4. Brigadier General （陆军、空军或海军陆战队）准将。

5. Army of the Cumberland 坎伯兰军，美国南北战争时，在阿巴拉契亚山脉以西联邦的主要军队之一，原本称为“俄亥俄军”。

6. Postmaster General 邮政总局局长。

7. John Wanamaker 约翰•沃纳梅克(1838.7.11～1922.12.12)，美国商人，生于美国宾夕法尼亚州费城，被认为是百货商店之父。1875年他购买了一个废弃的铁路仓库，并将它改建成一个大商场——沃纳梅克氏，一般认为这是美国第一家百货商店。1889年，沃纳梅克被美国总统本杰明•哈利森任命为美国邮政总局局长，任期到1893年结束，在此期间，他进行了行之有效的改革，大大提升了邮政服务的效率。

8. World Columbian Exposition 芝加哥哥伦布纪念博览会，亦称芝加哥世界博览会，是于1893年在美国芝加哥举办的世界博览会，以纪念哥伦布发现新大陆400周年。

9. the U.S. Post Office 美国邮政署，亦称美国邮政总局，是美国联邦政府的独立机构。

10. R. O. Smith R•O• 史密斯，美国的一位邮票设计师。

11. Marcus W. Baldwin 马库斯•W•鲍德温(1853.3.31～1925.7.15)，美国著名雕刻家，创作了许多作品。

12. Clair Aubrey Houston 克莱尔•奥布里•休斯敦，20世纪初美国财政部铸印局多才多艺的首席邮票设计师。在邮票雕刻和印制局工作21年，设计了诸多美国邮票。

13. Adolph A. Weinman 阿道夫• A•温曼(1870.12.11～1952.8.8)，美国雕刻家和建筑雕塑家，出生于德国卡尔斯鲁厄。

14. John Herron Art Institute 约翰•赫伦艺术学院，印第安纳大学的一所学院。招收攻读包括美术、视觉传达设计、视觉艺术、艺术教育和艺术史等学士和硕士学位课程的学生。该学院还是赫伦画廊所在地，展出当地和全国各地艺术家的当代艺术作品，

15. Charles Parker 查尔斯•帕克，美国一位著名摄影师。

16. AMERIPEX'86 1986年国际集邮展，为纪念美国集邮协会和芝加哥集邮协会成立100周年，1986年5月22日至6月1日在美国伊利诺伊州罗斯蒙特奥黑尔博览会/会议中心举办的第8届国际集邮展览。

17. Rosemont 罗斯蒙特， 美国伊利诺伊州东北部库克县的一个镇，是该地区一个主要的商业中心以及黄金走廊的重要组成部分。

18. Jerry Dadds 杰里•戴德兹， 优秀版画家，在马里兰州巴尔的摩创建了自己的工作室。为企业、政府部门、机构、广告公司、书籍、杂志和日历等创作了许多作品。

19. Baltimore 巴尔的摩，美国大西洋沿岸重要的海港城市，它位于切萨皮克湾顶端的西侧，离美国首都华盛顿仅有60多公里，港区就在帕塔帕斯科河的出海口附近。从这里经过海湾出海到辽阔的大西洋还有250公里的航程，但由于港口附近自然条件优越，切萨皮克湾又宽广，航道很

深，万吨级远洋轮可直接驶入巴尔的摩港区。这个港口属于马里兰州，向来是美国五大湖区、中央盆地与大西洋上联系的一个重要出海口。

20. Old Glory 古老的光荣。它是美国国旗的爱称，美利坚合众国的国旗旗面由13道红白相间的宽条构成，左上角还有一个包含了50颗白色小五角星的蓝色长方形。50颗小星代表了美国的50个州，而13条间纹则象征着美国最早建国时的13块殖民地。红色象征勇气，白色象征真理，蓝色则象征正义。这面旗帜俗称“星条旗”(Stars and Stripes)，正式名称为“合众国旗”(The Flag of the United States)。
21. the Mega Stamp Show 巨型邮票展。
22. Richard Sheaff 理查德•谢夫，1983年到2008年，理查德•谢夫担任公民邮票咨询委员会的设计顾问。在这个岗位上，他负责设计或在艺术方面指导业已发行的美国邮票共有300多枚。作为一个艺术总监，他还负责指导和监督设计师、插图画家 、研究人员和生产人员。

中文译文
Suggested Translation

1 一百六十多年来，美国邮票票面图样中最常出现的一个主题就是美国总统。在1847年美国邮局发行的首批两枚邮票上，乔治•华盛顿(George Washington)和本杰明•富兰克林(Benjamin Franklin)是其描绘的主题。这两枚邮票开创了美国普通邮票设计一代又一代人遵循的先例，即采用已故政治家的肖像。

2 本杰明•哈里森（1833.8.20～1901.3.13）是美国第23任总统，任期从1889年到1893年。哈里森出生于俄亥俄州北本德(North Bend)，21岁时搬到印第安纳州印第安纳波利斯(Indianapolis)，在那里他参与了印第安纳州的政治事务。在美国南北战争期间哈里森担任坎伯兰军(Army of the Cumberland)的准将。

3 在本杰明 • 哈里森以及美国邮政总局局长约翰 • 沃纳梅克 (John Wanamaker) 的关怀下，美国第一套纪念邮票面市并在 1893 年伊利诺伊州芝加哥世界哥伦布纪念博览会 (World Columbian Exposition) 首次发行。沃纳梅克最初向哈里森、美国国会和美国邮政总局介绍了发行全国首枚纪念邮票的想法。与国会普遍的想法相反，沃纳梅克 (Wanamaker) 预测，纪念邮票能为国家创造所需要的收入。此后不久，美国的首批纪念邮票在当时举办世界哥伦布纪念博览会发行，两者都是为了纪念哥伦布发现美洲 400 周年。为了展示他对发行纪念邮票的信心，沃纳梅克 (Wanamaker) 用自己的钱购买了价值一万美元的邮票。哈里森也出席了世界哥伦布纪念博览会和相关仪式并发表讲话。他说："我以美国政府和美国人民的名义谨此邀请世界上所有的国家参加以纪念一个人类历史上最卓越，并永远为人类造福的事件。"本届博览会历时数月。结束时，仅发行纪念邮票的收入就超过四千多万美元。从那时起，美国邮政局就定期发行纪念邮票。哈里森四次出现在普通邮票上，两次出现在纪念邮票上。

4 第一枚纪念本杰明•哈里森的邮票为1902年版13美分的邮票，1902年11月18日发行，距离其去世不到两年的时间；为美国邮政总局发行的首枚13美分邮票，也是向公众发布的1902至1903年系列邮票中的第一枚。邮票根据哈里森夫人提供的照片由R•O•史密斯(R. O. Smith)设计，马库斯•W•鲍德温(Marcus W. Baldwin)完成凸版制作。

5 1926年版哈里森的邮票由克莱尔•奥布里•休斯敦(Clair Aubrey Houston)完成凸版制作。他以1902年版邮票所采用的哈里森的照片作为形象设计的基础。

6 1938年版24美分哈里森的邮票灵感来自在约翰•赫伦艺术学院(John Herron Art Institute)展出的由阿道夫• A•温曼(Adolph A. Weinman)的半身像。

7 1959年版12美分哈里森的形象源于查尔斯•帕克(Charles Parker)拍摄的照片。

8 哈里森22美分的纪念邮票于1986年5月22日作为纪念美国总统系列邮票的一个组成部分发布，在伊利诺伊州罗斯蒙特(Rosemont)举行的86'国际集邮展(AMERIPEX'86)期间首次发行。马里兰州巴尔的摩(Baltimore)的艺术家杰里•戴德兹(Jerry Dadds)设计了四张包含36枚邮票的小型张。戴德兹还运用木刻的风格设计邮票。他设计的邮票中只有一枚是纪念哈里森的。

9 美国邮政总局于2003年4月3日在纽约州纽约巨型邮票展上发行一枚37美分的古老光荣(Old Glory)纪念邮票。该邮票由理查德•谢夫(Richard Sheaff)设计，描绘了一枚1888年总统大选徽章，本杰明•哈里森的照片就位于其中心位置。

24 Stephen Grover Cleveland and the *Statue of Liberty*①

斯蒂芬·格罗弗·克利夫兰总统与自由女神像

格罗弗·克利夫兰 总统及第一夫人简介

斯蒂芬·格罗弗·克利夫兰(Stephen Grover Cleveland, 1837.3.18～1908.6.24)，第22(1885～1889)和24任美国总统(1893～1897)，是唯一一位担任了两个非连续任期的总统，也是美国内战后第一位当选总统的民主党人。在他任期内，自由女神像竖立在纽约市。他被人认为是独立、诚实的总统。他在反腐败、反政党分赃等方面做出了较大贡献，但他也镇压工人罢工，否决过一些例如给灾民分发种子等的福利法案，还否决了照顾内战老兵的法案。对外，他反对扩张，实行孤立主义。他在当选前是一位律师，卸任后，他曾在一家人寿保险公司供职。

弗朗西斯·福尔索姆·克利夫兰(Frances Folsom Cleveland, 1864.7.21～1947.10.29)，克利夫兰总统的夫人。他们结婚时，克利夫兰49岁，而弗朗西斯·福尔索姆只有22岁。最年轻的第一夫人——克利夫兰夫人成为报界最感兴趣的话题。这使两口子很苦恼，他们以沉默对待谣言。1888年克利夫兰竞选失败，她警告白宫人员四年以后还会回来。事实证明她是对的。克利夫兰死后她于1913年又与考古学教授托马斯·J·普雷斯顿结婚。1930年大萧条时期，她曾领导美国针织业工会为穷人缝补衣服。

经典原文
Original Text

1 On Oct. 28, 1886, President Stephen Grover Cleveland dedicates the Statue of Liberty in New York Harbor.

2 The statue's full name was Statue of Liberty Enlightening the World. It had been a gift from French citizens to their American friends in recognition of the two countries' commitment to liberty and democracy and their alliance during the *American Revolutionary War*②, which had begun 110 years earlier. The 151-foot copper statue was built in France and shipped to New York in 350 separate parts. It arrived in the city on June 17, 1886, and over the next several months was reassembled while electricians worked to wire the torch to light up at night.

3 As President Cleveland accepted the statue on behalf of American citizens, he declared "we will not forget that liberty here made her home; nor shall her chosen altar be neglected." The statue quickly became a symbol of America's humanitarianism and willingness to take in the world's "tired, poor and huddled masses" — in the words of the poem by *Emma Lazarus*③ inscribed on the monument's pedestal — who yearned for freedom and a better life.

4 "Lady Liberty" was originally intended to work as a functional lighthouse and, from 1886 to 1901, the statue was operated by *the United States Lighthouse Board*④. In 1901, *the War Department*⑤ took over its operation and maintenance. The statue and the island on which it stands, now known as *Liberty Island*⑥, were together proclaimed a national monument by *President Calvin Coolidge*⑦ on October 15, 1924, and, in 1933, *the National Park Service*⑧ assumed oversight of the monument. In 1982, *President*

Words & Expressions

dedicate [ˈdedikeit] *vt.* 致力，为…举行落成典礼（或仪式）

in recognition of 承认…而，为酬谢

liberty [ˈlibəti] *n.* 自由，许可

reassemble [ˌriːəˈsembl] *vt.* 重新装配，重新召集

electrician [ˌilekˈtriʃən] *n.* 电工，电气技师

altar [ˈɔːltə] *n.* 祭坛，圣坛，圣餐台

humanitarianism [hjuːˌmæniˈteəriənizəm] *n.* 人道主义，博爱主义

take in 接受，理解，拘留，欺骗，让…进入，改短

pedestal [ˈpedistəl] *n.* 基架，基座，基础

yearn for 极想，渴望

maintenance [ˈmeintənəns] *n.* 维护，维修，保持，生活费用

proclaim [prəuˈkleim] *vt.* 宣告，公布，声明，表明，赞扬

oversight [ˈəuvəˌsait] *n.* 疏忽；监督；失察

Ronald Reagan[9] established a commission tasked with restoring the deteriorating Lady Liberty in time for a centennial celebration in 1986. A joint French-American preservation and rehabilitation group cleaned the statue and replaced the glass and metal torch with gold leaf. The original torch is on display in the statue's lobby.

5 Today, the Statue of Liberty is a major tourist attraction, hosting as many as 5 million people every year. Although access to the statue's crown was restricted following the September 11, 2001, terrorist attacks, tourists can still visit Liberty Island, and the statue's pedestal observation deck and museum.

deteriorate [diˈtiəriəreit] *v.* 退化，恶化

centennial [senˈteniəl] *adj.* 一百年的 *n.* 百年纪念

preservation [ˌprezəˈveiʃən] *n.* 保存，保留

rehabilitation [ˈriːhəˌbiliˈteiʃən] *n.* 复原

lobby [ˈlɔbi] *n.* 大厅，休息室，会客室，游说议员的团体

access [ˈækses] *n.* 进入，通路

crown [kraun] *n.* 王冠，花冠，王权，顶点

observation deck 观景台

背景知识注释 Background Notes

1. Statue of Liberty 等同于Statue of Liberty Enlightening the World，自由女神像，全名为“自由女神铜像国家纪念碑”，正式名称是“照耀世界的自由女神”，于1886年10月28日矗立在美国纽约市海港内的自由岛的哈德逊河口附近，被誉为美国的象征。创作者是弗雷德里克•奥古斯特•巴托尔迪。1984年，它被列入世界遗产名录。
2. American Revolutionary War 美国革命战争，或称美国独立战争(American War of Independence，1775～1783)，是大英帝国和其北美十三州殖民地的革命者，以及几个欧洲强国之间的一场战争。这场战争主要是始于为了对抗英国的经济政策，但后来却因为法国、西班牙及荷兰加入战争对抗英国，而使战争的范围远远超过了英属北美洲之外。1783年订定的《巴黎条约》承认了美国的独立，因为许多殖民地的居民逃离那十三个殖民地并在北方安顿下来，这场战争同时也为日后加拿大的建立做了准备。
3. Emma Lazarus 爱玛•拉扎露丝，1849年出生于纽约一个犹太人家庭。她有六个兄弟姊妹，她是老四。她从小爱好写作。小小年纪，就写了很多诗歌剧本，还出了一本作品集。她懂几门外语，包括法语、德语、意大利语。她最著名的代表作品是十四行诗《新巨人》(The New Colossus)。

4. the United States Lighthouse Board　美国灯塔委员会，隶属美国联邦政府财政部，于1852年和1910年之间负责全美所有灯塔和导航设备的建设和维护。

5. the War Department　美国战争部，1789年创建。1947年9月18日，该部更名为“美国陆军部”。它是美国国防部的三个军种部委之一。该部由陆军部长（即一名文官）领导，负责美国陆军的行政性(非作战)事务。该部的最高军事首长为陆军参谋长。

6. Liberty Island　自由岛，旧称Bedloe’s Island，是一个由美国联邦政府所有，由美国国家公园管理局管理的纽约港岛屿，坐落于纽约州和新泽西州边界的新泽西州一侧，邻近纽约州纽约市曼哈顿和新泽西州泽西市。世界文化遗产自由女神像屹立在此岛上。自由岛这个名称虽然自20世纪早期就已经开始使用，但直到1956年才成为正式名称。

7. President Calvin Coolidge　卡尔文•柯立芝总统，美国第30任总统。

8 .the National Park Service　美国国家公园管理局。

9. President Ronald Reagan　罗纳德•里根总统，美国第40任总统。

中文译文
Suggested Translation

1 1886年的10月28日，总统斯蒂芬•格罗弗•克利夫兰为纽约港的自由女神像落成揭幕。

2 雕像的全名是：照耀世界的自由女神，为法国公民赠送给他们的美国朋友的礼物，以彰显这两个国家为追求自由和民主所做的努力以及在美国革命战争期间所结成的联盟。这场革命战争发生在此前110年。在法国建造的这尊151英尺的铜质雕像，被拆分为350个独立的部分运往纽约。 1886年6月17日铜像抵达纽约，并在接下来的几个月里被进行重新组装。电工们忙着为火炬安装照明线路以便在夜间能将它点亮。

3 克利夫兰总统代表美国公民接受了这尊雕像。他宣称：“我们不要忘记自由已在这里安家落户，也不要冷落她所选择的圣坛。”这尊雕像迅速成为美国践行人道主义以及乐于接受世界各地芸芸众生的象征。“让那些因为渴求自由并追求美好生活，而历经长途跋涉业已疲惫不堪、身无分文的人们，相互依偎着投入我的怀抱吧！”。爱玛 • 拉扎露丝 (Emma Lazarus) 诗歌里的这些词句被刻在雕像的底座上。

4 “自由女神”最初被打算用做一个多功能的灯塔。1886年至1901年，雕像由美国灯塔管理委员会管理。1901年，战争部接管其运行和维护工作。1924年10月15日卡尔文·柯立芝总统宣布雕像及其坐落的岛屿——如今称为自由岛，一起成为自由女神铜像国家纪念碑。1933年它改由美国国家公园管理局监管。1982年，罗纳德·里根总统成立了一个委员会，负责整修日见恶化的自由女神像，以迎接1986年的百年庆典。一个美法联合保护和修复小组的成员清扫了雕像，并用金箔包装的火炬替换了玻璃和金属的火炬。原来的火炬则在雕像的大厅里展出。

5 如今，自由女神像每年接待多达500万人，成为一个主要的旅游景点。尽管2001年9月11日恐怖袭击以后欲登女神冠冕观景台(the statue’s crown)受到限制，但游客们仍然可以访问自由岛、雕像的基座观景台以及博物馆。

25 U.S. President William McKinley Assassinated 又一个遇刺身亡的美国总统——威廉·麦金莱

威廉·麦金莱 总统及第一夫人简介

威廉·麦金莱(William Mckinley, 1843.1.29～1901.9.14)，第25任美国总统(1897～1901)。他18岁从军，以少校军衔退伍，先后当过律师、县检察官、众议员和州长，1897年当选为总统。执政后，他采取提高关税和稳定货币的政策，加上其他措施，使美国的经济有了很大起色，他因此被称为“繁荣总统”。对外，他发动了美西战争。他最后在布法罗被枪杀身亡，享年58岁，是美国立国后被刺身亡的第三位总统。

艾达·萨克斯顿·麦金莱(Ida Saxton McKinley, 1847.6.8～1907.5.26)，第25任美国总统威廉·麦金莱的妻子，与总统育有两个女儿。艾达结婚前在她父亲的银行里当出纳员。艾达生性脆弱，还有些神经质，由于母亲和两个妹妹在短时间内相继死亡，她悲痛欲绝，健康也受到影响，最终发展成癫痫病，完全有赖于丈夫的照顾。总统对夫人的耐心、忠诚、爱护和关注，为当时首都人士津津乐道。总统被暗杀后，麦金莱夫人痛不欲生，健康日益恶化。

经典原文
Original Text

Words & Expressions

in the heat 在高温下

unbeknownst [ˌʌnbiˈnəunst] *adj.* 不知的

anarchist [ˈænəkist] *n.* 无政府主义者

1 On September 6, 1901, U.S. President William McKinley spent the morning visiting *Niagara Falls*① with his wife before returning to *the Pan-American Exposition*② in *Buffalo*③, New York in the afternoon to spend a few minutes greeting the public.

2 By about 3:30 p.m., President McKinley stood inside *the Temple of Music*④ building at the Exposition, ready to begin shaking the hands of the public as they streamed into the building. Many had been waiting for hours outside in the heat for their chance to meet the President. Unbeknownst to the President and the many guards who stood nearby, among those waiting outside was 28-year-old anarchist *Leon Czolgosz*⑤ who was planning to kill President McKinley.

3 At 4 p.m. the doors to the building were opened and the mass of people waiting outside were forced into a single line as they entered the Temple of Music building. The line of people thus came up to the president in an organized fashion, with just enough time to whisper a "Nice to meet you, Mr. President," shake President McKinley's hand, and then be forced to continue along the line and out the door again.

4 President McKinley, the 25th president of the United States, was a popular president who had just started his second term in office and the people seemed clearly glad to get a chance to meet him. However, at 4:07 p.m.. Leon Czolgosz had made it into the building and it was his turn to greet the President.

5 In Czolgosz's right hand, he held *a 32 caliber Iver-Johnson revolver*⑥, which he had covered by wrapping

a handkerchief around the gun and his hand. Although Czolgosz's swaddled hand was noticed before he reached the President, many thought it looked like it covered an injury and not that it was hiding a gun. Also, since the day had been hot, many of the visitors to see the President had been carrying handkerchiefs in their hands so that they could wipe the sweat off their faces.

6 When Czolgosz reached the President, President McKinley reached out to shake his left hand (thinking Czolgosz's right hand was injured) while Czolgosz brought up his right hand to President McKinley's chest and then fired two shots.

7 One of the bullets didn't enter the President — some say it bounced off of a button or off the President's sternum and then got tucked into his clothing. The other bullet, however, entered the President's abdomen, tearing through his stomach, pancreas, and kidney. Shocked at being shot, President McKinley began to sag as blood stained his white shirt. He then told those around him, "Be careful how you tell my wife."

8 Those in line behind Czolgosz and guards in the room all jumped on Czolgosz and started to punch him. Seeing that the mob on Czolgosz might easily and quickly kill him, President McKinley whispered either, "Don't let them hurt him" or "Go easy on him, boys."

9 President McKinley was then whisked away in an electric ambulance to the hospital at the Exposition. Unfortunately, the hospital was not properly equipped for such a surgery and the very experienced doctor usually on premises was away doing a surgery in another town. Although several doctors were found, the most experienced

swaddle [ˈswɔdl] *vt.* 用襁褓包，束缚

sternum [ˈstəːnəm] *n.* 胸骨

tuck [tʌk] *vt.* 卷起，挤进，用某物舒适地裹住，使隐藏

abdomen [æbˈdəumen] *n.* 腹部，下腹，腹腔

pancreas [ˈpænkriəs] *n.* 胰腺

kidney [ˈkidni] *n.* 肾，肾脏

sag [sæg] *vi.* 下垂；下降；萎靡

stain [stein] *vt.* 沾污，败坏，给…着色

whisk [hwisk] *vt.* 拂，掸，搅拌，挥动

on premises 在屋内

doctor that could be found was *Dr. Matthew Mann*⑦, a gynecologist. The surgery began at 5:20 p.m..

10 During the operation, the doctors searched for the remains of the bullet that had entered the President's abdomen, but were unable to locate it. Worried that continued searching would tax the President's body too much, the doctors decided to discontinue looking for it and to sew up what they could. The surgery was completed a little before 7 p.m..

11 For several days, President McKinley seemed to be getting better. After the shock of the shooting, the nation was excited to hear some good news. However, what the doctors did not realize was that without drainage, an infection had built up inside the President. By September 13 it was obvious the President was dying. At 2:15 a.m. on September 14, 1901, President William McKinley died of gangrene. That afternoon, Vice President Theodore Roosevelt was sworn in as President of the United States.

12 After being pummeled right after the shooting, Leon Czolgosz had been arrested and taken to police headquarters before nearly being lynched by the angry crowds that surrounded the Temple of Music. Czolgosz readily admitted that he was the one who had shot the President. In his written confession, Czolgosz stated, "I killed President McKinley because I done my duty. I didn't believe one man should have so much service and another man should have none."

13 Czolgosz was brought to trial on September 23, 1901. He was quickly found guilty and sentenced to death. On October 29, 1901, Leon Czolgosz was electrocuted.

gynecologist [ˌgainiˈkɔlədʒist] *n.* 妇科医生

tax [tæks] *vt.* 向…课税，使负重担

drainage [ˈdreinidʒ] *n.* 排水，废水

gangrene [ˈgæŋgriːn] *n.* 坏疽

pummel [ˈpʌməl] *vt.* 击，打，用拳头连续揍

police headquarters 警察总部

lynch [lintʃ] *vt.* 以私刑处死

electrocute [iˈlektrəkjuːt] *vt.* 施以电刑，以电刑处死，使触电致死

背景知识注释
Background Notes

1. Niagara Falls　尼亚加拉瀑布。它位于加拿大安大略省和美国纽约州的交界处，是北美东北部尼亚加拉河上的大瀑布，也是美洲大陆最著名的奇景之一。它与伊瓜苏瀑布、维多利亚瀑布并称为世界三大跨国瀑布。尼亚加拉瀑布一直吸引人们到此度蜜月、走钢索横越瀑布或者坐木桶漂游瀑布。
2. the Pan-American Exposition　泛美博览会，即1901年5月1日至11月2日在美国纽约布法罗举办的世界博览会。
3. Buffalo　布法罗，又译“水牛城”，是美国纽约州西部的一座城市，位于伊利湖东端、尼亚加拉河的源头，是纽约州第二大城市(仅次于纽约市)、伊利县首府。对岸为加拿大伊利堡。泛美博览会当年在布法罗举办主要原因是那时布法罗是美国第八大城市而且是最重要的铁路枢纽城市。
4. the Temple of Music　音乐殿堂，为1901年在纽约布法罗参观泛美博览会修建的音乐厅和礼堂。建筑风格和博览会的其他大多数建筑一致，但博览会结束后就拆除了。
5. Leon Czolgoz　即Leon Frank Czolgosz 里昂•弗兰克•乔戈什(1873.5～1901.10)，刺杀美国总统威廉•麦金莱的凶手。在生命的最后几年里，他自称受到了无政府主义者诸如埃玛•戈尔德曼与亚历山大•贝克曼的巨大影响。
6. a 32 caliber Iver-Johnson revolver　埃尔文•约翰逊军火公司制造的0.32口径左轮手枪。Iver-Johnson 埃尔文•约翰逊军火公司是1871年至1993年间美国的军火、自行车和摩托车生产商。公司以其创办人——在挪威出生的埃尔文•约翰逊的名字命名。
7. Dr. Matthew Mann　马太•曼博士，一名妇科医生。

中文译文
Suggested Translation

1 1901年9月6日，美国总统威廉•麦金莱花了一上午的时间和他的妻子参观尼亚加拉大瀑布(Niagara Falls)，然后于下午回到纽约州布法罗(Buffalo)泛美博览会(the Pan-American Exposition)，以便能腾出点时间与公众见面。

2 下午3时30分左右，麦金莱总统站在博览会音乐殿堂大楼(the Temple of Music)内，准备与鱼贯而入的市民握手。许多人为了有机会拜见总统已经在炎热中等待了几个小时。等候的人群中28岁的无政府主义者里昂•乔戈什(Leon Czolgosz)正在预谋刺杀麦金莱总统。对此，总统以及站在他身边的许多卫兵全然不知。

3 下午 4 时，殿堂的门开了。等候在外面的人群排成一列进入音乐殿堂。他们次序井然地走到总统跟前，每个人仅有足够的时间轻声说一句：“很高兴见到您，总统先生！”握握麦金莱总统的手，随即又随着队伍走到门外。

4 麦金莱总统为美国第25任总统。此时其第二个任期伊始，人气极高。人们有机会见到他，似乎都非常高兴。然而，下午4时7分，里昂·乔戈什进入了大楼。该轮到他问候总统了。

5 乔戈什(Czolgosz)的右手握着一把0.32口径的左轮手枪，但枪和手用一块手帕包裹着。尽管在他走到总统跟前时人们还是注意到他缚着的手，但是许多人认为这似乎是用于包扎伤口的而不是用来藏枪支的。此外，由于天气炎热许多来看总统的游客手中都拿着手绢以便能擦拭脸上的汗水。

6 乔戈什走到总统跟前时，麦金莱总统伸出手来握着他的左手(认为乔戈什的右手受伤了)，而乔戈什却举起右手对准麦金莱总统的胸部连开两枪。

7 一颗子弹未穿入总统的体内——有些人说它击中了纽扣或总统的胸骨然后弹开落到了总统的衣服里。然而，另一颗子弹射进了总统的腹部，穿过他的胃、胰腺和肾脏。麦金莱总统受惊后开始慢慢倒了下去，鲜血染红了他的白衬衫。这时，他告诉周围的人：“你们告诉我的妻子时小心点。”

8 乔戈什身后的人们和殿堂里的警卫全都扑向乔戈什并开始揍他。见到乔戈什身上愤怒的人群可能三下两下就将其置于死地，麦金莱总统低声说：“别让他们伤害他”、“放过他，孩子们。”

9 麦金莱总统随即被电动救护车迅速送往博览会附近的一所医院。不幸的是，医院没有适当的装备，无法进行手术，而医院那位通常在岗又经验丰富的医生外出到另一个城镇做手术了。尽管找来了几位医生，但是最有经验的乃是妇科医生马太·曼博士(Dr. Matthew Mann)。手术在下午5时20分开始。

10 在手术过程中，医生搜寻进入总统腹部的子弹，但都未能找到。因为担心继续搜索会对总统身体造成太多伤害，医生们决定停止寻找并尽其所能进行缝合。手术在下午7时之前结束。

11 一连几天，麦金莱总统的伤情似乎日渐好转。在经受枪击事件的冲击之后，听到一些好消息，国民都很兴奋。然而，医生并没有意识到由于没有实施引流导致总统体内已经产生了感染。9月13日总统显然已经奄奄一息。1901年9月14日凌晨2时15分威廉•麦金莱死于坏疽。副总统西奥多•罗斯福(Theodore Roosevelt)宣誓就任美国总统。

12 开枪之后，里昂・乔戈什 (Leon Czolgosz) 当即被猛揍一顿，随后被逮捕并带到警察局总部。音乐殿堂周围愤怒的人群几近将其施于私刑。乔戈什很快就承认是他开枪射击总统的。在书面供词中，乔戈什说："我之所以杀了麦金莱总统是为我尽了自己的责任。我认为有的人不应当拥有那么多的工作而有的人却一无所有。"

13 1901年9月23日，乔戈什被送上法庭受审。他很快就被判有罪，并被判处死刑。1901年10月29日，里昂•乔戈什(Leon Czolgosz)被施以电刑而死。

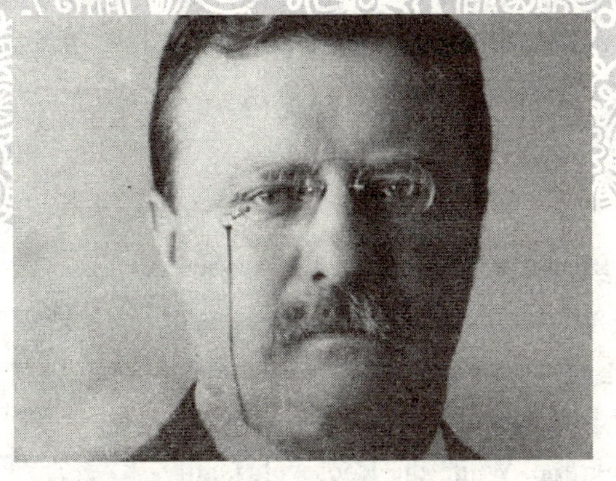

26 President Theodore Roosevelt's Family Pets and the Rough Riders 西奥多·罗斯福总统的家庭宠物与莽骑兵

西奥多·罗斯福 总统及第一夫人简介

西奥多•罗斯福(Theodore Roosevelt, 1858.10.27～1919.1.6)，第26任美国总统(1901～1909)，人称“老罗斯福”，昵称“泰迪(Teddy)”，曾任海军副部长，1900年当选副总统。1901年总统威廉•麦金莱(William McKinley)被无政府主义者刺杀身亡，西奥多•罗斯福继任成为美国总统，时年42岁，是上任时最年轻的美国总统。西奥多•罗斯福在总统任期内，对美国国内的主要贡献是建立资源保护政策，保护了森林、矿产、石油等资源；建立公平交易法案，推动劳资和解。对外奉行门罗主义，实行扩张政策，建设强大军队，干涉美洲事务。他的独特个性和改革主义政策，使他成为美国历史上最伟大的总统之一。

艾蒂斯•克米特•卡罗•罗斯福(Edith Kermit Carow Roosevelt, 1861.8.6～1948.9.30)，第26任美国总统西奥多•罗斯福的第二任妻子，与总统育有四儿一女。艾蒂斯是罗斯福在纽约的邻居，是他妹妹凯瑟琳的挚友。她是他青梅竹马的伙伴。成年后，两人对书籍和大自然有共同爱好。后来罗斯福到哈佛大学读书，并和艾丽司•李相爱，和艾蒂斯的来往遂告中断。在他第一任妻子去世后一年，罗斯福在妹妹的住处偶然碰到艾蒂斯小姐，与她重叙旧好。罗斯福夫人沉默寡言，治家有方。作为第一夫人，她改变了每周举办音乐爱好者招待会的惯例，花费47万美元改建白宫使它成为总统所说的“共和国首脑简朴而有尊严的寓所”。此外，她一直与政界和外交界人士保持亲密的朋友关系，是一位出色的外交活动家。她与英国外交官斯普林•里斯的友情，改变了美国的历史。

经典原文
Original Text

1 When Roosevelt was a young boy he had been sick with asthma. In order to get well he spent a lot of time outdoors building up his strength and learning about animals. Since he loved animals, it was no surprise that his six children loved them too. While the Roosevelt family lived in the White House, the children collected many pets, including a badger, a bear, a raccoon, cats, dogs, rats, guinea pigs, snakes, and a calico pony named Algonquin. During the summers, the children and Mrs. Roosevelt often stayed at their home in *Long Island* ①, New York. While they were away from their father, he often sent them letters. Roosevelt wrote one to his son *Theodore Jr.* ② who had not yet learned to read.

2 President Roosevelt seemed to enjoy the family's numerous pets just as much as his children. Roosevelt also enjoyed writing letters to his friends and telling them about his children's animals. Here's an example:

3 To Mrs. Elizabeth Stuart Phelps Ward White House, Oct. 20, 1902.

4 "At this moment, my small daughter being out, I am acting as a nurse to two wee guinea pigs, which she feels would not be safe in the room with me — and if I can prevent it I do not intend to have wanton suffering inflicted on any creature."

Words & Expressions

asthma [ˈæsmə] *n.* 哮喘，气喘

badger [ˈbædʒə] *n.* 獾

raccoon [rəˈkuːn] *n.* 浣熊，浣熊毛皮

guinea pig [ˈgini pig] *n.* 天竺鼠

calico [ˈkælikəu] *n.* 有斑纹(或斑点)的动物

pony [ˈpəuni] *n.* 矮种马，小马

wee [wiː] *adj.* 很小的，微小的，很早的

wanton [ˈwɔntən] *adj.* 淘气的，顽皮的，无意义的，无缘无故的，怀恶意的

inflict [inˈflikt] *vt.* 施予打击，使遭受痛苦，使承受负担，使受处罚，加刑

safari [sə'fɑːri] *n.* (尤指在东非的)旅游，游猎，科学考察，长途徒步的旅游或考察

specimen ['spesimin] *n.* 样品，抽样，标本，样本，实例

known for 因…而出名

bully ['buli] *adj.* 第一流的，特好的

slang [slæŋ] *n.* 俚语，行业用语

push through 完成，挤着穿过

big-game refuges 大型猎物禁猎区

5 Although Roosevelt loved animals, he also liked to go hunting. As his boys grew up they often went with their dad on hunting trips. When he was no longer president, Roosevelt went on safaris to Africa and *Brazil* ③ to gather natural specimens for *the Smithsonian Institution*④. His son, *Kermit* ⑤, went on the African safari with him.

6 Roosevelt was known for his endless energy. *Buffalo Bill* ⑥ called him "a cyclone" and Mark Twain called him "an earthquake." As a young man he spent two years as a cowboy on his ranch in *the Dakota Territory*⑦. When Spain and the U.S. went to war in 1898, he organized a *Volunteer Cavalry*⑧ (an army unit on horseback), which was called "*the Rough Riders*⑨." How do you think Roosevelt did in the war?

7 Roosevelt came back from the Spanish-American War as a national hero. He liked to say, "We had a 'bully' fight." "Bully" was a slang word at the time that meant "first-rate" or "splendid." Another phrase he liked to use when facing a problem was "never around, always through."

8 Roosevelt was a very determined president. During his term, he forced coal mine owners to negotiate with striking miners, pushed through laws to conserve land and won *the Nobel Peace Prize*⑩ for helping to end *a war between Japan and Russia in 1905* ⑪.

9 Roosevelt's love of nature and wildlife inspired him to help conserve land and create national parks. While he was president, he created 51 national parks, four big-game refuges, and the first national game reserve. He also added 43 million acres of national forest. When Roosevelt believed in something he worked hard to promote it. He believed that the only thing worth doing in life was hard

work for a worthy cause.

背景知识注释
Background Notes

1. Long Island 长岛，一座位于北美洲大西洋岸的岛屿，行政上属于美国纽约州的一部分。长岛长190公里，宽约20～30公里，它从纽约港伸入北大西洋。

2. Theodore Jr. 小西奥多•罗斯福（1887.12.13～1944.7.12），西奥多•罗斯福的第二个孩子，他是西奥多•罗斯福与艾蒂斯•卡罗的第一个孩子，曾在哈佛大学就读，做过商人、政治家、士兵、作家。

3. Brazil 巴西联邦共和国，它是拉丁美洲最大的国家，人口居世界第五，面积居世界第五。巴西的官方语言为葡萄牙语。足球是巴西人文化生活的主流。巴西是2014年世界杯足球赛主办国家，巴西城市里约热内卢是2016年夏季奥林匹克运动会举办城市。

4. the Smithsonian Institution 史密森学会，美国一系列博物馆和研究机构的集合组织。该组织囊括19 座博物馆、9座研究中心、美术馆和国家动物园以及1.365亿件艺术品和标本，也是美国唯一一所由美国政府资助、半官方性质的第三部门博物馆机构，还拥有世界最大的博物馆系统和研究联合体。管理和经费来源于美国政府拨款、其他捐助以及自身商店和杂志销售盈利。

5. Kermit 克利姆特•罗斯福（1998.10.10～1943.6.4），西奥多•罗斯福的第三个孩子；西奥多•罗斯福与艾蒂斯•卡罗的第二个儿子。曾在哈佛大学就读，做过商人、执政官、士兵。

6. Buffalo Bill 水牛比尔，William Cody的绰号，他是1846～1917年美国西部拓荒时代的传奇性人物，传说他曾在17个月中杀掉水牛4,280头。他最为人所知的身份可能是作为蛮荒西部 (wild west) 的代表人物，

7. the Dakota Territory 达科他领土，存在于1861年3月2日至1889年11月2日。最后一分为二，分裂为南达科他和北达科他两个州加入美国。

8. Volunteer Cavalry 自愿骑兵队，马背上的军队。

9. the Rough Riders 莽骑兵团，1898年，麦金莱总统在美西战争中招募的三个骑兵团中的第一骑兵团，也是这三个团中唯一参加过战斗的一个团。战士多为印第安人、大学生运动员、牛仔和牧场主。西奥多•罗斯福为其第二任团长。

10. the Nobel Peace Prize 诺贝尔和平奖，是五个诺贝尔奖中的一个。根据诺贝尔的遗嘱，和平奖应该颁给"为促进民族团结友好、取消或裁减常备军队以及为和平会议的组织和宣传尽到最大努力或做出最大贡献的人"。

11. a war between Japan and Russia in 1905 即Russo-Japanese War 日俄战争(1904.2.8～1905.9.5)，是日本与沙皇俄国为了侵占中国东北和朝鲜，在中国东北的土地上进行的一场战争。

中文译文
Suggested Translation

1 还是个小男孩时，罗斯福饱受哮喘折磨。为了能够康复，他花了很多时间从事户外活动以增进体魄并学习有关动物的一些知识。由于他热爱动物，所以他的六个小孩也喜欢动物。当罗斯福一家住在白宫时，孩子们收养了许多宠物，包括獾、熊、浣熊、猫、狗、鼠、天竺鼠、蛇及一匹名为阿尔贡金 (Algonquin) 斑点花色的小马。夏季时，罗斯福的妻子及孩子们常常留在他们位于纽约长岛的家中。当罗斯福跟他的家人分隔两地时，他时常写信回家。罗斯福曾写信给他的儿子小西奥多 (Theodore Jr.)，可他那时还不会阅读呢。

2 与他的孩子一样，罗斯福总统似乎非常喜爱家中为数众多的宠物。罗斯福还喜欢写信给他的朋友，告诉他们关于他小孩养的宠物的事儿。这儿有一份范例：

3 致白宫华德太太 (Mrs. Elizabeth Stuart Phelps Ward)，1902年10月20日

4 “这时，我的小女儿正在室外，而我则负责照顾两只小型天竺鼠，但她觉得它们跟我同在一室并不安全；假如可以预防的话，我绝对不会故意伤害任何生物的。”

5 罗斯福热爱动物，也喜欢狩猎。他的儿子长大后常跟他一起出外狩猎。卸任后，为了帮助史密森尼博物馆 (Smithsonian Institution) 收集自然标本，罗斯福曾参加非洲及巴西的狩猎旅行。他的儿子柯密(Kermit)也跟他一起参加了非洲的狩猎旅行。

6 罗斯福以拥有无穷精力而著称。野牛比尔(Buffalo Bill)称呼他为“一阵旋风”，而马克•吐温则形容他为“一场地震”。罗斯福年轻时，他在位于达科他领地(the Dakota Territory)他自己家的牧场里当了两年的牛仔。1898年西班牙及美国开战时，他组织了一队名为“莽骑兵”(the Rough Riders)的自愿骑兵 (Volunteer Cavalry)。

7 美西战争之后，罗斯福以国家英雄的形象凯旋。他喜欢把这场战事形容为“一场 Bully 战事”，Bully 是当时的一个俚语，意指“第一流”或“杰出的”；面对问题时，他喜欢说的另一句话是“绝不回避，永远面对”。

8 罗斯福总统行事非常果断。在其任期内，他强迫煤矿老板与罢工的矿工达成了协议、推行保存土地的相关法律，并因居中调停1905年的日俄战争而获得诺贝尔和平奖。

9 罗斯福对自然及野生生物的热爱激励着他保护土地及兴建国家公园。在其总统任内，他兴建了51座国家公园、四座大型猎物禁猎区及第一座国家动物保护区。他还增加了4,300万英亩的国家森林。当罗斯福相信某件事时，他会不遗余力地去推动它。他相信生命中唯一值得做的就是为有意义的事情奋斗。

27 The Taft Smile Upon the Future
塔夫脱总统面对未来的微笑

威廉·霍华德·塔夫脱 总统及第一夫人简介

威廉•霍华德•塔夫脱(William Howard Taft, 1857.9.15～1930.3.8)，第27任美国总统(1909～1913)。塔夫脱在总统任期内虽然政绩平平，但一直勤勤恳恳，做了不少工作，如：逐步采取年度预算，建立邮政储蓄体系，鼓励保护自然资源，大力推行反托拉斯法等。塔夫脱还曾担任过律师、地方检察官、州高级法院法官、司法部副部长、法庭庭长、法学教授、美国第一任菲律宾总督等。1921年，沃伦•G•哈定总统任命塔夫脱为美国首席大法官。他也是唯一担任过首席大法官的前总统。塔夫脱的很多家庭成员也从过政。他的儿子和孙子都当过参议员。他的重孙子鲍伯•塔夫脱曾当过俄亥俄州的州长(1999～2007)。

海伦·路易斯·赫伦·内莉·塔夫脱 (Helen Louise Herron "Nellie" Taft, 1861.6.2～1943.5.22)，第27任美国总统威廉·霍华德·塔夫脱的妻子，与总统育有两子一女。婚前曾在中学教书。她是第一位在总统就职典礼日随着丈夫乘车穿过宾夕法尼亚大街的总统夫人(此前为前总统伴随新总统行进)。塔夫脱夫人入住白宫两个月后，突患中风，不能言语，一直没有完全恢复。从此，她只能适度参加接待活动。

经典原文 Original Text

1 Taft adored children. He joked that he had laid *YMCA*① cornerstones "the world over." The finest sights during his 1909 tour were the 150,000 children of *Chicago*② who lined the streets, the 20,000 children of *Salt Lake*③ who greeted him, and a like number at *Portland*④, Oregon, who formed, first, a "living flag," then spelled "T-A-F-T" with placards. Taft was moved to tears. "You call your city the 'City of Roses' because of the beautiful flower," he told the children of Portland, "but I look now upon 20,000 human roses."

2 To Kansas school children Taft said, "You are obedient children, aren't you?" "Sure," they yelled in chorus. "I hope my coming here has given you part of a vacation for one day." "You bet it has!" "So, you owe me something, don't you?"

3 A small scandal arose when some newspapers got hold of the story of a rambunctious boy who stepped in the Presidential soup at a banquet. Taft squelched the story and upheld the boy's honor with an official "certification" that the boy did not disturb his soup. "I do not want to spoil a good story," the President said, "but it seems hardly fair that the kid should be forever charged with the thing that he did not do..."

4 One child was overjoyed when Taft was elected President. He wrote, "I am a boy eleven years old and I am big and fat like you. The boys at my school call me Taft and when you were elected they hauled me around in an old buggy and had a reception with me representing you."

5 Four years later, children again gave Taft their

Words & Expressions

adore [ə'dɔː] *vt.* 崇拜，敬爱，爱慕，敬仰，疼爱

cornerstone ['kɔːnəˌstəun] *n.* 奠基石，要素，柱石，基础

like [laik] *adj.* 同样的，相似的

placard ['plækɑːd] *n.* 布告，招贴，海报

scandal ['skændəl] *n.* 丑事，丑行，丑闻

get hold of 把握，抓住，得到

rambunctious [ræm'bʌŋkʃəs] *adj.* 狂暴的，骚乱的，无秩序的，难于控制的

step in 插手，介入，干涉

squelch [skweltʃ] *vt.* 压碎，击碎，使缄默，使无言

uphold [ʌp'həuld] *vt.* 举起，支撑，维护，认可，维持

overjoy [ˌəuvə'dʒɔi] *vt.* 使狂喜，使万分高兴

haul [hɔːl] *vt.* 拖，拉，强曳

buggy ['bʌgi] *n.* 童车，婴儿车，小货车，旧汽车

electoral support. One wrote, "I have read in the paper that this is your birthday. It is my birthday too and I am eleven years old today. I wish I were ten years older so that I could vote for you. I wish you a happy birthday and hope you will be elected President again. I would like to come to see you sometime. I am going to be a lawyer when I am a man."

6 That lawyerly ambition must have warmed the Judge President's heart, but Taft received one of the sweetest endorsements ever during the 1912 Massachusetts primary: "I am your little cousin, *Betty B. Higgins*⑤. Your sixth grandfather, Deacon Samuel Chapin, was my seventh great-grandfather, so one-ninth of you and one-tenth of me are alike, but ten-tenths of me hopes that nine-ninths of you will be President again."

7 Shortly before leaving office, Taft received a visit from a little girl from Wyoming who had refused to leave the city without a kiss from the President. The mother pleaded with the White House to grant the request of the obstinate child. Soon after, Taft's appointment calendar read, "Phyllis Westrand, *Lander*⑥, Wyo., (to be kissed)." He told her, "So you want to be kissed by the President... Well, I hope you will remember that."

electoral [iˈlektərəl] *adj.* (有关)选举的，选民的，选举人的，选举者的

lawyerly [ˈlɔːjəli] *adj.* 律师的

endorsement [inˈdɔːsmənt] *n.* 背书，批准，认可，赞同，担保

deacon [ˈdiːkən] *n.* 执事，会使

obstinate [ˈɔbstinit] *adj.* 固执的，倔强的，顽固的

appointment calendar 预约日程记录本

背景知识注释
Background Notes

1. YMCA （全称为Young Men's Christian Association) 基督教青年会，是基督教性质的国际性社会服务团体。已具有160多年的历史。它以基督“为世人服务”的精神，根据社会人群(尤其是弱势群体)的需要，从事各种各样的社会服务工作。这些服务工作以“促进大众德、智、体、群全面成长”的理念为导向，服务人群不分性别、年龄、国籍、种族和宗教信仰。服务工作有平民教育、体育康乐、营地服务、社区服务、青少年工作、难民工作、就业服务等等，一些青年会还开设有价格低廉的旅舍和宾馆。“基督教青年会”不是一个传教组织，也不是一个慈善机

构。它主要以传递爱心为使命，倡导和推动承担社会责任及促进社会和谐。中国基督教青年会创建于1895年，并存在至今。

2. Chicago　芝加哥，位于美国中西部，属伊利诺伊州，东临密歇根湖，是美国仅次于纽约市和洛杉矶的第三大城市。芝加哥地处北美大陆的中心地带，为美国最重要的铁路、航空枢纽。芝加哥同时也是美国最为重要的金融、文化、制造业、期货和商品交易中心之一。芝加哥常见的别名有："第二城"、"风城"，"芝城"等。

3. Salt Lake　盐湖城，美国犹他州的首府及最大城市，名列美国西部内陆城市的第三位，仅次于丹佛和菲尼克斯。它周围的高山海拔达到3,582米。以紧靠大盐湖而得名。

4. Portland　波特兰，位于美国的俄勒冈州，波特兰气候温和，阳光充沛，风景秀丽，别称是"玫瑰之城"。波特兰是美国最大的城市之一，也是美国重要的经济中心。

5. Betty B. Higgins　贝蒂•B•希金斯，支持塔夫脱总统连任的一位小朋友。

6. Lander　兰德市，是位于兰德怀俄明州中部弗里蒙特县的一个城市，为弗里蒙特县的县治。

中文译文
Suggested Translation

1 塔夫脱喜欢孩子。他开玩笑说他已经为世界各地的基督教青年会(YMCA)奠定了基石。1909 年他出巡时遇到的最为壮观的景象是 15 万名芝加哥儿童站立在街道两旁夹道欢迎他们的到来；盐湖城 (Salt Lake) 有两万名儿童热烈欢迎他的到来；俄勒冈州波特兰 (Portland) 近两万名儿童高举标语首先形成一面飘扬的旗帜然后又拼写成他的名字"T-A-F-T"。塔夫脱感动得热泪盈眶。"你们叫你们的城市'玫瑰之城'，因为这美丽的花朵，"他告诉波特兰的孩子们，"但是，我现在看到的这两万名学童犹如玫瑰。"

2 塔夫脱对堪萨斯的学童们说："你们是听话的孩子，不是吗？""当然，"他们齐声喊道。"我希望我的到来能给你们一天的假期。""当然有！""所以，您欠我们的，可不是吗？"

3 有些报纸曾抓住一位顽皮的男孩在一次宴会上弄脏了总统的汤这件事不放，于是流言蜚语传开了。总统制止了这样的传言并以官方的名义证明孩子并没有在他的汤里胡来以维护这位孩子的荣誉。"我不想糟蹋一个好故事，"总统说，"但是倘若那个孩子一直因一件他未曾做过的事情被指控，这似乎不公平……"

4 塔夫脱当选总统让一个孩子喜出望外。他写道："我是一个 11 岁的男孩，像您那样又壮又胖。学校里的孩子都叫我塔夫脱。当您当选总统的时候他们用一部老旧的车拉着我四处转并举行招待会让我代表您。"

5 四年以后，孩子们再次支持塔夫脱竞选。有位孩子写道："我在报纸上读到今天是您的生日。今天也是我的生日，我今年 11 岁了。我希望自己再长 10 岁，这样就能投您的票。祝您生日快乐，希望您将再次当选总统。我希望能来看您。长大以后我要当律师。"

6 那想当一名律师的雄心壮志一定温暖了这位法官总统的心。塔夫脱在 1912 年马萨诸塞州初选中收到了一份最贴心的支持——"我是您的小侄女，贝蒂 •B• 希金斯 (Betty B. Higgins)。您的第六代祖父，塞缪尔 • 查宾执事 (Deacon Samuel Chapin)，是我的第七代曾祖父，所以您有九分之一和我的十分之一相似。但是我十分之十期盼您九分之九能再次当选总统。"

7 即将卸任前，塔夫脱接见了一位来自怀俄明的小女孩。没得到总统的亲吻她就不离开那座城市。因此，孩子的母亲恳求白宫能满足这个固执的孩子的请求。不久，塔夫脱预约日程表上写着："怀俄明州兰德 (Lander) 菲利斯 • 韦斯特兰德 (Phyllis Westrand)。——被亲吻"。他告诉她："你想要总统的亲吻……嗯，那么，我希望你会记住它。"

28 Thomeas Woodrow Wilson — One of the Great Presidents of American History 托马斯·伍德罗·威尔逊——美国历史上最伟大的总统之一

托马斯·伍德罗·威尔逊 总统及第一夫人简介

托马斯·伍德罗·威尔逊 (Thomas Woodrow Wilson, 1856.12.28～1924.2.3)，第28任美国总统(1913～1921)。作为进步主义时代的一个领袖级知识分子，他曾先后任普林斯顿大学校长，新泽西州州长等职。1912年总统大选中，由于西奥多·罗斯福和威廉·塔夫脱的竞争分散了共和党选票，他以民主党人身份当选总统。迄今为止，他是唯一一名拥有哲学博士学位的美国总统，也是唯一一名任总统以前曾在新泽西州担任公职的美国总统。1962年历史学家对31位总统的投票排名中，威尔逊排名高居第4位，仅次于乔治·华盛顿、亚伯拉罕·林肯和富兰克林·罗斯福。

埃伦·路易斯·阿克森·威尔逊(Ellen Louise Axson Wilson, 1860.5.15～1914.8.6)，第28任美国总统威尔逊的第一任妻子，与总统育有三女。埃伦是一位对艺术、音乐和文学有修养的女性。成为第一夫人后，他在白宫三楼开辟了一个画室，把她的画捐赠给慈善团体。她还安排了她的两个女儿在白宫举行婚礼。1914年她死于肾病。艾迪斯·博林·盖尔特·威尔逊(Edith White Bolling Galt Wilson，1872.10.15～1961.12.28)原为珠宝商诺尔曼·盖尔特的妻子，1905年盖尔特去世。1915年由总统的堂妹海伦将诺尔曼介绍给总统。作为第一夫人，她在第一次世界大战期间严格遵守联邦定量供应制，为民众树立了榜样。1919年9月总统中风后，她小心翼翼地甄审所有国家大事，决定哪些至关重要，必须让卧床不起的总统过目。1924年总统去世后，她成为伍德罗·威尔逊基金会的负责人。1938年她的回忆录问世。

经典原文
Original Text

Words & Expressions

consecutive [kən'sekjutiv] *adj.* 连续的，连续不断的

suffrage ['sʌfridʒ] *n.* 投票，投票权，选举权

inauguration [iˌnɔːgju'reiʃən] *n.* 就职，就职典礼，开幕，开幕仪式

inaugural [i'nɔːgjurəl] *adj.* 就职典礼的，就任的

1 "He is one of the great presidents of American history," said *Rabbi*[①] *Stephen A. Wise*[②] of Woodrow Wilson. Born on December 28, 1856, in *Staunton*[③], Virginia, Thomas Woodrow Wilson started his career as a university professor. He went on to serve as president of *Princeton University*[④] and then ran as governor of New Jersey in 1910. Two years later, he ran for president on the Democratic ticket and won. Wilson became the 28th president of the United States, serving two consecutive terms in the White House, from 1913 to 1921. During his time in office, Wilson faced many challenges at home and abroad, and face them he did.

2 The issue of women's suffrage (right to vote) confronted Wilson right from the start. *The National Women's Party*[⑤] organized a suffrage parade in Washington, D.C., the day before Wilson's inauguration. Drawing away the crowds from inaugural events, leaders hoped to put pressure on the new president to pay attention to women's rights. It is said that when Wilson arrived in town he found the streets empty, instead of full with welcoming crowds, and was told that everyone was on *Pennsylvania Avenue*[⑥] watching the parade. Before the end of his second term in 1920, Wilson and Congress approved *the 19th Amendment*[⑦],

giving women the right to vote.

3 In foreign policy, Wilson faced a greater challenge than any president since Abraham Lincoln. Deciding whether or not to involve the U.S. in World War I severely tested his leadership. Initially reluctant to send soldiers overseas, Wilson met increased pressure. On April 6, 1917, the United States went to war with Germany. Less than a year later, on January 8, 1918, Wilson made his famous "*Fourteen Points*⑧" address, introducing the idea of a *League of Nations*⑨. The purpose of the international organization was to preserve peace. Wilson promoted his plan tirelessly, as U.S. troops contributed to an earlier than expected cease-fire in 1918.

4 For his efforts, Wilson was awarded the 1919 Nobel Peace Prize, but the award was bittersweet. Congress opposed U.S. entry into the League. The strain of his campaigning and the disappointment of Congress's resolution weakened him. He returned to Washington in a state of collapse and shortly suffered a thrombosis (a blood clot in a blood vessel) that impaired control over the left side of his body. Wilson and his second wife, *Edith Bolling Galt Wilson*⑩— who continued work in the White House when Wilson was ill — retired in Washington, D.C., in 1921. Wilson died three years later, and he is memorialized in many ways, including this 1918 footage of the president in a New York parade encouraging Americans to participate in *Liberty Loans*⑪ to support the war effort.

contribute to 是…的部分原因，促成，有助于，起作用

cease-fire [ˈsiːsˈfaiə] *n.* 停火，停战，停火协议，停火命令

bittersweet [ˈbitəswiːt] *adj.* 又苦又甜的

strain [strein] *n.* 种，族，应力，张力，压力

thrombosis [θrɔmˈbəusis] *n.* 血栓形成，交通堵塞

clot [klɔt] *n.* 凝块

impair [imˈpeə] *vt.* 损害，损伤

memorialize [miˈmɔːriəlaiz] *vt.* 纪念，庆祝

footage [ˈfutidʒ] *n.* 英尺长度，连续镜头

背景知识注释
Background Notes

1. Rabbi 拉比，犹太人中的一个特别阶层，主要为有学问的学者，是老师，也是智者的象征，他们经常与常人接触、解答他们的疑惑。他们是一群观察生活、思考生活从而获得智慧的人。
2. Stephen A. Wise 即Stephen Samuel Wise 斯蒂芬•塞缪尔•怀斯，匈牙利裔的美国宗教领袖，激进的犹太复国主义者且是世界犹太人议会的创始人（1936年）。
3. Staunton 斯汤顿，美国弗吉尼亚州西北部的一个独立城市，也是奥古斯塔县县治。它的面积为51.0平方公里，成立于1908年1月16日，城名纪念州长威廉•古奇的妻子利贝卡•斯汤顿。
4. Princeton University 普林斯顿大学，位于美国新泽西州的普林斯顿，是美国一所著名的私立研究型大学，八所常春藤盟校之一。学校于1746年在新泽西州伊丽莎白镇创立，是美国殖民时期成立的第四所高等教育学院，当时名为“新泽西学院”，1747年迁至新泽西州，1756年迁至普林斯顿，并于1896年正式改名为普林斯顿大学。
5. The National Women's Party （缩写为NWP）全国妇女党，成立于1913年，是美国20世纪初争取女性权力的团体，当时美国仅有男性有投票权，该团体主要为女性争取身为美国公民的基本平等权利，并于1920年促使美国通过宪法修正案，保障妇女的选举权力。
6. Pennsylvania Avenue 宾夕法尼亚大道，是华盛顿哥伦比亚特区的一条街道，联结白宫和美国国会大厦，是官方游行和民间抗议的地点，也是重要的通勤路线，是美国公路系统的一部分。
7. the 19th Amendment 即the Nineteenth Amendment to the United States Constitution 美国宪法第十九修正案，一般简称第十九修正案(Amendment XIX)。此修正案赋予了美国妇女选举权。
8. Fourteen Points 十四点和平原则， 由美国总统伍德罗•威尔逊于1918年1月提出。它在国际关系中被视为理想主义的典范之一。
9. League of Nations 国际联盟，简称国联，是《凡尔赛条约》签订后组成的国际组织。其宗旨是减少武器数量、平息国际纠纷及维持民众的生活水平。在存在的26年中，国联曾协助调解某些国际争端和处理某些国际问题。不过国联缺乏军队武力，所以要依赖大国援助，尤其是在制裁某些国家的时候。二战结束以后，随着各国矛盾的发展和激化，国联走向破产的境地，最后被联合国取代。
10. Edith Bolling Galt Wilson 艾迪斯•博林•盖尔特•威尔逊(1872.10.15～1961.12.28)，美国总统伍德罗•威尔逊的第二任妻子，美国1915年至1921年间的第一夫人。因为在1919年10月她的丈夫威尔逊总统身患严重中风后所发挥的作用被称为“隐身总统”和“第一位管理白宫的女人”，也被称为“美国的第一位女性总统”。
11. Liberty Loans 自由公债，美国政府在第一次世界大战时发行的五种完全由认购者自愿承购的政府公债的一种。

中文译文
Suggested Translation

1 “他是美国历史上最伟大的总统之一。”当斯蒂芬•怀斯拉比 (Rabbi Stephen A. Wise) 谈到伍德罗•威尔逊时，他是这样认为的。托马斯•伍德罗•威尔逊于1856年12月28日在弗吉尼亚州的史坦顿 (Staunton) 出生。他本来是一名大学教授，后来成为普林斯顿大学的校长，然后于1910年当选为新泽西州的州长。两年之后，他成为民主党的总统候选人，并且赢得选举。威尔逊是美国的第28任总统，从1913年到1921年连续担任两届。在其任内，威尔逊面临来自国内外的许多难题，但他还是勇敢地解决了这些问题。

2 有关女性投票权的议题从威尔逊上任之初就开始酝酿。当时全国妇女党 (National Women's Party) 在威尔逊就职的前一天，在华盛顿特区举办了一场投票权大游行。这场游行吸引了许多原本要观看就职活动的群众，带领游行的领队想对这位新总统施压，希望他能够重视女性投票权的问题。据说，当威尔逊到达的时候，街道空荡荡的，连一个欢迎他的人都没有。后来才有人跟他说，群众都跑去宾州大道看游行了。直到1920年，在威尔逊第二任总统任期即将结束之前，他和国会一致通过美国宪法第19号修正案，赋予了妇女投票的权力。

3 在外交政策上，威尔逊也面临了自亚伯拉罕•林肯总统之后最严厉的挑战。美国究竟是否卷入第一次世界大战这一问题是对威尔逊的领导能力的严峻考验。一开始，威尔逊并不愿意派兵到海外参加战争，但是他却感受到越来越大的压力。1917年4月6日，美国对德国宣战。过了不到一年的时间，在1918年的1月8日，威尔逊发表了著名的“十四点原则”(Fourteen Points) 演说，向全世界提出了成立“国际联盟”(League of Nations) 的构想。这个国际组织的目的是维持世界和平。威尔逊不屈不挠地推动这个构想，而由于美国军队的介入，战争也在1918年早于预期实现停火。

4 因为他的努力，威尔逊得到了1919年的诺贝尔和平奖，但是对他而言，这却是苦乐参半的。国会反对美国加入国际联盟。因为竞选期间的压力，以及对国会决议案的阻挠感到失望，威尔逊回到华盛顿之后，整个人身心俱疲。不久之后，他罹患血管栓塞疾病，整个左半身都无法自由行动。威尔逊的第二任妻子艾迪斯•博林•盖尔特•威尔逊 (Edith Bolling Galt Wilson) 在他生病之后，仍然在白宫服务，两人都在1921年退休。威尔逊于三年之后去世，各界都以不同的方式对他表示追忆，包括放映1918年他在纽约参加鼓励美国民众购买“自由公债”(Liberty Loan) 以支持战事的游行等一系列影片。

29 President Warren Gamaliel Harding and Sex, Scandal and Death in the White House
沃伦·甘梅利尔·哈定总统与白宫的性、丑闻和死亡

沃伦·甘梅利尔·哈定 总统及第一夫人简介

沃伦•甘梅利尔•哈定 (Warren Gamaliel Harding, 1865.11.2～1923.8.2)，第29任美国总统(1921～1923)。哈定的父亲乔治•哈定在南北战争时应征入伍，后来教过书，从过医；母亲菲比是个医生。哈定在农村长大，曾当过小报记者。他与弗洛伦斯•克林•德沃尔夫于1891年结婚，婚后，弗洛伦斯经营报纸来支持哈定投身政界。哈定1921年当选为总统，1923年因心脏病突发于任内病逝。他当选总统前曾先后担任俄亥俄州议会参议员(1899～1903)、俄亥俄州副州长和联邦参议员(1915～1921)等职。

弗洛伦斯•克林•哈定(Florence Kling Harding, 1860.8. 15～1924.11.21)，第29任美国总统沃伦•哈定的妻子。她年轻时与邻家男生尤金•德沃尔夫(Eugene deWolfe)私奔后，曾随丈夫姓德沃尔夫，但两人一起不久便以离婚收场，与哈定再婚时弗洛伦斯带着一个孩子。她泼辣干练，运筹帷幄，操持办报业务，而她的丈夫则在政界打拼。哈定突然去世后，她也因肾炎变得非常虚弱，不到16个月之后就去世了。

经典原文
Original Text

1 In the rankings of American Presidents, Warren Gamaliel Harding often comes in first... from the bottom.

2 Even though Harding was elected in the biggest landslide up to that point... and even though he and his dog *Laddie Boy*① remained immensely popular in office... Harding today is remembered (if at all) for his womanizing, and for the scandals that engulfed his administration after he died suddenly in 1923 — poisoned, some believe, by his wife.

3 But in Warren Harding's hometown of *Marion*②, Ohio, the favorite son gets more favorable treatment.

4 Harding home tour guide (or docent) *Sherry Hall*③ sees it as her job to set the record straight, or try to.

5 "He was not poisoned, as you might hear," Hall told *Rocca*④. "His wife did not kill him. That was a totally made-up story."

6 In fact, said Hall, Warren and Florence Harding were very much a team during the 1920 presidential campaign, when the world beat a path to Warren Harding's doorstep. Literally!

7 "It was not unusual for 10,000 people to gather before the house," said Hall.

8 Hollywood stars came to Marion... athletes, too. *Al Jolson*⑤ even wrote a song for the campaign, and played

Words & Expressions

ranking [ˈræŋkiŋ] *n.* 等级，级别，地位，排名

landslide [ˈlændslaid] *n.*压倒性胜利；滑坡，塌方，泥石流

up to that point 直到那个时候

womanize [ˈwumənaiz] *vi.* 沉溺女色

engulf [inˈgʌlf] *vt.* 吞没，淹没，席卷，使陷入

docent [dəuˈsent] *n.* 讲解员，向导

set the record straight 澄清问题，弄清真相，纠正误解

made-up *adj.* 捏造的，制成的，化妆过的

literally [ˈlitərəli] *adj.* 照着原文，逐字地，准确地，不加夸张地

Warren Harding's porch.

9 *Trella Romine*[⑥], 95 years young, had a front row seat: "When I was four years old, I shook hands with Harding, right over the banister out there," she told Rocca. "You want to shake hands with the hand that shook hands with Harding?"

10 "Wow! Amazing!" he replied.

11 "I was scared, you know, but when I looked up at his face, it was such a kind face," said Romine. "So I just stuck out my hand and made history."

12 "I'm sorry to go all tabloid on you, but do you think Warren Harding was a womanizer?" Rocca asked.

13 Romine took the Fifth.

14 There's little doubt that Harding was at best negligent in supervising his administration. Several of his appointees, including a cabinet member, went to jail.

15 But students from *Harding High*[⑦] prefer to accentuate the positive.

16 "His presidential election was the first election that women voted in," said one girl.

17 "He was one of the presidents that helped start getting veterans health benefits," said one boy.

18 And trivia buffs, take note: President Harding was the only president to be elected on his birthday.

19 He was always described as being a very natty dresser. Sherry Hall displayed some of Harding's wardrobe, his golf clubs, his briefcase, his cigars, and even his shoes. The president with *matinee idol*[⑧] looks had the biggest feet of any *Oval Office*[⑨] occupant.

20 Among his accomplishments, Harding was the

banister [ˈbænistə] *n.* 栏杆，扶手

tabloid [ˈtæblɔid] *adj.* 通俗的，庸俗的，耸人听闻的，简短的

womanizer [ˈwumənaizə] *n.* 沉溺于女色的人，玩弄女人的人

take the Fifth 拒绝作危害自己的证词，拒绝回答，避而不谈

negligent [ˈneglidʒənt] *adj.* 玩忽的，疏忽的，过失的，漫不经心的，马虎的

accentuate [ækˈsentjueit] *vt.* 强调，重读

trivia [ˈtriviə] *n.* 琐事

buffs [bʌfs] *n.* 爱好者

natty [ˈnæti] *adj.* 整洁的，漂亮的，利落的，灵巧的

dresser [ˈdresə] *n.* 服装师，穿着讲究的人，服饰漂亮的人，好打扮的人

matinee [ˌmætˈnei] *n.* 午后场

idol [ˈaidəl] *n.* 偶像

occupant [ˈɔkjupənt] *n.* 占有人，占用人，居住者

first president to visit Alaska. He died on the way back. Thousands lined the streets to mourn as his body made its way home to Marion, where the town built a monument to him.

21 When President Harding died, the scandals that would define his presidency hadn't yet come to light... he was still a popular guy. Hence the size of the monument. This thing is big!

22 A bit grandiose, right? Until you consider that Warren Gamaliel Harding was a small town boy who made it to the White House. No matter what, THAT'S a big deal.

mourn [mɔːn] *vi.* 哀伤，悲哀，凭吊，哀悼

come to light 暴露，真相大白，众所周知

grandiose [ˈgrændiəus] *adj.* 雄伟的，壮丽的，浮夸的，炫耀的，自以为是的

背景知识注释
Background Notes

1. Laddie Boy　莱迪•波依，哈定的爱犬。在其执政期间远近闻名。它很忠诚。在内阁会上有自己的手工雕刻的椅子可坐。白宫为它举行过生日晚会并邀请附近的狗参加。报纸刊登过对它的“采访”。它是第一条全国性报纸经常报道的“第一狗”。据称，哈定总统去世前它因预知了主人即将到来的死亡连续嚎叫了三天。
2. Marion　马里恩，位于美国俄亥俄州中部的一个城市，是马里恩县的县治所在，县名纪念美国独立战争军官法兰西斯•马里恩。
3. Sherry Hall　雪莉•霍尔，哈定故居的导游。
4. Rocca　罗卡，造访哈定故居的游客。
5. Al Jolson　艾尔•乔森，1886年3月26日出生于路易斯安那州。他是20世纪初期百老汇舞台和后来银幕上最有名的歌星和演员之一，他热情奔放的表演风格使他成为当时最伟大的表演者。他那精湛的表演技艺和出众的歌唱天赋也使得他在百老汇的音乐史上占有重要的一席之地。
6. Trella Romine　特雷乐•罗密尼，是哈定的同乡。
7. Harding High　这里指哈定高中，位于俄亥俄州沃伦市的一所公立高中。他们的吉祥物是掠袭者(the Raider)。
8. matinee idol　受女观众欢迎的男明星。
9. Oval Office　白宫椭圆形办公室，位于白宫西翼，是美国总统的正式办公室。椭圆形办公室的地毯上印着美国总统徽章，总统杜鲁门是第一位使用美国总统徽章地毯的总统。那时美国总统

徽章是以单一颜色配以地毯不同的深浅度显示出来的。艾森豪威尔和肯尼迪亦继续使用这款地毯。近年的总统都设计不同款式的地毯以配合不同的内部装修。但总统奥巴马却继续使用乔治•布什于2001年设计的地毯。

中文译文
Suggested Translation

1 在美国总统的排名中，沃伦•甘梅利尔•哈定经常排名"第一"——排名倒数第一。

2 尽管哈定那时候在选举中取得了压倒性的胜利……尽管他和他的狗莱迪•波依(Laddie Boy)在其任内时讨人喜欢……人们今天能够回忆起的只是哈定沉溺于女色，以及他1923年突然去世之后他的政府所深陷的种种丑闻；而有些人认为他是被他妻子毒死的。

3 但是在沃伦•哈定的家乡俄亥俄州马里恩(Marion)，这位他们最喜爱的儿子得到了更为宽厚的对待。

4 哈定故居的导游雪莉•霍尔(Sherry Hall)认为她的工作就是澄清事实，或者力图做到这一点。

5 "你可能会听到他是被毒死的，其实不是这样的。"霍尔告诉罗卡 (Rocca)。"他的妻子并没有杀死他。这是一个完全虚构的故事。"

6 事实上，霍尔(Hall)说，沃伦和佛罗伦萨•哈定夫妇在1920年总统大选中相互呼应配合密切，上天开辟了一条一直延伸到沃伦•哈定家门口的道路。确实如此。

7 "他们的房子前聚集了 10,000 人是常事。"霍尔 (Hall) 说。

8 好莱坞明星来到马里恩(Marion)……运动员也来了。艾尔•乔森(Al Jolson)甚至为竞选写了一首歌，并且在哈定家的门廊里表演。

9 特雷乐 • 罗密尼 (Trella Romine)，95 岁，坐在前排座位上："4 岁时，我曾与哈定握过手，就在外面的栏杆上，"她告诉罗卡 (Rocca)。"你想握与哈定握过的手吗？"

10 "哇！太神奇了！"他回答说。

11 "我吓坏了，你知道，但是当我抬头看着他的脸时我发现，那真是一张慈祥的脸，"罗密尼 (Romine) 说，"所以我只是伸出我的手，创造了历史。"

12 "很抱歉，都是问你低俗的事情。你认为沃伦 • 哈定是个好色之徒吗？"罗卡 (Rocca) 问道。

13 罗密尼(Romine)避而不谈。

14 毫无疑问，哈定对于自己的政府确实疏于监管。他任命的几位官员，包括一名内阁成员，都进了监狱。

15 但哈定高中的学生更喜欢彰显其积极的一面。

16 “他的总统选举是第一次妇女也参加投票的选举。”一个女孩说。

17 “他是帮助启动退伍军人医疗保险的总统之一。”一个男孩说。

18 而对于那些热衷琐事的人，请注意：哈定总统是唯一一位在自己生日当天当选总统的。

19 他一直是一个非常注重衣着整洁的人。雪莉•霍尔(Sherry Hall)展示了哈定的一些衣柜、他的高尔夫球棒、他的公文包、他的雪茄、甚至他的鞋子。总统，有着让女戏迷着迷的长相，他的双脚可是入主白宫的人中最大的。

20 哈定是第一位访问阿拉斯加(Alaska)的总统。这也是他的成就之一。他死在回来的路上。当他的遗体被运回马里恩(Marion)时成千上万人在街道两旁表示哀悼。马里恩为他建立了一个纪念堂。

21 哈定总统去世时，那些足以为他的总统生涯定位的丑闻尚未大白于天下…他仍然是一个深受欢迎的人。这些都决定了纪念堂的大小。那个纪念堂可够大的！

22 有点浮华，对吗？可你应考虑：沃伦•甘梅利尔•哈定是一位来自小城镇的男孩，但他却能问鼎白宫。无论如何，这可不容易。

30 Calvin Coolidge's Humor
卡尔文·柯立芝总统的幽默

卡尔文·柯立芝 总统及第一夫人简介

卡尔文•柯立芝(Calvin Coolidge, 1872.7.4～1933.1.5)，第30任美国总统(1923～1929)。佛蒙特州律师出身，在马萨诸塞州政界奋斗多年后成为州长。1920年大选时作为沃伦•哈定的竞选伙伴成功当选第29任美国副总统。1923年，哈定在任内病逝，柯立芝随即递补为总统。1924年大选连任成功。政治上，他主张小政府，以古典自由派保守主义闻名。柯立芝在任内一扫哈定时期政治丑闻的阴霾，恢复了公众对白宫的信任，故离任时威望极高。

格雷丝•安娜•古德休•柯立芝(Grace Anna Goodhue Coolidge, 1879.1.3～1957.7.8)，美国第30任总统卡尔文•柯立芝的妻子，与总统育有两子。婚前为一聋哑人学院唇读法讲师。其活泼的性格和迷人的风度与柯立芝正好相得益彰，两人十分恩爱。作为第一夫人，她是很受公众喜爱的女主人。柯立芝去世后，她继续从事聋哑人工作。二战期间，她热心于红十字会和民防工作。

经典原文
Original Text

1 Humorous stories about Calvin Coolidge are legion. Most of these are true. Others have been told so many times that they masqueraded as truth, making it difficult to separate fact from fabrication. They are being offered here for your information. The truth of some of the more suspicious ones, I leave to your own judgment and investigation. All, however, have gone into creating the *patchwork quilt*[①] of humor that is Coolidge:

2 **SHORT NOTICE** Coolidge went to visit Grace's parents in *Burlington*[②], Vermont for the first time. Her father asked if he was up there on some law business. Coolidge said:"No, I'm up here to ask for permission to marry Grace." He gave him a startled look and said:"Does she know yet?" Coolidge said:"No, but she will soon."

3 **THE WEDDING PARTY** The night before their wedding, a party was held. One of Grace's friends arrived late and saw Coolidge standing very quietly in the corner alone. Knowing that she taught the deaf and dumb she said:"Is that young man standing there by himself in the corner one of your pupils?"

4 **DARN IT** After the Coolidges were married, Coolidge had about fifty pairs of socks that needed mending. He told Grace there would be more later. She asked him if he married her just to get his socks mended. He told her: "No, but I find it might handy."

5 **GRACE'S COOKING** Grace Coolidge did all the cooking and housework in their home. Coolidge used to drop one of her biscuits on the floor and stamp his foot to emphasize the thud. He said they were awful hard. The first

Words & Expressions

legion [ˈliːdʒən] *adj.* 大量的，大批的，众多的

masquerade [ˌmæskəˈreid] *v.* 化装，伪装

fabrication [ˌfæbriˈkeiʃən] *n.* 制造，建造，装配，制作；虚构，捏造的托词

startled [ˈstaːtld] *adj.* 受惊吓的

the deaf and dumb 聋哑人

handy [ˈhændi] *adj.* 方便的，手巧的

thud [θʌd] *n.* 重击，砰的一声

time Grace made an apple pie, it came out tough. After she offered it to a couple of her friends, he asked them: "Don't you think the road commissioner would be willing to pay my wife something for her recipe for pie crust?"

6 **YOU BET** Probably the most frequently told story about Coolidge is the one where an important hostess told him why he had to talk to her: "You must talk to me Mr. Coolidge. I made a bet today that I could get more than two words out of you." Coolidge told her: "You lose." When he was Governor of Massachusetts, a woman asked him if he had participated in athletics while he was at *Amherst*[③]. He said: "Yes, I held the stakes."

7 **PAYDAY** Soon after Coolidge took office, he received his first paycheck which was "delivered with a flurry" by a messenger from *the Treasury Department*[④]. Coolidge told him solemnly "Call again." (Coolidge's salary as President was $75,000 per year.)

8 **RING FOR SERVICE** Once in a while, Coolidge would press all the buttons on his desk, which made bells ring all over the White House, and have everybody come running for the fun of it.

9 **SIN** On Sundays, Coolidge went to church. According to a famous story told about him, after he had returned from the service Mrs. Coolidge asked him what the sermon had been about. "Sin", he said. "Well, what did the minister say about it?" she asked. Coolidge said: "He was agin it." Coolidge said he had heard that story many times and that it would be funnier if it were true.

10 **NOT A WORD** Governor *Channing Cox*[⑤] of Massachusetts visited Coolidge at the White House and said that with all the communications Coolidge had, he

commissioner [kə'miʃənə] *n.* 被授权者，委员，专员，干事，负责公路的专员

pie crust 派皮，大馅饼皮

stake [steik] *n.* 桩，标桩，支柱，篱笆桩，赌金，赌注

flurry ['flʌri] *n.* 慌张，疾风，飓风，骚动

solemnly ['sɔləmli] *adj.* 庄严地，严肃地

sermon ['səːmən] *n.* 布道，讲道

agin [ə'gin] *prep./adv.* 反对

didn't seem to be pressed for time. Cox said back home in Massachusetts he was always seeing people and was fighting all the time to get ahead, so he could get some real work done. Coolidge told him:"Channing, the trouble is you talk back."

11 **CIGARS** The President was a regular cigar smoker. He rarely bought any, as they were usually given to him. On one occasion, *Senator Freylinghuysen*⑥ of New Jersey was a White House guest. He told the President he was having some *Havanas*⑦ made for him in *Cuba*⑧, but he didn't have them yet since there had been a delay in printing his initials on the bands. Coolidge told him:"Well Joe, you know I don't smoke the bands."

12 **FISH FEAR ME** Coolidge was fishing in Wisconsin while vacationing. He was asked how many fish he thought were in the river. Coolidge said:"About forty-five thousand. I haven't caught them all yet, but I've intimidated them."

13 **DEPRESSION** After Coolidge announced he didn't intend to seek a second term of his own, he and Mrs. Coolidge had lunch in *Woodstock*⑨, Vermont with the famous theatrical figure *Otis Skinner*⑩ and his wife. Mrs. Skinner said to him: "I wish it were you that we were able to vote for in November! It would be the end of this terrible Depression." Coolidge said:"Yeah, but it would be the beginning of mine!"

talk back 顶嘴，反驳

initials [i'niʃəl] *n.* 首字母 *adj.* 最初的，原始的，第一的

vacation [və'keiʃən] *vi.* 休假，度假 *n.* 休假，假期

intimidate [in'timideit] *vt.* 使畏惧，恫吓，恐吓

theatrical [θi'ætrikəl] *adj.* 剧场的，戏剧的

背景知识注释
Background Notes

1. patchwork quilt 百纳被，即拼布。拼布(PATCHWORK)主要分生活拼布和艺术拼布。

2. Burlington 伯灵顿，美国佛蒙特州最大的城市，为该州最大的城市和进口港。

3. Amherst 阿默斯特，美国东部马萨诸塞州西边的一个小镇。虽是小镇却四通八达，很方便；美国历史上著名的女诗人爱米莉就出生、成长在这里，并在此地出了名。

4. the Treasury Department 美国财政部(全称为United States Department of the Treasury)，美国政府一个内阁部门，管理美国政府的收入。

5. Channing Cox 钱宁•考克斯(1879.10.28～1968.8.20)，生于新罕布什尔州曼彻斯特，是马萨诸塞州共和党政治家，第49任马萨诸塞州州长。

6. Senator Freylinghuysen 即Joseph Sherman Frelinghuysen, Sr. 老约瑟夫•谢尔曼•弗里林海森(1869.3.12～1948.2.8)， 新泽西州共和党参议员(1917～1923)。弗里林海森家族为美国显赫的政治世家，共有六人先后担任参议员和众议员。

7. Havana 哈瓦那，古巴共和国的首都，经济、文化中心，也是西印度群岛中最大的城市和著名良港。哈瓦那大学为哈瓦那的著名高等学府。大部分古巴华人华侨也居住在哈瓦那。

8. Cuba 古巴，正式名称为古巴共和国，是美洲加勒比海北部的一个群岛国家。

9. Woodstock 伍德斯托克，位于美国佛蒙特州中部，是温莎县的县治。

10. Otis Skinner 奥蒂斯•斯金纳(1858.6.28～1942.1.4)，美国19世纪末期和20世纪早期著名的演员。

中文译文
Suggested Translation

1 有关卡尔文•柯立芝幽默的故事不胜枚举。其中大部分是真实的，有一些则因反复流传而成了假戏真唱，以致真伪难辨。下面这些故事在此供你传阅，其中有一些令人生疑的地方由你们自己判断并核实。然而，柯立芝的幽默就是由所有这些五光十色的故事拼凑而成的。

2 **临时通知** 柯立芝第一次上佛蒙特州伯灵顿(Burlington)去拜访格雷斯的父母。她的父亲问他是不是为了一些法律上的业务来的。柯立芝说："不，我来这里是为了请求允许与格雷斯结婚的恩典。"格雷斯的父亲大吃一惊，看了他一眼说："她知道了吗？"柯立芝说"不，但是很快她就会知道。"

3 **婚礼** 婚礼前夜，正举行一个晚会。格蕾丝的一位朋友来晚了，看到柯立芝独自静悄悄地站在角落里。因为知道格蕾丝是教聋哑人的，所以她问道："独自站在角落里的那个年轻人是你的学生吗？"

4 **不会吧** 柯立芝夫妇婚后不久，柯立芝有50来双袜子需要缝补。他告诉格蕾丝以后还会更多。她问他和她结婚的目的是否就是叫她缝这些破袜子。他说："不，但是我发现这样挺方便的。"

5 **格雷斯的烹饪术** 家中的家务活和三餐都由格雷斯•柯立芝(Grace Coolidge)负责。柯立芝常让一块饼干掉到地上然后再用脚踩来加强"砰砰"的撞击声。他说，这些饼干都很

硬。格雷斯第一次做出来的苹果馅饼很硬。她让一些朋友品尝。后来，他问她们："你认为那个负责公路的专员愿意出资购买我太太制作馅饼皮的配方吗？"

6 **当然** 可能人们经常讲的有关柯立芝的故事有：一次一位地位显赫的女主人要他和她谈话。"柯立芝先生，你必须与我谈话。今天我跟别人打了赌，说至少我能让你说出三个字来。"柯立芝告诉他"你输（了）。"当他任马萨诸塞州州长时，有位妇女问他在阿默斯特 (Amherst) 时是否参加过体育运动。他说："当然，我下注了。"

7 **发薪日** 柯立芝上任后不久，即收到头一次总统薪金支票。这是由财政部一位信使急急忙忙送来的。柯立芝神情严肃地对他说："再来一次。"（柯立芝的总统薪金是每年 75,000 美元。）

8 **按铃召唤** 柯立芝有时会按按桌上所有的铃。这时白宫上下一片铃声。每个人都循着铃声跑来，乐趣无穷。

9 **罪孽** 星期天柯立芝都会上教堂。一个有关他的著名的故事讲到：一次他去教堂礼拜回来，柯立芝太太问他布道的内容。"罪孽，"他说。"那么，牧师讲了些什么？"她问道。柯立芝说："他对此并没有什么反感。"柯立芝说那个故事他听过多次，倘若它是真的就更有趣了。

10 **一言不发** 马萨诸塞州州长考克斯 (Cox) 到白宫看望柯立芝时说，尽管柯立芝有那么多的社交活动，但他似乎没有感到时间的紧迫。考克斯说回到马萨诸塞州他总是得看望一些人并不断地抗争以便获得成功，所以他得干一些实事。柯立芝告诉他："钱宁 (Channing)，麻烦在于你回话了。"

11 **雪茄** 总统经常抽雪茄。他很少买，因为都是人家送给他的。有一次，新泽西州佛里林海森 (Freylinghuysen) 参议员到白宫做客。他告诉总统他有些哈瓦那雪茄，是专门在古巴为柯立芝制作的。但不巧的是，还得耽搁些时间来印刷写着总统名字首字母的平板商标。"哦，乔 (Joe)。"柯立芝说："你知道我是不抽那种牌子的。"

12 **鱼被我吓坏了** 柯立芝度假期间在威斯康星州钓鱼。有人问他认为河里有多少鱼。柯立芝说："约 45,000。我还没有把它们全部逮住。但是我已经把这些鱼吓坏了。"

13 **大萧条** 在柯立芝宣布他不打算寻求第二个任期后，他和夫人在佛蒙特州伍德斯托克 (Woodstock) 和著名演员奥蒂斯·斯金纳 (Otis Skinner) 及他的妻子共进午餐。斯金纳太太对他说："我希望 11 月投票选的是你。那就会结束这场可怕的大萧条了。"柯立芝说，"是的。但是那将会是我的大萧条的开始。"

31 Herbert Clark Hoover and the World's Most Exclusive Club 赫伯特·克拉克·胡佛总统与世界上独一无二的俱乐部

赫伯特·克拉克·胡佛 总统及第一夫人简介

赫伯特·克拉克·胡佛(Herbert Clark Hoover, 1874.8.10～1964.10.20)，第31任美国总统(1929～1933)。他出生于爱荷华州，毕业于斯坦福大学。1897年，胡佛与罗·亨利结婚。后来，胡佛被一家公司雇用去了澳大利亚和中国。他曾任哈定和柯立芝两届总统的商务部长，其间打出“经济现代化”的旗号推动政府干预经济。1928年大选，此前从未经选举而担当政府职位的胡佛轻松赢得了党内提名，并在国内一片欣欣向荣的乐观气氛中完胜民主党候选人当选总统。他是美国迄今为止由内阁部长直接升为总统的最后一人。

卢·亨利·胡佛(Lou Henry Hoover, 1874.3.29～1944.1.7)，第31任美国总统赫伯特·克拉克·胡佛的妻子，与总统育有两子。亨利受过良好的教育，婚后成为胡佛的贤内助。她语言天赋极佳，精通中文，在白宫为防偷听她和胡佛总统有时讲中国话。她对拉丁文也有很深的研究。一战期间，她曾协助丈夫对比利时难民提供救济。胡佛在哈定和柯立芝总统内阁任职期间，她任全国女童子军主席。当了第一夫人后，她经常招待客人，成为20世纪社会活动家。她成功地扩大第一夫人的交际范围，为罗斯福夫人铺平了道路。

经典原文 Original Text

1 It was one of those moments that, in a mere second or two, changed American history.

2 On January 20, 1953, at the inaugurationof President *Dwight Eisenhower*①, *Harry Truman*② greeted Herbert Clark Hoover on the platform. "I think we ought to organize a former presidents club," Hoover suggested.

3 "Fine," Truman replied. "You be the President of the club. And I will be the Secretary."

4 Up to that moment, *the Presidents Club*③was more an idea than an institution. Some sitting presidents consulted with their predecessors, but beyond sharing war stories, there were limits to what a former president could do unless he applied for a new job, like congressman (*John Quincy Adams*④) or *Supreme Court justice*⑤(*William Howard Taft* ⑥).

5 But with the coming of the modern, post-war age, the Presidents Club became an actual fraternity, an abiding alliance between sitting and former presidents born of the experiences they had shared, the mistakes they avoided and the opportunities they seized. Presidents can do more together than apart, and they all know it, and so they join forces as needed, to consult, complain, console, pressure, protect, redeem.

6 In the case of Hoover and Truman, they did much more.

Words & Expressions

sitting ['sitiŋ] *adj.* 坐着的，现任的，停落的，蹲伏的

predecessor ['priːdisesə] *n.* 前任者，前辈

fraternity [frə'təːniti] *n.* 兄弟关系，兄弟情谊，博爱，兄弟会，互助会

abiding [ə'baidiŋ] *adj.* 持久的，永久的，持久不变的

born of 源于，出生于

console [kən'səul] *vt.* 安慰，慰问，抚慰

in the case of 就…来说，至于

7 Truman had been in office for a matter of weeks in the spring of 1945 when newspapers began warning of the next disaster: "the most stupendous feeding problem in history," as the *New York Times* described the hideous famine facing 100 million European civilians who had suffered through years of living in a war zone. Aware of the objections of many in the White House, Truman secretly mailed a letter to the still despised Hoover, inviting him back to the White House for the first time since *Franklin Roosevelt* [7]'s inauguration 12 years before. The two men met on May 28, 1945; Hoover, an engineer by training who had been revered for his relief work following World War I, laid out for Truman what it would take to get the food from countries that had it to those that needed it, a massive logistical challenge on which millions of lives depended.

8 The austere Republican Hoover left the meeting skeptical that the novice Democrat Truman would do anything so radical as enlist a political enemy in a joint mission. "Nothing more would come of it," Hoover concluded in his memo of the encounter.

9 But he was wrong. In the year that followed, Truman enacted one Hoover recommendation after another, and sent the 71 year-old former President on a 50,000 mile mission around the world: With Truman's encouragement, Hoover, the man many Democrats revile to this day, met with seven kings, 36 Prime Ministers and *the Pope*[8]. He gave 42 press conferences. When he was in *Cairo*[9] in April of 1946, he and Truman did a joint radio broadcast exhorting Americans to conserve food: "The saving of these human lives is far more than an economic necessity to the recovery of the world," Hoover said. It was "a part of the moral and

a matter of 大约，…的问题

hideous [ˈhidiəs] *adj.* 极丑陋的，可怕的，令人厌恶的，令人沮丧的

famine [ˈfæmin] *n.* 饥饿，饥荒时期，奇缺

civilian [siˈviljən] *n.* 平民，百姓

despise [diˈspaiz] *vt.* 轻视，藐视，蔑视，鄙视，看不起

revere [riˈviə] *vt.* 尊敬，尊重，崇敬

lay out 展示，安排，花钱，为…划样，提议

logistical [ləˈdʒistikl] *adj.* 后勤方面的，运筹的，逻辑的

austere [ɔˈstiə] *n.* 严肃的，苛刻的，严格律己

skeptical [ˈskeptikəl] *adj.* 怀疑的，不可知论的

novice [ˈnɔvis] *n.* 新手

enlist [inˈlist] *vt.* 使入伍，征募，谋取

memo [ˈmeməu] *n.* 备忘录

enact [iˈnækt] *vt.* 使成为法律，通过，制定

revile [riˈvail] *vt.* 辱骂，谩骂

exhort [igˈzɔːt] *vt.* 规劝，激励，敦促，吁求，恳请

spiritual reconstruction of the world."

10 And it worked; by the end of that summer, Truman could announce that America had shipped five and a half million tons of grain to the ravaged regions of Europe, thereby keeping the nations promise and forestalling a humanitarian catastrophe. "Every molecule in my body yells at me that it is tired," Hoover told a friend. "I am going away for a rest."

11 "Yours was a real service for humanity," Truman wrote privately to Hoover. By that time the two had battled enough common enemies to have seeded something like a friendship. "I know that I can count upon your cooperation if developments at any time in the future make it necessary for me to call upon you again."

12 And he did. Truman had discovered in Hoover a most surprising ally, whose commitment to serving the country and strengthening the presidency was undiminished by the fact that at that point the White House was occupied by a Democrat. Hoover helped Truman sell the idea of European relief to a skeptical Republican Congress. Even more important, he oversaw that radical overhaul of the Executive Branch: As a result of their partnership, the Hoover Commission, which Congress created, Truman sanctioned, and Hoover chaired, produced the greatest transformation of the presidency in history, a concentration of power that ultimately yielded *the CIA*[10], *the National Security Council*[11], *the Council of Economic Advisors*[12], *the General Services Administration*[13], a unified *Defense Department*[14], and much more.

13 And so it went: an unexpected partnership had produced a new kind of power — certainly a new kind of

ravage ['rævidʒ] *vt.* 毁坏，破坏，掠夺

forestall [fɔː'stɔːl] *vt.* 预防，阻止

catastrophe [kə'tæstrəfi] *n.* 大灾难，大祸，惨败

molecule ['mɔlikjuːl] *n.* 分子，微粒，一点儿

yell [jel] *vi.* 呼喊，叫喊，尖叫

count upon 料想，依靠，指望

call upon 号召，要求，拜访

ally ['ælai] *n.* 同盟者；同盟国

undiminished [ˌʌndi'miniʃt] *adj.* 不减的，未衰落的，没有降低的

overhaul ['əuvəhɔːl] *n.* 彻底检修，详细检查

sanction ['sæŋkʃən] *n.* 认可，批准，允许，支持，赞助

yield [jiːld] *vt.* 屈服，出产，放弃

peerage. It was an arrangement that favored them both; by 1951, Truman and Hoover ranked three and five on *Gallups* ⑮ list of *Most Admired Men* ⑯. So as they watched Eisenhower on *the Capitol* ⑰ steps preparing to take over the chair both had occupied, it was natural that they would recognize the particular value of a working alliance between sitting and former presidents.

14 Not every president who followed would share their willingness to collaborate; but it was already clear that used wisely, the Presidents Club could function as an instrument of presidential power. For all of the clubs self-serving habits and instincts, when it is functioning at its best, it can serve the president, help solve his problems, and the nation's, even save lives.

peerage [ˈpiəridʒ] *n.* 贵族，贵族地位，贵族阶级

collaborate [kəˈlæbəreit] *vi.*合作，通敌

self-serving *adj.* 自私的，自私自利的，只顾自己的

instinct [ˈinstiŋkt] *n.* 直觉，本能，天性

at one's best 处于最佳状态

背景知识注释 Background Notes

1. Dwight Eisenhower　德怀特•艾森豪威尔，第34任美国总统。
2. Harry Truman　哈里•杜鲁门，第33任美国总统。
3. the Presidents Club　总统俱乐部，美国总统俱乐部最初起源于1953年艾森豪威尔总统的就职仪式，两位政治上的对手前总统胡佛和杜鲁门摒弃前嫌，重归于好。但那时，总统俱乐部还停留在概念意义上，并没有太多实际行动。杜鲁门之后，历任总统开始越来越多地和前辈们沟通，向他们咨询或告知重大决策。于是，人们看到：在肯尼迪宣布封锁古巴那天早上，他打电话给艾森豪威尔通报了这一决定；克林顿在任时，经常抽出时间与尼克松研讨俄罗斯和中国问题；而在本•拉登被击毙的那个夜晚，小布什和克林顿第一时间就从奥巴马那里收到了这条好消息。进入21世纪，美国总统俱乐部的成员们密切关注对方的情况，包括健康情况。他们的助手保持着密切的电话和邮件联系。因此，总统俱乐部并非严格法律意义上的团体，它所折射出的更多是历任美国领导人的传承，代表了一种“向长者请教”的传统。
4. John Quincy Adams　约翰•昆西•亚当斯，第6任美国总统门罗政府时期的国务卿，其外交思想与实践对美国早期外交产生了深远的影响。

5. Supreme Court justice　最高法院法官，美国最高法院法官是由总统任命的，但这不意味着法官要在政治上对总统效忠。最高法院同行政部门权力相当。法官的职责是权衡法律和宪法保障的权利，而非支持任何政治观点。

6. William Howard Taft　威廉•霍华德•塔夫脱，第27任美国总统。作为政界要人、国家元首，他曾从美国的利益出发，力倡向东方国家推行基督教文明。

7. Franklin Roosevelt　富兰克林•罗斯福，第32任美国总统，美国历史上唯一一位连任四届的总统。

8. the Pope　教宗，是罗马的主教，也是天主教会的领袖，根据耶稣在世时留下的教导来领导普世的大公教会。

9. Cairo　开罗，是埃及首都，古称优努（通道）。现在的开罗地区，阿拉伯穆斯林占多数，科普特基督徒也占有较大比例。

10. the CIA　即 Central Intelligence Agency 中央情报局，是美国最大的情报机构，主要任务是公开和秘密地收集和分析关于国外政府、公司和个人，政治、文化、科技等方面的情报，协调其他国内情报机构的活动，并把这些情报报告到美国政府各个部门的工作。它也负责维持大量军事设备，这些设备在冷战期间用于推翻外国政府，和对美国利益构成威胁的反对者。中央情报局总部设在弗吉尼亚州的兰利。中央情报局的地位和功能相当于英国的军情六处和以色列的摩萨德，是美国情报体系中唯一一个独立的情报部门。

11. the National Security Council　国家安全委员会，美国于 1947年根据《国家安全法》设立国家安全委员会，由总统任主席，副总统、国务卿、财政部长、国防部长为法定的正式成员。参谋长联席会议主席和中央情报局局长分别以军事顾问、情报顾问身份法定列席会议。此外，总统可以根据需要指定有关人员列席会议。国家安全委员会的日常工作，由总统的国家安全事务助理负责主持。国家安全委员会的职责主要是在一切有关国家安全政策的统一与协调方面，向总统提出建议，协助总统制定、审查并协调与国家安全有关的内政、外交及军事政策。世界上设置国家安全委员会的，除美国之外，还有巴西、智利、南非、土耳其、泰国和马来西亚等国。

12. the Council of Economic Advisors　（缩写为 CEA）美国总统经济顾问委员会，是美国总统办事机构的一部分，由一组经济学家组成并为美国总统提供相关咨询，它为白宫提供了大量的经济政策。

13. the General Services Administration　（缩写为 GSA）美国总务管理局，联邦政府的一个独立部门，负责为联邦机构提供办公室、办公用品和交通服务等。该局还负责制定联邦政府的节省开支政策。

14. Defense Department　美国国防部(简称DOD或DoD)，是美国联邦行政部门之一，主要负责统合国家安全与武装力量(美军)，它的总部大楼是五角大楼(The Pentagon)，因此人们也常用五角大楼代称。

15. Gallups　(Gallup,GeorgeHorace，1901～1984) 乔治•盖洛普，是美国数学家，抽样调查方法的创始人、民意调查的组织者，他几乎是民意调查活动的代名词。盖洛普是一个不同寻常的、正直的人。尽管他深入总统大选民意测验这一工作，但他从不参与投票，而且从不为任何政治上的竞争者工作。

16 Most Admired Men 盖洛普民意调查美国人最敬佩的男性。它是1948年以来每年年底美国所进行的一次年度民意调查。被调查的美国人会被问到：当今世界上在世的哪位男性和女性你最钦佩？然后公布排名前十位的名单。

17. the Capitol 即United States Capitol 美国国会大厦，别称国会山庄，是美国国会所在地，位于美国首都华盛顿的国会山，坐落在华盛顿国家广场(National Mall)东端。由于电视报道美国政府做出决定时多出现的是国会大厦，加之经常配合有“白宫方面宣布”的言辞，且其风格巍峨挺拔，导致不了解的人在很长一段时间内将国会大厦误认为是白宫——美国总统官邸暨办公室。另外，公众可免费参观国会大厦，但每天的名额有限，也可旁听参议院或众议院议事。

中文译文
Suggested Translation

1 这是众多改变历史的瞬间之一。

2 1953年1月20日，新任总统德怀特•艾森豪威尔的就职典礼在白宫举行，哈里•杜鲁门在台上对一起出席典礼的赫伯特•克拉克•胡佛致意问候——“我想我们应该组织一个前总统俱乐部。”胡佛这时候建议道。

3 “好极了”，杜鲁门回应道：“你就任这个俱乐部的主席，而我担任秘书就好了。”

4 直到那一刻，总统俱乐部一直只是一个想法和概念，而并不是一个真实存在的机构。在此之前，一些在职的总统也会向他的前任咨询，寻求建议。但囿于法律限制，除了互诉苦衷外，前总统并不能做更多的事情。除非这位前总统拥有一个新的职务，比如国会议员（约翰•昆西•亚当斯），或者最高法院大法官（威廉•霍华德•塔夫脱）。

5 但是，随着战后时代的到来，总统俱乐部逐渐成为一个实际存在的互助会，一个前任和现任总统间持久的联盟，一个源自于他们曾共同享有的经验、早先避免过的错误以及原本曾把握的机会的联盟。总统们深知，他们结成联盟比单独行动能做更多的事情，于是他们同心协力，以益于相互咨询、抱怨、慰藉、增压、保护彼此的利益以及履行各自的义务。

6 而在胡佛和杜鲁门之间，他们则做得更多。

7 1945年的春天，报纸上已经开始警告下一场可能到来的灾难——史上最严重的食物短缺问题。《纽约时报》描述，有多达1亿的、在战区煎熬数年刚刚走出战争灾难的欧洲人，将面临可怕的饥荒。为此杜鲁门在办公室焦躁不安了数周。最终杜鲁门秘密地给胡佛发了一封信，邀请胡佛返回白宫任职，尽管他深知此举会招致白宫幕僚的反对。此时的胡佛仍受尽轻视，自富兰克林•罗斯福就任总统以来，他已有12年未曾踏入白宫。1945年5月28日，两个人会面了。胡佛，这个受过良好训练的工程师，曾经由于一战后的救济工作而备受褒扬。他

给杜鲁门建议将食物从富裕的国度转移到短缺的国家，这在后勤补给上是一个巨大挑战，但无数人会从中受益。

8 严谨的共和党人胡佛在会面结束离开时，对民主党总统新手杜鲁门是否敢任用一名政敌来帮助自己感到十分怀疑。“仅止于此，不会再有下文了。”胡佛在他的备忘录中对这次会面评价道。

9 然而，胡佛这回却错了。在随后的一年里，杜鲁门接连地实施胡佛所提出的建议，并委派他踏上了五万公里的环球历程。带着杜鲁门的鼓励，胡佛，这个至今仍遭受民主党人唾骂的人，会见了 7 位国王、36 名总理以及罗马教皇，召开了 42 场记者招待会。1946 年 4 月，他在开罗与杜鲁门总统一起在广播里呼吁美国民众贮存食物。“挽救这些人的生命远不止是出于复苏世界经济的需要，它更是这个世界道德和精神重建中的一部分。”胡佛说道。

10 他们的行动果然奏效了。1946 年的夏天，杜鲁门宣布美国已经运输了 550 万吨的粮食到欧洲的重灾区，维持了这些国家的希望，避免了人道主义上的大灾难。此时如释重负的胡佛对一位朋友说道：“我身体的每一个细胞都感觉到疲乏了，我需要离开好好休息一下。”

11 “你的所作所为诠释了人道主义的真正内涵。”杜鲁门在给胡佛的私信中写道。到那时，这两个共同面对种种艰难挑战的人已经酝酿出了惺惺相惜的友谊。“我知道，在未来的任何时候，倘若事态发展到需要的地步，我会再次得到你的协助。”

12 而杜鲁门确实得到了，他发现了胡佛这个最意外的盟友。胡佛的可贵之处在于，作为一个共和党人，他没有因为白宫被民主党人盘踞而降低自己服务国家协助总统执政的意愿。胡佛帮助杜鲁门向抱有疑虑的共和党控制的国会兜售了欧洲救济法案。更重要的是，他全面监督了行政部门的彻底改组：由于两人的伙伴关系，杜鲁门批准了由国会提议组建的胡佛委员会。胡佛担任主席，推动了历史上总统职权最重大的转变，权力得到集中，最终产生了中央情报局、国家安全委员会、经济顾问委员会、美国总务管理局以及统一的国防部等部门。

13 就这样，一段意外的伙伴关系塑造了一个新的权力模式。1951年，在最受尊敬人物的民意测试中，杜鲁门和胡佛分列第三位和第五位。所以当他们看到艾森豪威尔在国会大厦的台阶上准备接管总统职位时，很自然地，他们就认识到现任总统和前任总统之间建立工作联盟的特别价值。

14 在杜鲁门之后的总统里，并不是所有的人都有着如他俩那般的合作意愿。但很显然的是，倘若运用得当，总统俱乐部可以成为一个很好的施政工具。尽管它具有所有社团的通病——自私自利的习惯和本能，然而当它运行在最佳状态时，它可以为总统所用，帮助解决总统的难题，帮助解决国家的问题，甚至是拯救生命。

32 Franklin Deleno Roosevelt and His *Fireside Chats*[①]

富兰克林·德拉诺·罗斯福总统与他的炉边谈话

富兰克林·德拉诺·罗斯福 总统及第一夫人简介

富兰克林·德拉诺·罗斯福 (Franklin Delano Roosevelt, 1882.1.30 ~ 1945.4.12)，第 32 任美国总统 (1933 ~ 1945)。美国历史上唯一蝉联四届 (1933.3.4 ~ 1937.1.20，1937.1.20 ~ 1941.1. 20，1941.1. 20 ~ 1945.1.20，1945.1.20 ~ 1945.4.12，第四届未任满) 的总统。富兰克林·罗斯福在 20 世纪的经济大萧条和第二次世界大战中扮演了重要的角色，被学者评为是美国最伟大的三位总统之一，同华盛顿和林肯齐名。美国第 26 任总统西奥多·罗斯福是富兰克林·罗斯福的远房堂叔。富兰克林·罗斯福是第一位将飞机作为交通工具的美国总统。1943 年他到摩洛哥参加卡萨布兰卡会议，为了避免乘坐客轮可能遭到纳粹德国潜艇袭击的威胁，他搭乘了世界航空的波音 314 “狄克西快艇号”，飞行了 5,500 英里抵达目的地。

安娜•埃莉诺•罗斯福(Anna Eleanor Roosevelt, 1884.10.11～1962.11.7)，美国第32任总统富兰克林•德拉诺•罗斯福的妻子，与总统育有四儿一女。小时候，她腼腆怕事。1921年罗斯福患病后，她耐心护理他，并激励他。为了弥补罗斯福的行动不便，她克服了羞怯，为他出面活动。她是第一个在实质问题上有影响的第一夫人。第二次世界大战后她出任美国首任驻联合国大使，并主导起草了联合国的《世界人权宣言》。她是女性主义者，亦大力提倡保护人权。总之，她是一位不同寻常的第一夫人。她不是以传统的白宫女主人的形象，而是作为杰出的社会活动家、政治家、外交家和作家被载入史册的。

经典原文
Original Text

1 "I never saw him—but I knew him. Can you have forgotten how, with his voice, he came into our house, the President of the United States, calling us friends..."— *Carl Carmer*[①], April 14, 1945.

2 In the midst of *the Great Depression*[②], America in 1933 was suffering. One-third of its workforce was unemployed, every bank had been closed for eight days, and the public was barely surviving through a combination of barter and credit.

3 On Sunday evening, March 12, a troubled nation sat down by its radio sets to listen to their president. With his calm and reassuring voice, President Franklin Delano Roosevelt (FDR) explained how the nation was going to recover from the current banking crisis.

4 That evening marked the beginning of the historic Fireside Chats, thirty radio addresses that covered issues like the renewed Depression and America's role in World War II. In his Fireside Chats, Roosevelt shared his hopes and plans for the nation and invited the American people to "tell me your troubles."

5 Roosevelt took special care in preparing each aspect of his Fireside Chats and made his addresses accessible and understandable to ordinary Americans. In order to attract a peak national audience, the Chats were broadcast on all

Words & Expressions

barter [ˈbɑːtə] *n.* 易货贸易，以货易货，交换

credit [ˈkredit] *n.* 信贷，赊销，赊欠

reassuring [ˌriəˈʃuriŋ] *adj.* 安心的，可靠的，鼓气的

cover [ˈkʌvə] *vt.* 包括，采访，报导，涉及

renew [riˈnjuː] *vt.* 使更新，续借，复兴，重申

accessible [əkˈsesəbl] *adj.* 易接近（或进入）的，可使用（或得到）的

national networks around 10:00 p.m. Eastern time—early enough that Easterners were still awake but late enough that even people on the West Coast would be home from work.

6 The Chats were relatively brief, ranging in length from fifteen to forty-five minutes. In addition, FDR and his speechwriters always used basic language when preparing the Fireside Chats. Eighty percent of the words FDR chose were among the 1000 most commonly used words in the English vocabulary.

7 He also relied on stories, anecdotes, and analogies to explain the complex issues facing the country. For example, he used a baseball analogy to describe the first two months of the New Deal: "I have no expectations of making a hit every time I come to bat. What I seek is the highest possible batting average, not only for myself, but for the team."

8 The radio addresses strove to turn listeners into a unified nation of active citizens. FDR was confident in the programs his government put forth, but he reminded the American people that only they could ultimately bring about the desired results.

9 He believed the American citizens — individually and together — could bring about change. By referring to his audience in terms of "you" and "we," FDR constructed a sense of national identity, encouraged individual participation, and forged an intimate relationship between the president and the public.

10 The success of the Fireside Chats is evidenced by the millions of letters that flooded the White House. Americans from all walks of life wrote FDR, and many of these letters were written within days, even hours, of hearing their beloved president over the radio. In these

anecdote [ˈænikdəut] *n.* 轶事，逸事，趣闻

analogy [əˈnælədʒi] *n.* 类似，相似性，比拟，比喻，模拟，类推

make a hit 获得成功

bat [bæt] *vt.* 用球棒击球，击球率达

batting average 击球率

strive [straiv] *vi.* 努力，尽力，力争

put forth 提出，发表，起航，长出，放出

individually [ˌindiˈvidjuəli] *adj.* 个别地，分别地，各个地，各自地

evidence [ˈevidəns] *vt.* 证明

all walks of life 各行各业，各界人士

letters, people often wrote about how they felt during these radio addresses, as if FDR entered their homes and spoke to each of them.

11 They also expressed their praise, appreciation, and confidence in their leader and friend. People also wrote of listening to the speeches with a group of friends or relatives, illustrating their collective appeal. Through these letters, Roosevelt became better acquainted with the views of his public and became even more aware of the power of radio.

12 With almost 90% of all households owning radios at the end of his presidency, it made sense that Roosevelt would choose radio addresses as his means of connecting with the public. And FDR did connect with the public in a way no other president had before.

13 Not only did his Fireside Chats speak to the people on a personal level and encourage their individual participation, but they also made listeners feel part of a larger whole; a united nation that would overcome the tough times it faced.

14 As a conversation between the people and their president, the Fireside Chats provided a portrait of America during one of its most difficult times and how its leader reminded the Americans of their dreams, their hopes, and the promise of democracy.

appreciation [əˌpriːʃiˈeiʃən] *n.*赏识，赞赏，重视 感激

household [ˈhaushəuld] *n.* 全家人，一家人，家庭，户

make sense 有意义，讲得通，言之有理

背景知识注释
Background Notes

1. **Fireside Chats** 炉边谈话，1933 年 3 月 12 日即罗斯福就职总统后的第 8 天，他在总统府楼下外宾接待室的壁炉前接受美国广播公司、哥伦比亚广播公司和共同广播公司的录音采访，工作人员在壁炉旁装置扩音器。总统说：希望这次讲话亲切些，免去官场那一套排场，就像坐在自己的家里，双方随意交谈。哥伦比亚广播公司华盛顿办事处经理哈里·布彻说：既然如此，那就叫

"炉边谈话"吧，于是就此定名。罗斯福在其 12 年总统任期内，共做了 30 次炉边谈话，每当美国面临重大事件之时，他都用这种方式与美国人民沟通。在罗斯福上任后雷厉风行地推动第一次新政时，这种方法的作用表现得最为突出。今日美国总统的周六例行讲话始于当年的"炉边谈话"。第一次每周例行的电台演讲是在里根总统当政的 1982 年 4 月 3 日。奥巴马入主白宫之后又将这一例行讲话改为视频演说。美联社戏称这一演说新模式为"管边谈话"(Tubeside Chats)。

2. Carl Carmer　卡尔·卡梅(1893.10.16～1976.9.11)，出生于纽约科特兰。美国20世纪40年代和50年代最畅销书的作家之一。

3. the Great Depression　大萧条，指1929年至1933年之间全球性的经济大衰退。大萧条的影响比历史上任何一次经济衰退都深远。这次经济萧条是以农产品价格下跌为起点的：首先发生在木材的价格上(1928)；但更大的灾难是在1929年到来的，加拿大小麦的过量生产，美国强迫压低所有农产品产地基本谷物的价格。不管是欧洲、美洲还是澳洲，农业衰退由于金融的大崩溃而进一步恶化，尤其在美国，一股投机热导致大量资金从欧洲抽回，随后在1929年10月发生了令人恐慌的华尔街股市暴跌。在所有国家中，经济衰退的后果是大规模失业：美国1,370万，德国560万，英国280万(1932年的最大数据)。大萧条对拉丁美洲也有重大影响，使得一个几乎被欧美银行家和商人企业家完全支配的地区失去了外资和商品出口。

中文译文
Suggested Translation

1 "我从来没有见过他——但我知道他。你怎么会忘记作为美国总统的他，随着他的声音，传到我们的家中，他称我们为朋友……"——卡尔·卡梅，1945年4月14日。

2 在大萧条中，1933年的美国饱受煎熬。三分之一的劳动力失业，所有的银行被迫关闭了八天，而公众只得通过以物易物和借贷赊欠勉强度日。

3 3月12日，周日晚上，陷入困境的国民坐在收音机旁聆听他们的总统的讲话。富兰克林·德拉诺·罗斯福总统以其平静而坚定的声音向人们解释国家将何以从当时的金融危机中恢复过来。

4 那天晚上，标志着具有历史意义的炉边谈话的发端。这些炉边谈话，即30次广播讲话，涉及如何缓解大萧条以及美国在二战中的作用。在炉边谈话中，罗斯福谈到了他对国家的希望以及振兴国家的计划，并邀请美国民众"告诉我你们的烦恼"。

5 对于这些炉边讲话所涉及的方方面面，罗斯福都做了精心准备，以便普通的美国民众

都能听得到并听得懂这些讲话。为了吸引全国尽可能多的听众，谈话通过全国所有的广播网络在东部时间下午10:00左右播出。这样东部的人们尚未上床休息而西部的人们则已经下班回到家中能赶得上听这些讲话。

6 每次的炉边谈话时间都相对较短——长度从15分钟到45分钟不等。此外，富兰克林•德拉诺•罗斯福（FDR）及其演说撰稿人准备炉边谈话时总是使用基本的文字。罗斯福所选用的词语80%来自英语最常用的1,000个词汇。

7 他还借助故事传说、奇闻趣谈和推理类比等来解释国家所面临的复杂问题。例如，他用棒球来类比描述执行新政最初的两个月："每次击球，我并不期望能一炮打响。我所追求的是最高的打击率，不仅是为自己，而是为了球队。"

8 广播讲话竭力使听众成为一个团结的国家里主动且活跃的公民。罗斯福对自己政府提出的计划充满自信，但他提醒美国人民只有他们自己才可能最终带来期望的结果。

9 他坚信美国公民——无论是个人或是整体——都能带来改变。通过称听众"你们"或"我们"，富兰克林•德拉诺•罗斯福(FDR)构建了一种民族认同感，鼓励个人参与，并形成了一种总统与公众休戚与共的关系。

10 数以百万计的信件涌入白宫就是炉边谈话喜获成功的明证。来自社会各界的美国民众写信给富兰克林•德拉诺•罗斯福(FDR)。在这些信件中，许多是在聆听他们自己心爱的总统的声音后几天内甚至几个小时内写就的。在这些信中人们经常写到他们收听这些广播讲话的感受——犹如富兰克林•德拉诺•罗斯福走进他们的家庭与他们每个人促膝谈心。

11 他们也表达了自己对自己的领袖与朋友的赞美之心、感激之情和无比信任。人们还写到他们是如何与一群朋友或亲戚聆听这些讲话的，阐明他们共同的诉求。通过这些信件，罗斯福对公众的意见更加了解了，也更为清楚地认识到广播的力量。

12 在罗斯福总统任期行将结束时，几乎90%的家庭都拥有收音机。因此，罗斯福选择广播讲话作为他与公众联系的手段，意义重大。罗斯福与公众接触的方式确实是之前的其他总统所未曾采用的。

13 他的炉边谈话不仅在个人层面上与民众交谈，并鼓励他们参与，也让听众觉得自己是一个更大的整体——一个众志成城、必将能够穿越所面临的艰难时刻的国家——的一部分。

14 炉边谈话，作为民众和他们的总统之间的对话，是美国在其最为艰难困苦的时期的一幅画卷。它展示了国家的领导人是如何提醒美国人民去追求他们的梦想、实现他们的希望以及践行对民主的承诺的。

33 The Real Story behind the "S" of the Name of President Harry S. Truman 哈里·S·杜鲁门总统名字中"S"背后的真实故事

哈里·S·杜鲁门 总统及第一夫人简介

哈里·S·杜鲁门(Harry S. Truman, 1884.5.8 ～ 1972.12.26)，第34任美国副总统(1945)，随后接替因病逝世的富兰克林·德拉诺·罗斯福总统，成了第33任美国总统(1945 ～ 1953)，绰号"Give 'Em Hell Harry"。杜鲁门总统在任期内的1945年对日本使用原子弹使第二次世界大战迅速结束。他1947年提出"杜鲁门主义"，1948年批准以扶植欧洲为目的的"马歇尔计划"。相比前任总统，杜鲁门的支持度不算高，但他谨慎果断的性格令他在面对险峻的国际情势时，能够成功接受许多艰巨的挑战。他1953年卸任回乡，1972年12月26日在堪萨斯城病故，著有回忆录两卷《决定的年代》、《试验和希望的年代》和《公民先生》。尽管他最后在1952年被迫放弃竞选连任，但今日的历史学者仍视他为最出色的美国总统之一。

伊丽莎白·维吉尼亚·华莱士·杜鲁门(Elizabeth Virginia Wallace Truman, 1885.2.13～1982.10.18)，昵称贝丝·杜鲁门(Bess Truman)，美国第33任总统哈利·S·杜鲁门的妻子，与总统育有一儿一女。贝丝•杜鲁门是历史上最长寿的美国第一夫人，死时享年97岁，比最长寿的美国总统杰拉尔德•福特——93岁还长寿。当了第一夫人以后，她不像她的前辈那样积极从事政治活动，并且停止了罗斯福夫人开创的第一夫人记者招待会。她更喜欢邀请密苏里的老朋友来打桥牌。

经典原文
Original Text

1 Harry Truman's S was from his grandfathers' names, Shipp and Solomon.

2 Truman did not have a middle name, but he did have a middle initial. Truman explained that the S was a compromise tribute to his grandfathers, Anderson Shipp Truman and Solomon Young. For years there has been a controversy over whether or not the S should have a period after it; the Harry S. Truman Library does use the period, as does *the Government Printing Office*①, but many people don't, because the initial doesn't stand for a name.

3 Truman did not have a middle name, only a middle initial. It was a common practice in southern states, including Missouri, to use initials rather than names. In Truman's autobiography, he stated, "I was named for... Harrison Young. I was given the diminutive Harry and, so that I could have two initials in my given name, the letter S was added. My Grandfather Truman's name was Anderson Shippe Truman and my Grandfather Young's name was Solomon Young, so I received the S for both of them." (Anderson's name was also spelled Shipp.) He once joked that the S was a name, not an initial, and it should not have a period, but official documents and his presidential library all use a period. Furthermore, the Harry S. Truman Library has numerous examples of the signature written at various times throughout Truman's lifetime where his own use of

Words & Expressions

initial [iˈniʃəl] *n.* 首字母 *adj.* 开始的，最初的，原始的，

compromise [ˈkɔmprəmaiz] *n.* 妥协，和解，折中，妥协方案

tribute [ˈtribju:t] *n.* 贡品，贡金礼物，颂辞，称颂

autobiography [ˌɔ:təubaiˈɔgrəfi] *n.* 自传

diminutive [diˈminjutiv] *n.* 昵称，爱称 *adj.*缩小的，微小的

initial [iˈniʃəl] *n.* 首字母 *adj.* 字首的，最初的

a period after the “S” is conspicuous. The *Associated Press Stylebook*② has called for a period after the S since the early 1960s, when Truman indicated he had no preference. The use of a period after his middle initial is not universal, however; the official White House biography does not use a period after his name.

4 Truman’s bare initial caused an unusual slip when he first became President and had to take the oath of office. At a meeting in *the Cabinet Room*③ *Chief Justice*④ *Harlan Stone*⑤ began reading the oath by saying “I, Harry Shipp Truman...”! Truman responded using his actual name: “I, Harry S. Truman...”

conspicuous [kən'spikjuəs] *adj.* 明显的，显著的

preference ['prefərəns] *n.* 偏爱，较喜欢

slip [slip] *n.* 失误，疏漏，口误，笔误

actual ['æktʃuəl] *adj.* 实际的，现实的，真实的，当前的

背景知识注释
Background Notes

1. the Government Printing Office （缩写为GPO）政府印刷局，1860年，国会通过《1860年印刷法》，政府印刷局随之建立，主要负责整合政府信息的印刷和出版。1861年3月4日，政府印刷局局长同林肯总统同一天宣誓就职。

2. *Associated Press Stylebook* 《美联社写作指南》。美国没有类似中国的语言文字管理部门，但很多严肃的美国媒体都有自己的写作规范，其中最著名的当属《美联社写作指南》。它被称为美国新闻从业者的“圣经”。因此，它成了记者写作的基本指导工具。

3. the Cabinet Room 内阁会议室，位于白宫西翼，毗邻椭圆形办公室，外边是白宫玫瑰花园，为内阁部长和总统顾问开会的地方。

4. Chief Justice （全称为Chief Justice of the United States）美国首席大法官，美国联邦政府司法部门的领袖并主管美国最高法院。首席大法官是美国最高司法官员，领导最高法院的事务并在弹劾美国总统时主持参议院。同时，按近现代传统，首席大法官还主持美国总统的宣誓仪式，但这样的做法没有《美国宪法》和任何法律作依据。

5. Harlan Stone 哈伦•斯通（1872.10.11～1946.4.22），美国律师、政治家，曾任美国总检察长、美国最高法院大法官和美国首席大法官。

中文译文
Suggested Translation

1 哈里·S·杜鲁门名字中的"S"来自其祖父的名字，希普(Shipp)和所罗门(Solomon)。

2 杜鲁门没有中间名，但他却有一个中间的首字母。杜鲁门解释说，这个"S"是对他两位祖父安德森·希普·杜鲁门(Anderson Shipp Truman)和所罗门·杨(Solomon Young)表示敬意的一种折中的方案。多年来对于"S"之后是否应该加一个圆点一直争论不休。哈里·S·杜鲁门总统图书馆与政府印刷局都使用圆点，但很多人不这样做，因为这个首字母并不代表一个名字。

3 杜鲁门没有中间名，只有一个中间的首字母。使用首字母而不是名字这样的做法在美国南方的一些州，包括密苏里州，颇为普遍。在杜鲁门的自传中，他写道："家人给我取名为哈里森·杨。我的昵称是'哈里'。所以在我的名字里有两个首字母，字母'S'是加进去的。我的祖父杜鲁门的名字为安德森·希普·杜鲁门(Anderson Shipp Truman)。我的外祖父杨的名字叫所罗门·杨(Solomon Young)，所以我采用了他们两个人的S。"(安德森的名字也被拼写为希普[Shipp]。)他曾开玩笑说那个"S"是个名字，不是首字母。因此，后面不应当有个圆点。但是，官方文件和他的总统图书馆都使用圆点。此外，哈里·S·杜鲁门图书馆拥有无数杜鲁门一生不同时期的签字的例证：在"S"之后他自己使用了圆点，这是显而易见的。20世纪60年代早期《美联社写作指南》就呼吁在"S"之后使用圆点。当时杜鲁门表示他没有偏好。然而，在其中间名字的首字母之后使用圆点并不普遍。白宫官方的传记在他的名字后面就没有使用圆点。

4 当杜鲁门首次出任总统进行宣誓时，他名字中不带圆点的首字母造成了非比寻常的口误。在内阁会议室的会议上，首席大法官哈伦·斯顿(Harlan Stone)开始朗读誓词时说道："我，哈里·希普·杜鲁门……"。杜鲁门则以他实际的名字回应："我，哈里·S·杜鲁门……"

34 A Tough Decision under Time Pressure by President Eisenhower 艾森豪威尔总统迫在眉睫的艰难抉择

德怀特·大卫·艾森豪威尔 总统及第一夫人简介

德怀特•大卫•艾森豪威尔(Dwight David Eisenhower, 1890.10.14～1969.3.28)，第34任美国总统(1953～1961)，昵称为艾克(Ike)，陆军五星上将。在美军历史上，艾森豪威尔是一个充满戏剧性的传奇人物。他曾获得很多个第一。美军共授予10人五星上将军衔，他是晋升得“第一快的一个”；他出身“第一穷”；他是美军统率最大战役行动的第一人；他是第一个担任北大西洋公约组织盟军的最高统帅；他是美军退役高级将领担任哥伦比亚大学校长的第一人；他是美国惟一一个当上总统的五星上将。艾森豪威尔酷爱高尔夫球运动，据统计，他在任职总统期间共打过800多次高尔夫球。

玛米•热纳瓦•杜德•艾森豪威尔(Mamie Geneva Doud Eisenhower, 1896.1.14～1979.11.1)，美国第34任总统德怀特•大卫•艾森豪威尔的妻子，与总统育有一子。他们在总统任期结束退休以前共搬了28次家。作为第一夫人，她是一位对私事三缄其口，但对人和蔼可亲的女主人。有一段时期，她因患病影响了身体平衡，走路不太稳，就有人造谣说她酗酒。1961年她和艾森豪威尔总统一起退休，到宾夕法尼亚的葛底斯堡，住在他们第一个永久性的家中。

经典原文
Original Text

1 In the spring of 1944, General Dwight David. Eisenhower, *the Allied Supreme Commander in Europe*①, had to make one of the most important decisions of World War II and time was quickly running out. Hundreds of thousands of *Allied troops*②, sailors, and airmen awaited his orders to begin *Operation Overlord* ③, the invasion of Europe. Eisenhower had already delayed Overlord for a month and postponed other military operations to allow the Allies enough time to build and gather together the landing craft they needed. He set a date, June 5, 1944, and told his officers and men to be ready. Still, there was one factor beyond the Allies' control.

2 The Allied planners knew they could not control the weather for *D-Day*④ ("D-Day" was the first day of any military operation during the war. The expression "D-Day" has come to mean the greatest single Allied operation of World War II, the invasion of *Normandy*⑤). Late on the evening of June 2, 1944, Eisenhower, his top generals, and British Prime Minister *Winston Churchill* ⑥ met to review the weather forecast. The news was not good—D-Day, June 5, promised cloudy skies, rain, and heavy seas. Eisenhower decided to wait another day to see whether the forecast might improve. Less than 24 hours before the scheduled invasion Eisenhower gathered his advisers again. The forecast indicated that the rain would stop and there would be breaks in the clouds by mid-afternoon on June 5.

Words & Expressions

run out 用完，耗尽，跑出，到期，伸向

the landing craft 登陆艇

promise ['prɔmis] *vt.* 允诺，许诺，给人以…的指望或希望，预示

heavy seas 波涛汹涌的海面

in motion 在开动中，在运转中

amphibious [æmˈfibiəs] *adj.* 两栖的，水陆两用的，具有双重性的

armada [ɑːˈmɑːdə] *n.* 舰队

beachhead [ˈbiːtʃhed] *n.* 滩头堡，登陆场，滩头阵地

3 Eisenhower decided to change the date for D-Day to June 6. He knew that the tides would not favor an invasion again for nearly two weeks, long enough for the Germans to possibly learn of the Allies' plan. Eisenhower gave the order and set in motion the largest amphibious invasion in world history; an armada of over 4,000 warships, nearly 10,000 aircraft, and about 160,000 invasion troops. The hard fought invasion was a success—Eisenhower had won his gamble with the weather. Within 2 months, Allied forces broke out from their Normandy beachheads and began the long heroic struggle to liberate Europe from *Nazi* ⑦ tyranny.

背景知识注释 Background Notes

1. the Allied Supreme Commander in Europe　欧洲战区盟军的最高司令官。
2. Allied troops　盟军，即同盟国军队。同盟国是第二次世界大战爆发之后，部分国家为抵抗轴心国的侵略而组成的联盟。
3. Operation Overlord　大君主作战，即霸王行动，是盟军于二次世界大战期间为反攻纳粹德国人侵欧洲西北部的代号。行动展开于诺曼底登陆的1944年6月6日(亦称为D-day)。
4. D-Day　D日，是美军常用军事术语，和D日同样常用的另一个军事术语是H小时(H- hour)。这两个字母用来表示特定作战与行动的开始时间。这种表示有两个意义，第一是表示作战时间尚未确定，第二表示行动计划高度保密。D与H两个字母分别源于它们所代表的单词——D即Day，H即Hour，通常，D日用来表示攻击日，H小时则表示作战开始的具体时间。在一次特定的作战行动中，D日和H小时都是唯一的。
5. Normandy　诺曼底，是法国的一个地区。著名的诺曼底登陆战役发生在1944年6月6日6时30分，是第二次世界大战中盟军在欧洲西线战场发起的一场大规模攻势。这场战役在1944年8月19日结束。
6. Winston Churchill　温斯顿•丘吉尔爵士(1874.11.30～1965.1.24)，英国政治家、演说家、军事家和作家，曾于1940年至1945年出任英国首相，任期内领导英国在第二次世界大战中联合美国等国家对抗德国，并取得了最终胜利；并自1951年至1955年再度出任英国首相。丘吉尔被认为是20世纪最重要的政治领袖之一，对英国乃至于世界均影响深远。此外，他在文学上也有很高的成就，曾于1953年获诺贝尔文学奖。在2002年，BBC举行了一个名为“最伟大的100名英国人”

的调查，结果丘吉尔获选为有史以来最伟大的英国人。

7. Nazi　纳粹党，德国法西斯政党。纳粹是德语Nationalsozialist（民族社会主义者）一词的缩写词Nazi的汉语音译。

中文译文
Suggested Translation

1 1944年春天，身为欧洲战区盟军的最高司令官艾森豪威尔将军(General Dwight D. Eisenhower)必须做出第二次世界大战中最重要的决定，而且已经迫在眉睫了。数以千计的盟军部队、水手及空军士兵正在等待他的命令，准备开始进攻欧洲的霸王行动。艾森豪威尔已经将该作战行动延迟了一个月并延缓了其他的军事作战，目的是让盟军有足够的时间建造及搜集他们所需的登陆船只。他设定了一个日期：1944年6月5日，并要求他的军官及士兵做好准备。然而，仍有一个因素是盟军无法掌控的。

2 盟军的计划者知道他们无法控制D-Day的天气。“D-Day”是战时用来指发动任何军事攻击的第一天。“D-Day”这个词语现在已用来指第二次世界大战中盟军最伟大的作战行动：诺曼底攻击。1944年6月2日深夜，艾森豪威尔、他的高级将领及英国首相温斯顿•丘吉尔 (Winston Churchill) 开会评估天气预报。然而消息并不乐观——6月5日这个D-Day似乎是个多云、有雨及海面风高浪大的日子。艾森豪威尔决定再等一天，看看天气是否会变好；离预定的作战时间只剩下不到24小时的时候，艾森豪威尔再次聚集他的顾问开会。预报显示雨会停止且6月5日午后天空将云消雾散。

3 艾森豪威尔决定将D-Day改为6月6日。他知道接下来有两个星期的时间，潮汐将不适合用于发起攻击，而两个星期的时间可能会让德国获悉盟军的计划。艾森豪威尔下达作战命令并开始发动世界历史上最大的两栖作战攻击。这项任务总共动员了超过4,000艘战舰、将近10,000架飞机及约160,000攻击部队。这次艰苦卓 绝的作战行动获得了巨大成功——艾森豪威尔赢得了这场与天气进行的赌局。在两个月的时间里，盟军在诺曼底滩头阵地实现突破并开始旷日持久、有如史诗般的英勇奋战，以解放纳粹暴政下的欧洲。

35 JFK's Humor Broke the Ice
肯尼迪总统的幽默打破僵局

约翰·菲茨杰拉德·肯尼迪 总统及第一夫人简介

约翰•菲茨杰拉德•肯尼迪(John Fitzgerald Kennedy, 1917.5.29～1963.11.22)，第35任美国总统(1961～1963)通常被称做约翰•F.•肯尼迪(John F. Kennedy)、JFK或杰克•肯尼迪(Jack Kennedy)。美国著名的肯尼迪家族成员，他的执政时间从1961年1月20日开始到1963年11月22日在达拉斯遇刺身亡为止。肯尼迪在1946～1960年期间曾先后任众议员和参议员，并于1960年当选为美国总统，成为美国历史上最年轻的当选总统，也是美国历史上唯一信奉罗马天主教的总统和唯一获得普利策奖的总统。

杰奎琳•李•鲍维尔•肯尼迪•奥纳西斯(Jacqueline Lee Bouvier Kennedy Onassis, 1929.7.28～1994.5.19)，昵称杰基•肯尼迪(Jackie Kennedy)，第35任美国总统约翰•肯尼迪的夫人，与总统育有一儿一女。肯尼迪夫人是最受欢迎的第一夫人之一。但她不喜欢“第一夫人”这个称号，认为它像给马取的名字。虽然她生活中的所有细节都会暴露在媒体和公众的眼光之下，但她希望孩子们能过正常人的生活，她不允许曝光孩子们的照片，但当她外出时，肯尼迪会让白宫的摄影师为他们拍照。肯尼迪总统遇刺时她就在他的身边。她经受了肯尼迪可怕的死亡和全国庄严哀悼时刻所带来的哀痛。1968年她同希腊巨富亚里士多德•奥纳西斯结婚。1975年奥纳西斯去世。她后来在达波迪出版社当编辑。

经典原文
Original Text

1 More than fifty years ago, in late November 1960, Democrat John F. Kennedy was president-elect. The following January he took office as the 35th president of the United States, succeeding Dwight D. Eisenhower.

2 Shortly after taking the oath of office, JFK was asked what surprised him most. Said the 43-year-old president, "When we got into office, what surprised me most was that things were just as bad as we'd been saying they were during the presidential campaign."

3 Reporters and others in the room laughed, in response to a smiling President Kennedy.

4 *Bill Adler*①, who authored the book *The Kennedy Wit*, said that John F. Kennedy was a man with a keenly developed sense of humor. "Few men have displayed such wit in their speeches and writings," said Adler.

5 JFK used humor masterfully to charm the news media. He held 19 press conferences in 1961, 27 gatherings with the news media in 1962, and 18 press conferences in 1963, the year his life came to a tragic end. JFK had a keen grasp of domestic and foreign issues of the day.

6 Asked a reporter on July 17, 1963, "The Republican National Committee recently adopted a resolution saying you were pretty much of a failure. How do you feel about that?"

7 Replied President Kennedy, "I assume it passed

Words & Expressions

president-elect (尚未正式就职的)当选总统

succeed [sək'si:d] *vt.* 继承，接替，继…之后

in response to 响应，回答，对…有反应

author ['ɔ:θə] *vt.* 著（书），著作，写作，编写 *n.* 作者

masterfully ['ma:stəfuli] *adj.* 好支配人地，技巧熟练地

assume [ə'sju:m] *vt.* 承担，假定，采取，呈现

unanimously."

8 During a press conference in 1962, JFK was asked to comment on the press treatment of his administration. His reply, "Well, I'm reading more and enjoying it less."

9 Said JFK during a press conference in Paris on June 2, 1961, "I do not think it altogether inappropriate to introduce myself to this audience. I am the man who accompanied Jacqueline Kennedy to Paris, and I have enjoyed it."

10 During a speech in *Anderson*[2], Ind., Kennedy said, "I understand that this town suffered a misfortune this morning when a bank was robbed. I hope the *Indianapolis Star*[3] doesn't say, 'Democrats arrive and bank robbed.' If they do, please don't believe them."

11 In 1962, during a press conference, JFK responded seriously to a question about a difference of opinion from two of his top officials. At the center of the debate were *Orville Freeman*[4], former Minnesota governor who was U.S. secretary of agriculture, and future South Dakota Sen.. *George McGovern*[5] who headed *the Food for Peace Program*[6] during the Kennedy Administration, and who spoke this past spring at M State—*Fergus Falls*[7].

12 Question: "Mr. President, Secretary Freeman has said that it's impossible to expand the Food for Peace Program, and Mr. McGovern says it should be expanded. Have you been able to resolve this difference?"

13 President Kennedy: "Well, I think it should be expanded as we can. I think that Mr. Freeman's concern is with the regular markets of trade, that the Food for Peace Program should complement and not cut across it. I am hopeful that we can use our productive power. I think that Mr. McGovern and Mr. Freeman will be in balance by the

unanimously [ju'nænəməsli] *adv.* 全体一致地

treatment ['tri:tmənt] *n.* 待遇，对待，论述，讨论

inappropriate [ˌinə'prəupriət] *adj.* 不合适的，不相宜的，不相称的

Sen. （senator/senate/senior的缩写）议员

M State =Minnesota state 明尼苏达州

in balance 总而言之，总的来说，平衡

time they go before the Congress. I think they both have the same basic interests in using our food well and not having it wasted, in storage."

14 Later, JFK told summer interns working in Washington, "Sometimes I wish I just had a summer job here."

15 The book, *The Kennedy Wit*, shows a side of President Kennedy long forgotten by older Americans, and something not known by younger generations about JFK. Humor is part of President Kennedy's legacy.

intern [ˈintəːn] *n.* 实习生，实习医师

legacy [ˈlegəsi] *n.* 遗产；遗赠

背景知识注释 Background Notes

1. Bill Adler 比尔•艾德勒，美国音乐记者和评论家，1951年12月18日出生于纽约布鲁克林，自1980年代初期以来为推广街舞做了很大的努力。
2. Anderson 安德森，印第安纳州中东部麦迪逊县的县治。麦迪逊县成立于1823年，县名纪念第四任总统詹姆斯•麦迪逊。
3. *Indianapolis Star* 《印第安纳波利斯星》，1903年6月6日创办的一家每日晨报，分别于1975年和1991年两次获得普利策调查性报道奖。目前，它由甘尼特公司拥有。
4. Orville Freeman 奥维尔•弗里曼(1918.5.9～2003.2.20)，美国民主党政治家。1955年至1961年担任第29任明尼苏达州州长；1961年至1969年出任约翰•F•肯尼迪和林登•约翰逊总统的农业部部长；1960年弗里曼在全国民主党大会上为肯尼迪做主要提名演说。
5. George McGovern 乔治•麦戈文(1922.7.19～2012.10.21)美国历史学家、作家，前美国参议员，是1972年美国总统选举时民主党推选的候选人，在选举中败给了尼克松。
6. the Food for Peace Program 粮食换和平计划。
7. Fergus Falls 弗格斯•福尔斯，明尼苏达州西部奥特泰尔县的县治。奥特泰尔县成立于1858年3月18日，县名来自奥特泰尔湖和奥特泰尔河。

中文译文 Suggested Translation

1 五十多年前，在1960年11月下旬，民主党候选人约翰•F•肯尼迪当选总统。翌年1月，

他接替德怀特•D•艾森豪威尔就任美国第35任总统。

2 宣誓就职后不久，肯尼迪被问及最让他惊讶的是什么。43 岁的总统说："当我们走进办公室，最让我吃惊的是，形势糟透了，与我们竞选期间所说的没有两样。"

3 记者和房间里的其他人笑了起来，这是对微笑的肯尼迪总统的回应。

4 比尔•艾德勒(Bill Adler)——《肯尼迪的机智》一书的作者曾说约翰•肯尼迪是一位极为机敏幽默的人。"很少有人在他们的演讲和著作中表现出如此的智慧。"

5 约翰•菲茨杰拉德•肯尼迪(JFK)巧妙地使用幽默来吸引新闻媒体。1961年，他举行了19次记者招待会。1962年，他与新闻媒体相聚27次。1963年18次召开记者招待会。这一年，他的生命以一个悲惨的结局而告终。约翰•菲茨杰拉德•肯尼迪敏锐地把握了那个时代国内外的各种问题。

6 1963 年 7 月 17 日，记者问道："共和党全国委员会最近通过了一项决议，说你遭遇惨败。你觉得怎么样？"

7 肯尼迪总统回答说："我认为它获得一致通过。"

8 在 1962 年一个记者招待会上，约翰•菲茨杰拉德•肯尼迪被要求谈谈报界对他政府的评论，他的回答是："嗯，我所读的比以往多了，但是感兴趣的却比以前少了。"

9 1961 年 6 月 2 日约翰•菲茨杰拉德•肯尼迪在巴黎的一次记者招待会上说："我认为这样向各位听众介绍我自己并非完全不合适。我是那个陪同杰奎琳•肯尼迪 (Jacqueline Kennedy) 来巴黎的男人，而这样做让我陶醉。"

10 在印第安纳州安德森 (Anderson) 的一次讲话中，肯尼迪说："据我所知，这个小镇今天上午有个银行被劫，遭遇了不幸。我希望《印第安纳波利斯星报》(*Indianapolis Star*) 不要这样说：'民主党人来了，银行被抢。'如果他们这样说，请不要相信他们。"

11 1962年，肯尼迪在记者招待会上一本正经地回答有关他的两名高级官员意见相左这一问题。处于争辩中心的是：美国农业部长、前明尼苏达州州长奥维尔•弗里曼(Orville Freeman)和未来的南达科他州参议员、领衔肯尼迪政府"粮食换和平计划"的乔治•麦戈文(George McGovern)——在过去的那一年春季里他在明尼苏达州弗格斯•福尔斯(Fergus Falls)发表讲话。

12 问题："总统先生，弗里曼部长说不可能扩大'粮食换和平计划'，麦戈文先生说，应该扩大。你能解决这个分歧吗？"

13 肯尼迪总统说："好，我认为应该尽可能地扩大。我认为弗里曼部长关注的是普通的市场贸易。'粮食换和平计划'应当用于补充而不是切断这种贸易。我希望我们能利用我们的生产能力。我认为，麦戈文先生 (Mr. McGovern) 和弗里曼先生 (Mr. Freeman) 在提交国会之前意见能够趋于一致。在如何更好地使用我们的粮食而不让其在储存中浪费这一问题上，我认为他们的基本利益是相同的。"

14 后来，肯尼迪对在华盛顿工作的暑期实习生说："有时候，我希望我在这里干的只是一种暑期工作。"

15 《肯尼迪的机智》(*The Kennedy Wit*) 这本书展示了早被老一代美国人遗忘的肯尼迪总统的一面，而年轻一代所不了解的肯尼迪的幽默则是肯尼迪总统遗产的一部分。

36 Lyndon Baines Johnson and the Day Kennedy Died

林登·贝恩斯·约翰逊上任、肯尼迪遇刺的那一天

林登·贝恩斯·约翰逊 总统及第一夫人简介

林登·贝恩斯·约翰逊 (Lyndon Baines Johnson, 1908.8.27 ~ 1973.1.22)，第 36 任美国总统 (1963 ~ 1969) 和第 35 任副总统，也曾是国会参议员。他于 1908 年 8 月 27 日生于得克萨斯州中部草原。约翰逊家族曾参与了约翰逊城的建设。约翰逊在任时提出了与“新政”、“公平施政”、“新边疆”一脉相承的改革计划。主要功绩：通过老年保健医疗制度、医疗补助制度、民权法和选举权法。同时，他让美国积极介入越南战争，随着战争的拖延，他的声望持续下降。即使其外交政策有些失败，但约翰逊在美国总统中的排名不逊于某些史学家，这是因为他实施的国内政策成绩斐然。

克劳迪娅·阿尔塔·“小瓢虫”·泰勒·约翰逊 (Claudia Alta “Lady Bird” Taylor Johnson, 1912.12.22 ~ 2007.7.11)，美国第 36 任总统林登·贝恩斯·约翰逊的妻子，与总统育有两女。她还在摇篮中的时候，黑人保姆说了一句：“她美得像只瓢虫。”这使得“小瓢虫 (Lady Bird)”成了她的绰号。她以第一夫人的身份旅行过很多地方，推动了改善美国景观的运动。1965 年她帮助通过了

《公路美化法》。尽管她的活动很多，但她仍然认为第一夫人的主要责任是为总统在白宫创造一个"宁静岛"。约翰逊去世以后，她担任无线电、电报、电视企业公司的董事长及林登·约翰逊图书馆理事等职并且是国家公园顾问委员会成员，依旧跟过去一样活跃。

经典原文 Original Text

1 *Robert Caro*①, in the issue *The New Yorker* ②, told the story of Lyndon B. Johnson on the day he became President—the day, that was, when John F. Kennedy had been assassinated.

2 "As the procession drove farther into the canyon, the noise swelled and deepened, becoming louder and louder, so that the motorcade was driving through a canyon of cheers. Every time the President waved, the crowd on the sidewalk surged toward him, pressing back the lines of policemen, so that the passage for the cars grew narrower, and the lead car was forced to reduce its speed, from twenty miles an hour to fifteen, to ten, to five. Every time *Jackie*③ waved a white-gloved hand, shrieks of 'Jackie!' filled the air."

3 "A moment after the first shot, one of the agents on the *Queen Mary*④'s running board, *Clint Hill* ⑤, had sprinted after the limousine as it was accelerating, leaped onto its trunk, and grabbed one of its handholds. He was now lying spread-eagled across the trunk of the speeding vehicle, but he managed to raise his head and look down into the rear seat. Turning to the followup car, he made a thumbs down gesture."

4 "Johnson said later that he was rushed into the hospital so fast, his view blocked by the men around him, that he hadn't even seen the President's car, or what was

Words & Expressions

assassinate [əˈsæsineit] *vt.* 行刺，暗杀，毁谤，中伤

procession [prəˈseʃən] *n.* 队伍，一列，一排，列队行进

canyon [ˈkænjən] *n.* 峡谷

swell [swel] *vi.* 膨胀，鼓胀

motorcade [ˈməutəkeid] *n.* 一长列汽车，（汽）车队

surge [səːdʒ] *vi.* 激增，汹涌

the lead car 先导车

shriek [ʃriːk] *n.* 尖叫

running board 踏脚板

sprint [sprint] *vi.* 冲刺，全速奔跑

limousine [ˈliməzin] *n.* 豪华轿车，大型豪华轿车

grab [græb] *vt.* 攫取，抓取

handhold *n.* 握，手柄

spread-eagled [ˈspredˌiːgl] *adj.* 伸开四肢躺（或站）着的

followup 继而进行

thumbs down 表示反对或失败的手势

in it. *Lady Bird* ⑥, rushed along right behind him by her own cordon of agents, had seen, in "one last look over my shoulder," "a bundle of pink, just like a drift of blossoms, lying on the back seat. I think it was Mrs. Kennedy lying over the President's body."

5 "*Valenti* ⑦, watching those hands, saw that they were 'absolutely steady,' and Lyndon Johnson's voice was steady, too—low and firm—as he spoke the words he had been waiting to speak all his life. At the back of the room, crowded against a wall, *Marie Fehmer*⑧ wasn't watching the ceremony, because she was reading the oath to make sure it was given correctly. ('He taught you that, by George, you can do anything.')"

6 " 'It was a very, very hard thing to do,' Lady Bird Johnson recalled. 'Mrs. Kennedy's dress was stained with blood. One leg was almost entirely covered with it and her right glove was caked—that immaculate woman—it was caked with blood, her husband's blood. She always wore gloves like she was used to them; I never could. And that was somehow one of the most poignant sights… exquisitely dressed, and caked in blood.' "

7 "When the first calls came into George Hunt's office at *Life*⑨ reporting 'that Kennedy had been shot—at first, that's all: just that he had been shot,' *Russell Sackett* ⑩, an associate editor, recalled, the meeting broke up immediately, with editors and reporters running back to their offices."

8 "Valenti's initial feeling that this was a different man intensified; Johnson was suddenly 'something larger, harder to fathom' than the man he had thought he knew. In fact, for the first time in three years, he looked like the Lyndon Johnson of the Senate floor. Now he had suddenly come

cordon [ˈkɔːdən] *n.* 警戒线，哨兵线，封锁线，包围圈

bundle [ˈbʌndl] *n.* 捆（或包、扎）在一起的东西，包袱，包裹

drift [drift] *n.* 漂流，飘，飘游，漂流物，飘游物

oath [əuθ] *n.* 宣誓，起誓，誓言，誓约

stain [stein] *vt.* 玷污，染污 *n.* 污染处，污点

cake [keik] *vt.* 使结块 *n.* 糕，饼，蛋糕

immaculate [iˈmækjulət] *adj.* 洁白的，无污点的，纯洁的，清白的

poignant [ˈpɔinjənt] *adj.* 尖锐的，辛酸的，深刻的，切中要害的

exquisitely [ekˈskwizitli] *adj.* 精致地，精巧地，敏锐地

associate editor 副主编

intensify [inˈtensifai] *vt.* 使强烈，增强，加强，加剧

fathom [ˈfæðəm] *vt.* 追根究底，弄清…真相，彻底了解，洞察

to the very pinnacle of power. However he had got there, whatever concatenation of circumstance and tragedy—whatever fate—had put him there, he was there, and he knew what to do there."

9 "But, whatever the reasons, not long after *Robert Kennedy* [11] had been told that the brother he loved so deeply was dead his telephone rang again, and when Kennedy picked it up he found himself talking to a man he hated—who was asking him to provide details of the precise procedure by which he could, without delay, formally assume his brother's office."

pinnacle [ˈpinəkl] *n.* 顶点，小尖塔，尖顶，山顶，山峰

concatenation [kənˌkætiˈneiʃən] *n.* 联结，连锁，联系，一系列互相联系的事物或事件

precise [priˈsais] *adj.* 精确的，确切的，精密的

procedure [prəˈsi:dʒə] *n.* 过程，步骤

背景知识注释 Background Notes

1. Robert Caro　罗伯特•卡洛(1935.10.30～)，美国前总统林顿•约翰逊的传记作家，两次普利策奖的得主。《成为官僚》即他的1975年普利策奖获奖作品，同时获得了美国帕克曼奖。此书曾多次再版，成为美国两百多所高等院校规划专业的必读书。他的另一部作品《权力之路——林顿•约翰逊传》获得了美国国家图书奖。

2. *The New Yorker*　《纽约客》，也译作《纽约人》，是一份美国知识、文艺类的综合杂志，内容覆盖新闻报道、文艺评论、散文、漫画、诗歌、小说，以及纽约文化生活动向等，现由康得纳斯出版公司出版。《纽约客》不是完全的新闻杂志，然而它对美国和国际政治、社会重大事件的深度报道是其特色之一。

3. Jackie　杰基，肯尼迪夫人的昵称。

4. Queen Mary　玛丽皇后号，一艘退役邮轮的名字(1936～1967)，时为肯尼迪座驾的代号。

5. Clint Hill　克林特•希尔(1932～)，时为联邦特勤局特工，1975年退休。

6. Lady Bird　即Claudia Alta "Lady Bird" Taylor Johnson 克劳迪娅•阿尔塔•"小瓢虫"•泰勒•约翰逊(1912.12.22～2007.7.11)，美国第36任总统林登•约翰逊的妻子的绰号。

7. valenti　即Jack Valenti 杰克•瓦莱提(1921.9.5～2007.4. 26)，肯尼迪遇刺后，他参加了林登•约翰逊总统在"空军一号"上举行的就职仪式，被任命为约翰逊总统的特别助理并从达拉斯随约翰逊总统返回白宫。

8. Marie Fehmer　(1937～) 玛丽•费墨，她大学刚毕业，就被约翰逊选中。1962～1963年担任时任

副总统约翰逊的秘书，1963～1969年担任时任总统约翰逊的秘书。

9. Life 《生活杂志》，它是一本在美国发行的老牌杂志，一周发行一次，在美国家喻户晓，地位与《时代》杂志相差不远。

10. Russell Sackett 罗素•萨克特，时任《生活杂志》副主编。

11. Robert Kennedy 即Robert Francis "Bobby" Kennedy 罗伯特•弗朗西斯•肯尼迪(1925.11.20～1968.6.6)，通常被称做罗伯特•肯尼迪(Robert Kennedy)、巴比•肯尼迪(Bobby Kennedy)，人们也常以他的英文缩写R.F.K.称呼他。他是第35任美国总统约翰•肯尼迪的弟弟。在约翰•肯尼迪总统任内担任美国司法部长，肯尼迪总统被刺杀身亡后，他仍在继任的林登•约翰逊总统任内留任至1964年。1968年6月5日，他在民主党加州党内初选结束后，在洛杉矶国宾饭店举行记者会，在会后离场时遭到枪击受了重伤，一天之后因伤重死亡。

中文译文
Suggested Translation

1 在《纽约客》期刊中，罗伯特•卡洛(Robert Caro)曾给我们讲述了一个故事。故事发生的当天林登•贝恩斯•约翰逊(Lyndon B. Johnson)就任总统，而约翰•肯尼迪(John F. Kennedy)总统遇刺身亡。

2 “当车队驶入街道深处，喧哗声、呼喊声越来越大，车队几乎就在欢呼的人群中行驶。每当总统挥手致意，人群便潮水般地向他涌去，警察的警戒线只得被迫往后退。这使得车道越来越窄，先导车不得不放慢速度，从每小时 20 英里到 15 英里，再降至 10 英里，最后只有每小时 5 英里。杰基 (Jackie) 一挥动那戴着白色手套的手，‘杰基’、‘杰基’的尖叫声就在空中回荡。”

3 “在第一次枪响之后，玛丽皇后号(Queen Mary)的脚踏板上的特工克林特•希尔(Clint Hill)立马冲向总统的正在加速的座驾，跳上后备箱，然后抓住了一个门把手。虽然他已经全身横躺在后备箱上，但他还是能够抬起头并观察车后排座位上的情况。然后，他转头看向后面的车队，做出大拇指朝下的手势。”

4 “约翰逊 (Johnson) 后来说他赶紧冲进了医院，不过由于被身旁的人挡住了什么都看不见，甚至都没看到总统的车，或车里的东西。约翰逊夫人 (Lady Bird) 在其特工护卫下紧随其后看到了，‘从我的肩膀上方看了总统最后一眼，’‘一束粉红色，像一朵盛开的花，躺在后排座位上。我想当时应该是肯尼迪夫人正趴在总统的身体上。’”

5“瓦莱提 (Valenti)，注视着那双手，它们‘有力而又稳健，’当林登·约翰逊 (Lyndon Johnson) 说出他一生一直都在等待说的话时，他的声音亦低沉而又刚强。在房间的后面，靠墙站着的玛丽·费墨 (Marie Fehmer) 并没有观看这场仪式，因为她正在检查誓词，以便确保其准确无误。(‘是乔治 (George) 教会了你，一切皆有可能。’)”

6“‘这太令人难过了，’约翰逊夫人 (Bird Johnson) 回忆道。‘肯尼迪夫人 (Mrs. Kennedy) 的裙子沾满了血迹。一条腿上全是血，右手手套上的血迹已经凝固了，这个无暇的女人，血迹已经凝固了。这些血恰恰来自她的丈夫。她一直戴着手套就好像已经习惯了似的，换作我就脱下来了。这是我有生以来见过的最心酸的一幕：着装优雅却凝结在血液中。’”

7“罗素·萨克特 (Russell Sackett) 副主编回忆道，当最先打到他们《生活杂志》的乔治·亨特 (George Hunt) 办公室的电话响起时，当听到电话那头说‘肯尼迪 (Kennedy) 遇刺了——一开始，就这样：只是他中枪了’的时候，他们正在进行的会议立马解散，大家纷纷跑回各自的办公室。”

8“瓦莱提 (Valenti) 一开始的感觉是这是一个不一样的人，突然约翰逊变得比自以为认识的他‘更加强大，更加难以捉摸’。事实上，在这三年里他头一次看起来像参议院里的林登·约翰逊 (Lyndon Johnson)。现在他突然来到了权力的最巅峰。不管是不是这一连串事件和悲剧弄人，不管是不是命运使然，他就是达到了那一高度，他知道在那里该做什么。”

9“但是不管是什么原因，在罗伯特·肯尼迪 (Robert Kennedy) 被告知他深爱的哥哥去世的消息过后不久，他的电话铃又响了。电话中是他讨厌的一个人。那个人让他提供总统就职的详细过程，以便能够尽快正式接替他哥哥的职位。”

37 Richard Milhous Nixon and Watergate 理查德·米尔豪斯·尼克松总统与水门事件

理查德·米尔豪斯·尼克松 总统及第一夫人简介

理查德·米尔豪斯·尼克松 (Richard Milhous Nixon, 1913.1.9 ~ 1994.4.22)，第 37 任美国总统 (1969 ~ 1974)，也是第 36 任美国副总统 (1953 ~ 1961)。尼克松是美国历史上唯一当过两届总统和两届副总统的人，但也是唯一于在位期间以辞职的方式离开总统职位的美国总统。尼克松是登上《时代周刊》封面次数最多的人物——共 43 次成为《时代周刊》封面人物，并于 1968 年和 1972 年两度荣登“《时代周刊》年度风云人物”。

特尔玛·凯瑟琳·瑞安·“帕特”·尼克松(Thelma Catherine Ryan “Pat” Nixon, 1912.3.16～1993.6.22)，美国第37任总统理查德·尼克松的妻子，与总统育有两女。她之所以叫“帕特”是因为她生于圣帕特里克节的前一天，她还把这一天当做她的生日来庆祝。她是美国历史上旅行最多的第一夫人之一，也是第一位到过战区的第一夫人。1976年与1983年她两次患中风；1992年被确诊为肺癌。

经典原文
Original Text

1 The term "Watergate" has come to encompass an array of clandestine and often illegal activities undertaken by members of the Nixon administration. Those activities included "dirty tricks" such as bugging the offices of political opponents and people of whom Nixon or his officials were suspicious. Nixon and his close aides ordered harassment of activist groups and political figures, using the *FBI*①, *CIA*②, and *the Internal Revenue Service*③. The activities became known after five men were caught breaking into Democratic party headquarters at the *Watergate complex*④ in Washington, D.C. on June 17, 1972. The *Washington Post*⑤ picked up on the story; reporters *Carl Bernstein*⑥ and *Bob Woodward*⑦ relied on an informant known as "*Deep Throat*⑧"—later revealed to be *Mark Felt*⑨, associate director at the FBI—to link the men to the Nixon administration. Nixon downplayed the scandal as mere politics, calling news articles biased and misleading. As a series of revelations made it clear that Nixon aides had committed crimes in attempts to sabotage the Democrats and others, senior aides such as *White House Counsel*⑩ *John Dean*⑪ and *Chief of Staff*⑫ *H. R. Haldeman*⑬ faced prosecution.

2 In July 1973, White House aide *Alexander Butterfield*⑭ testified that Nixon had a secret taping system that recorded his conversations and phone calls in the Oval Office. These tapes were subpoenaed by *Watergate Special Counsel*⑮ *Archibald Cox*⑯. Nixon refused to release them, citing executive privilege. With the White House

Words & Expressions

encompass [inˈkʌmpəs] *vt.* 围绕，环绕，围住，包围

an array of 一排，一批，大量

clandestine [klænˈdestin] *adj.* 秘密的，私下的，偷偷摸摸的

bug [bʌg] *vt.* 装或暗设窃听器，通过窃听器窃听 *n.* 虫子，故障，窃听器

harassment [ˈhærəsmənt] *n.* 骚扰，扰乱，烦扰，烦恼事

break into 闯入

pick up on 注意到，了解

informant [inˈfɔːmənt] *n.* 提供消息(或情报)的人，报告者，告密者，检举者

downplay [ˌdaunˈplei] *vt.* 不予重视，将…轻描淡写

revelation [ˌrevəˈleiʃən] *n.* 揭露，展示，透露

sabotage [ˌsæbəˈtɑːʒ] *vt.* 妨害，对…采取破坏行动

prosecution [ˌprɔsiˈkjuːʃən] *n.* 起诉，检举，进行，经营

subpoena [səbˈpiːnə] *vt.* 传唤，传讯，命令交出

and Cox at loggerheads, Nixon had Cox fired in October in the "*Saturday Night Massacre* ⑰"; he was replaced by *Leon Jaworski* ⑱. In November, Nixon's lawyers revealed that an audio tape of conversations, held in the White House on June 20, 1972, featured an 18½ minute gap. *Rose Mary Woods* ⑲, the President's personal secretary, claimed responsibility for the gap, alleging that she had accidentally wiped the section while transcribing the tape, though her tale was widely mocked. The gap, while not conclusive proof of wrongdoing by the President, cast doubt on Nixon's statement that he had been unaware of the cover-up.

3 Though Nixon lost much popular support, even from his own party, he rejected accusations of wrongdoing and vowed to stay in office. He insisted that he had made mistakes, but had no prior knowledge of the burglary, did not break any laws, and did not learn of the cover-up until early 1973. On October 10, 1973, Vice President *Agnew* ⑳ resigned amid allegations—unrelated to Watergate—of bribery, tax evasion and money laundering from his tenure as Maryland's governor. Nixon chose *Gerald Ford* ㉑, Minority Leader of the House of Representatives, to replace Agnew.

4 On November 17, 1973, during a televised question and answer session with the press, Nixon said, "People have got to know whether or not their President is a crook. Well, I'm not a crook. I've earned everything I've got".

5 The legal battle over the tapes continued through early 1974, and in April 1974 Nixon announced the release of 1,200 pages of transcripts of White House conversations between him and his aides. *The House Judiciary Committee* ㉒, opened impeachment hearings against the President

at loggerheads 进行争论，吵架，与…相争

feature [ˈfiːtʃə] *vt.* 是…的特色

gap [gæp] *n.* 间隙，缺口，空白

allege [əˈledʒ] *vt.* 宣称，断言，提出…作为理由

transcribe [trænˈskraib] *vt.* 誊写，抄写，预录，录制，复制

mock [mɔk] *vt.* 嘲笑，讥笑，漠视，轻蔑

conclusive [kənˈklusiv] *adj.* 决定性的，最后的，确实的，

wrongdoing [ˈrɔŋduiŋ] *n.* 坏事，不道德的行为

cover-up [ˈkʌvəˌʌp] *n.* 掩盖，掩饰，攻守同盟

accusation [ˌækjuˈzeiʃən] *n.* 控告，指控，谴责

vow [vau] *n./v.* 发誓，郑重宣告

allegation [ˌæləˈgeiʃən] *n.* 主张，断言，辩解

evasion [iˈveiʒn] *n.* 逃避，回避，借口

money laundering 洗钱

tenure [ˈtenjə] *n.* 任期，占有

transcript [ˈtrænskript] *n.* 成绩单，抄本，副本，文字记录

impeachment [imˈpiːtʃmənt] *n.* 弹劾，控告，怀疑，指摘

hearings [ˈhiəriŋz] *n.* 听证会，倾听，听觉

on May 9, 1974, which were televised on the major networks. These hearings culminated in votes for articles of impeachment, the first being 27:11 in favor on July 27, 1974 on obstruction of justice. On July 24, the Supreme Court ruled unanimously that the full tapes, not just selected transcripts must be released.

6 Even with support diminished by the continuing series of revelations, Nixon hoped to win through. However, one of the new tapes, recorded soon after the break-in, demonstrated that Nixon had been told of the White House connection to the Watergate burglaries soon after they took place, and had approved plans to thwart the investigation. In a statement accompanying the release of the "*Smoking Gun*㉓Tape" on August 5, 1974, Nixon accepted blame for misleading the country about when he had been told of the truth behind the Watergate break-in, stating that he had a lapse of memory. He met with Republican congressional leaders soon after, and was told he faced certain impeachment in the House and had, at most, 15 senators prepared to vote for his acquittal—far fewer than the 34 he needed to avoid removal from office.

culminate[ˈkʌlmineit] *vi.* 到绝顶，达到高潮，达到顶点 *vt.* 使结束，使达到高潮

diminish [diˈminiʃ] *vt.* 使减少，使变小 *vi.* 减少，缩小，变小

thwart [θwɔːt] *vt.* 挫败，反对，阻碍，横过

a lapse of memory 记忆的错误

acquittal [əˈkwitəl] *n.* 宣判无罪，赦免，释放

背景知识注释

Back ground Notes

1. FBI（全称为 Federal Bureau of Investigation）美国联邦调查局，是世界著名的也是美国最重要的情报机构之一，隶属于美国司法部。"FBI"不仅是美国联邦调查局的缩写，还代表着该局坚持贯彻的信条——忠诚（Fidelity）、勇敢（Bravery）和正直（Integrity）。
2. CIA（全称为 Central Intelligence Agency）中央情报局，是美国政府的情报、间谍和反间谍机构，主要职责是收集和分析全球政治、经济、文化、军事、科技等方面的情报，协调美国国内

情报机构的活动，并把情报上报美国政府各部门。它也负责维持在美国境外的军事设备。中情局的根本目的是透过情报工作维护美国的国家利益和国家安全。

3. the Internal Revenue Service　国家税务局，隶属于美国财政部，于1862年起设立。

4. Watergate complex　水门综合大厦，是位于美国华盛顿哥伦比亚特区西北部的一座综合楼宇群，始建于1967年，与肯尼迪表演艺术中心毗邻，包括有三栋住宅楼、两栋办公楼和水门酒店。1972年水门事件发生于此，使得该地名声大噪。

5. *Washington Post*　《华盛顿邮报》，它是美国华盛顿哥伦比亚特区最大、最老的报纸。1970年代初通过揭露“水门事件”和迫使理查德•尼克松总统退职，《华盛顿邮报》获得了国际威望。

6. Carl Bernstein　卡尔•伯恩斯坦(1944.2.14～)，美国记者，是揭穿“水门事件”丑闻的两名《华盛顿邮报》记者之一。因此获得了1973年的普利策新闻奖。

7. Bob Woodward　鲍勃•伍德沃德(1943.3.26～)，美国记者，是揭穿“水门事件”丑闻的两名《华盛顿邮报》记者之一。因此获得了1973年的普利策新闻奖。

8. Deep Throat　深喉，或称“深喉咙”，是美国历史上“水门事件”中向《华盛顿邮报》透露幕后信息的秘密线人的代号。“深喉”的真实身份一直是个谜，直到 2005 年美国联邦调查局前副局长马克・费尔特承认他就是“深喉”。

9. Mark Felt　即William Mark Felt, Sr. 老威廉姆斯•马克•费尔特(1913.8.17～2008.12.18)，1970年代曾任联邦调查局副局长，在1972年的“水门事件”中，他就是向《华盛顿邮报》记者鲍勃•伍德沃德提供消息来源的秘密线人，后来被人称为“深喉”。他于2008年12月18日在睡梦中因心血管疾病离世，终年95岁。

10. White House Counsel　白宫法律顾问，其职责是向总统提供所有有关总统和白宫法律问题的咨询。

11. John Dean　即John Wesley Dean 约翰•迪恩(1938.10.14～)，1971年7月～1973年4月担任尼克松总统的法律顾问，因此深深卷入“水门事件”丑闻。现为作家和政治评论员。

12. Chief of Staff　即 White House Chief of Staff 白宫幕僚长，又被译为“白宫办公厅主任”，是美国总统办事机构的最高级别官员，同时亦是美利坚合众国总统的高级助理。白宫幕僚长是一个拥有很大权力的职位，常被称为“华盛顿第二最具权力的人”。

13. H. R. Haldeman　H•R•霍尔德曼(1926.10.27～1993.11.12)，1956年就开始担任尼克松的助手。因“水门事件”在狱中服刑18个月。

14. Alexander Butterfield 亚历山大•巴特菲尔德，他是H•R•霍尔德曼的老朋友，应邀于1969～1973年担任H•R•霍尔德曼的副手，“水门事件”的关键人物，但并未参与掩盖“水门事件”，因此没有被起诉。

15. Watergate Special Counsel　“水门事件”的特别顾问。

16. Archibald Cox　阿奇博尔德•考克斯，美国著名律师和法学教授，1973年担任“水门事件”的特别检察官。考克斯以他的信念和正直去追查尼克松总统的犯罪行为，这让他在后人皆知的

“星期六夜晚大屠杀”中被尼克松解雇，并最终导致了尼克松的中途下台。

17. Saturday Night Massacre　星期六夜晚大屠杀。在“水门事件”调查的过程中，1973年7月16日，尼克松的前助手亚历山大•巴特菲尔德向参议院特别调查委员会透露，从1970年以来，尼克松在白宫办公室端安装了录音装置，把自己同所有人的谈话都录了下来。“水门事件”检察官考克斯要求尼克松交出录音以供检查，但遭到拒绝。1973年10月20日，尼克松宣布开除考克斯(Archibald Cox)，撤销专事调查的特别检察官办事处。消息传出后，司法部长理查德森(Elliot Richardson)及副部长拉克尔(William Ruckelshaus)宣布辞职以示抗议，过了不到24小时，这几件事便以“星期六夜晚大屠杀”的标题被美国各家报纸、电视向全国做了报道。“星期六夜晚大屠杀”是政治大屠杀，是恐怖；但杀掉的，不是人命，而是乌纱帽。

18. Leon Jaworski　莱昂•沃斯基，1973年11月1日在考克斯10月20日被解职后，担任第二任“水门事件”的特别检察官。

19. Rose Mary Woods　罗丝•玛丽•伍兹，从1951年开始就担任尼克松的私人秘书，尼克松家人信得过的挚友。

20. Agnew　即Spiro Theodore Agnew 斯皮罗•西奥多•阿格纽，美国政治家，曾任马里兰州州长和第39任美国副总统，为美国历史上两个于任内辞职的副总统之一。

21. Gerald Ford　杰拉尔德•福特，第38任美国总统。

22. the House Judiciary Committee　众议院司法委员会，是美国众议院的一个常设委员会。它负责监督联邦法院、行政机构和联邦执法机构是否秉行公正，还负责弹劾联邦官员。 由于其工作性质，委员会的成员通常需有法律背景，但是并不是必须的。

23. Smoking Gun　冒烟的枪，源于夏洛克•福尔摩斯的侦探故事《格洛里亚斯科特号三桅帆船》，用于指确凿的证据。

中文译文
Suggested Translation

1 “水门事件”这个词语是指尼克松政府成员的一系列秘密且通常为非法的活动。这些活动包括诸如对政治对手的办公室以及对尼克松及其官员所怀疑的人进行窃听等“肮脏伎俩”。尼克松及其亲信下令运用联邦调查局、中央情报局与国家税务局对激进组织和政治人物进行骚扰。这些活动随着1972年6月17日五个人闯入位于华盛顿哥伦比亚特区水门综合大厦被抓而被曝光。《华盛顿邮报》了解到这件事。记者卡尔•伯

恩斯坦 (Carl Bernstein) 和鲍勃·伍德沃德 (Bob Woodward) 根据一个称为“深喉”的告密者——后来得知他是中央情报局的一名副局长——将那几个人与尼克松政府联系在一起。尼克松淡化这个丑闻，认为这仅仅是政治把戏，称新闻文章带有偏见并造成误导。随后揭露的一系列真相表明尼克松的助手企图对民主党和其他人实施破坏活动，业已构成犯罪。尼克松的高级幕僚诸如白宫法律顾问约翰·迪恩 (John Dean) 和幕僚长 H·R· 霍尔德曼 (H. R. Haldeman) 面临被起诉。

2 1973年7月，白宫助手亚历山大·巴特菲尔德(Alexander Butterfield)作证说，尼克松有一个秘密录音系统，记录了他在椭圆形办公室的谈话和电话。“水门事件”的特别顾问阿奇博尔德·考克斯(Archibald Cox)命令交出这些磁带。但尼克松以行政特权(executive privilege)为由拒绝交出。白宫与考克斯相持不下，于是，尼克松在10月“星期六夜晚大屠杀”中解雇了考克斯，取而代之的是莱昂·沃斯基(Leon Jaworski)。11月尼克松的律师透露，在1972年6月20日的一段白宫谈话的录音磁带中有18分半钟的空白。罗丝·玛丽·伍兹(Rose Mary Woods)，总统的私人秘书，声称对这段空白负责，她信誓旦旦地说那是在录制时不小心擦掉的，然而她编的故事成了众人的笑柄。这段空白虽然不能成为总统不法行为的确凿证据，然而也使人们对尼克松有关他对掩盖行为不知情的说明产生了怀疑。

3 虽然尼克松失去了民众以及甚至是来自他自己政党的支持，但他拒绝犯有不法行为的指控，并发誓要继续留任。他坚持说他曾犯了错误，但对非法闯入事先并不知情，他并没有违反任何法律，直到1973年初才得知出现掩盖真相的行为。1973年10月10日，阿格纽副总统(Agnew)因与“水门事件”无关的事情——在他担任马里兰州州长期间的贿赂、逃税和洗钱等行为——辞职。尼克松选择众议院少数党领袖杰拉尔德·福特(Gerald Ford)接替阿格纽。

4 1973 年 11 月 17 日，在一次电视直播的新闻发布会问答环节中，尼克松说：“人们应当知道他们的总统是否是一个骗子。嗯，我不是一个骗子。我所拥有的一切都是靠自己赢得的。”

5 有关磁带的法律之争一直持续到1974年初。1974年4月尼克松宣布公布1,200页他与他的助手们之间在白宫谈话的记录稿。众议院司法委员会于1974年5月9日开始举行弹劾总统的听证会，并通过主要网络电视直播。这些听证会最终以投票表决通过弹劾条款，第一项为妨碍司法公正，于1974年7月27日以27票对11票获得通过。7月24日，最高法院一致裁决必须交出完整的磁带，而不只是经过挑选的记录稿。

6 即使随着一些事情真相大白，人们对他的支持日渐减少，尼克松仍希望能赢得最终的胜利。然而，一段“擅自闯入”之后不久录制的新的录音带表明尼克松在事发后就被告知白宫与“水门事件”有牵连并批准阻挠调查的计划。在1974年8月5日“冒烟的枪带”(Smoking Gun Tape)曝光之后的声明中，尼克松说他记忆有误，承认对在得知“水门闯入”的真相之后仍然误导全国的指控。不久他与共和党国会领导人商谈并被告知他将面临国会不可避免的弹劾。最多只有15名参议员准备投票认定他无罪，远低于他避免被撤职所需要的34人。

38 Gerald Rudolph Ford—the Longest-lived U.S. President 杰拉尔德·鲁道夫·福特——美国最长寿的总统

杰拉尔德·鲁道夫·福特 总统及第一夫人简介

杰拉尔德·鲁道夫·福特(Gerald Rudolph Ford, Jr., 1913.7.14～2006.12.26)，第38任美国总统(1974～1976)和第40任副总统。1974年8月9日理查德·尼克松辞职后福特继任美国总统。他是美国历史上唯一一位未经选举就接任总统的人。福特执政期间，美国从越南撤军，《赫尔辛基协定》生效，但也面对美国国内通货膨胀、经济萧条、能源短缺等诸多的难题。由于在美国国会内民主党占多数，政府无法通过重要的法律。福特被迫用尽他的否决权。许多人对福特特赦尼克松也非常不满。在1976年大选中，民主党总统候选人吉米·卡特以微弱优势击败了福特。

伊丽莎白·安·布卢默·沃伦·福特(Elizabeth Ann Bloomer Warren Ford, 1918.4.18～2011.7.8)，美国第38任总统杰拉尔德·鲁道夫·福特的妻子，昵称贝蒂 (Betty)，与总统育有三儿一女。她原来学习舞蹈，1942年与家具商人威廉·沃伦结婚，但1947年离婚，这一年她和福特相识。1948年2月她接受福特的求婚。成为第一夫人后，她以推动女权运动、乳癌防治、反药物与酒精滥用等公益活动得到美国人民的深深敬重。

经典原文
Original Text

1 On December 26, 2006, Gerald Ford, the 38th President of the United States, died at his home in *Rancho Mirage*①, California, at 6:45 p.m. local time (02:45, December 27, *UTC*②). At 8:49 p.m. local time, President Ford's wife of 58 years, Betty Ford, issued a statement that confirmed his death:"My family joins me in sharing the difficult news that Gerald Ford, our beloved husband, father, grandfather and great grandfather has died at 93 years of age. His life was filled with love of God, his family and his country."

2 Ford's age at the time of his death was 93 years and 165 days, making him the longest-lived U.S. President. On December 30, 2006, Ford became the 11th U.S. President *to lie in state*③. The burial was preceded by a state funeral and memorial services held at the *National Cathedral*④ in Washington, D.C., on January 2, 2007. After the service, Ford was interred at his *Presidential Museum*⑤ in *Grand Rapids*⑥, Michigan.

3 Ford died on the 34th anniversary of President *Harry*⑦ Truman's death, thus becoming the second U.S. President to die on *Boxing Day*⑧. He was the last surviving member of *the Warren Commission*⑨. His wife, Betty Ford, died on July 8, 2011. Like her husband, Betty also died at age 93. They are the longest lived Presidential couple.

4 The State of Michigan commissioned and submitted a statue of Ford to *the National Statuary Hall Collection*⑩, replacing *Zachariah Chandler*⑪. It was unveiled on May 3, 2011 in *the Capitol Rotunda*⑫. On the proper right side

Words & Expressions

precede [priː'siːd] *vt.* 先于…，比…优先，比…重要

inter [in'təː] *vt.* 埋葬

commission [kə'miʃən] *n./ vt.* 委托，委任，任命

unveil [ʌn'veil] *vt.* 揭示，展露，揭去…的面纱，揭幕

the proper right side 右边正中间的位置

is inscribed a quotation from a tribute by *Thomas P. "Tip" O'Neill* [13], Speaker of the House during Ford's presidency: "God has been good to America, especially during difficult times. At the time of the Civil War, he gave us Abraham Lincoln. And at the time of Watergate, he gave us Gerald Ford—the right man at the right time who was able to put our nation back together again. " On the proper left side are words from Ford's swearing-in address: "Our constitution works. Our great republic is a government of laws and not of men. Here the people rule. "

5 Ford was the longest-lived U.S. President, his lifespan being 45 days longer than *Ronald Reagan* [14]'s. He was the third-longest-lived Vice President, falling short only of *John Nance Garner* [15], 98, and *Levi P. Morton* [16], 96. Ford had the third-longest post-presidency (29 years and 11 months) after *Jimmy Carter* [17] (31 years, 8 months and counting) and *Herbert Hoover* [18] (31 years and 7 months)

inscribe [in'skraib] *vt.* 雕，刻，题写，印，题赠

6 On November 12, 2006, upon surpassing Ronald Reagan's lifespan, Ford released his last public statement:

The length of one's days matters less than the love of one's family and friends. I thank God for the gift of every sunrise and, even more, for all the years He has blessed me with Betty and the children; with our extended family and the friends of a lifetime. That includes countless Americans who, in recent months, have remembered me in their prayers. Your kindness touches me deeply. May God bless you all and may God bless America.

背景知识注释
Background Notes

1. Rancho Mirage　兰乔•米拉奇，是美国加利福尼亚州南部里弗赛德县下属的一座城市。

2. UTC　（全称为Coordinated Universal Time）协调世界时，又称世界统一时间、世界标准时间或国际协调时间。

3. to lie in state　停放…接受公共瞻仰。

4. Natuinal Cathedral　即Washington National Cathedral 华盛顿国家大教堂，正式名称是圣彼得与圣保罗大教堂(the Cathedral Church of Saint Peter and Saint Paul)。

5. Presidential Museum　即Presidential library 总统博物馆/图书馆，一个由博物馆和图书馆组成的独特系统。它不是传统意义上的图书馆，它既是档案馆，又是纪念馆，既保存总统的档案文件，又收藏总统接受的赠品、个人物品、图书、艺术品以及货币、邮票等各种收藏品，因此，它实际上是一个集中保管总统档案文件和其他历史资料并提供服务的场所。

6. Grand Rapids　大急流城，又被译为“大瀑布城”。美国密歇根州西南部格兰德河岸的一个城市。19世纪末成为美国最大的家具制造中心之一，还有汽车零件、石油炼制、金属加工、化学、造纸、食品等工业。市博物馆展列有19世纪的家具。

7. Harry　即Harry Truman 哈里•杜鲁门，美国第16任总统。

8. Boxing Day　节礼日，为每年的12月26日，圣诞节次日或是圣诞节后的第一个星期日，是在英联邦部分地区庆祝的节日，一些欧洲国家也将其定为节日，叫做“圣士提反日”。这一日传统上要向服务业工人赠送圣诞节礼物。

9. the Warren Commission　即The President’s Commission on the Assassination of President Kennedy 总统特别调查肯尼迪遇刺事件委员会，俗称沃伦委员会(Warren Commission)。该委员会的非正式名称——沃倫委员会——系来自于该委员会的主席：美国首席大法官厄尔•沃伦。

10. the National Statuary Hall Collection　国家雕像展览厅，位于国会大厦，由各州捐赠的大理石或青铜雕像所组成，每个州只限两尊，以纪念他们各自历史上的名人。

11. Zachariah Chandler　撒迦利亚•钱德勒(1813.12.10～1879.11.1)，曾任美国第18任总统尤利塞斯•S•格兰特的内政部长(1875～1877)。

12. the Capitol Rotunda　美国国会大厦圆形大厅，位于国会大厦圆顶之下。每天都有成千上万的人参观。

13. Thomas P. “Tip” O’Neill　小托马斯•菲利普•“狄普”•奥尼尔(1912.12.9～1994.1.5)，美国政治家和美国众议院议长，一位直言不讳的自由派民主党人和众议院有影响力的成员，曾任职34年，是继萨姆•雷伯恩之后在美国历史上任职时间最长的众议院议长。

14. Ronald Reagan　罗纳德•里根，美国第40任总统。

15. John Nance Garner　此处指的是约翰•南斯•加纳四世(1868.11.22～1967.11.7)，绰号“仙人掌•杰克”(Cactus Jack)，美国政治家，曾于1931年至1933年间出任第44任美国众议院议长，并在1933年至1941年间出任第32任美国副总统。

16. Levi P. Morton　即Levi Parsons Morton 李维•帕森•斯莫顿(1824.5.16～1920.5.16)，纽约州众议员以及美国第22任副总统(1889～1893)，后来又成为纽约州第31任州长。

17. Jimmy Carter　吉米•卡特，第39任美国总统。

18. Herbert Hoover　赫伯特•胡佛，第31任美国总统。

中文译文
Suggested Translation

1 2006 年 12 月 26 日当地时间下午 6 时 45 分（国际协调时间 12 月 27 日 2 时 45 分）杰拉尔德・福特，第 38 任美国总统在其加利福尼亚州兰乔・米拉奇 (Rancho Mirage) 家中谢世。当地时间晚上 8 时 49 分，与福特总统结婚 58 年的妻子贝蒂・福特发表声明证实了他的死讯：“我的家人与我发布这一不幸的消息，我们深爱的丈夫、父亲、祖父和曾祖父去世了，享年 93 岁。他的一生中都充满了来自上帝、家庭以及国家的爱。”

2 福特辞世时的年龄为93岁又165天，这使得他成为美国历史上最长寿的总统。2006年12月30日，福特成为第11位接受公共瞻仰的美国总统。下葬之前，于2007年1月2日在华盛顿哥伦比亚特区举行国葬和悼念仪式；仪式之后，埋葬在密歇根州大急流城的福特总统博物馆。

3 福特逝世这一天正好是哈里•杜鲁门总统逝世34周年纪念日，他也成为第二位在节礼日辞世的美国总统。他还是最后一位离世的沃伦委员会成员。他的妻子，贝蒂•福特，2011年7月8日辞世。与她的丈夫一样，贝蒂也在93岁谢世。他们是最长寿的总统夫妇。

4 密歇根州向国家雕塑展览馆提交一尊委托制作的福特雕像，以取代撒迦利亚・钱德勒 (Zachariah Chandler)。2011 年 5 月 3 日该雕像在美国国会大厦圆形大厅揭幕。在其右边正中间刻着托马斯 •P• “狄普” • 奥尼尔 (Thomas P. “Tip” O’Neill)，福特担任总统期间众议院议长为表示敬意所写的一段话：“上帝从来就不亏待美国，特别是当这个国家陷入困境的时候。南北战争期间，他把亚伯拉罕•林肯赐给我们。‘水门事件’的时候，我们又有了杰拉尔德•福特。美国在关键时刻总是有人相助，把我们的国家重新聚集起来。”在其左边正中间则是福特就

职演讲的一段话：“我们的宪法是发挥作用的。我们伟大的共和国是一个法治而不是人治的政府。人民是这里的统治者。”

5 福特是美国最长寿的总统，他的寿命比罗纳德•里根长45天。他是第三位最长寿的副总统，仅次于约翰•南斯•加纳(John Nance Garner)——98岁和利维•P•莫顿(Levi P. Morton)——96岁。福特卸任后在世的时间是美国总统中第三长的(29年11个月)——排在吉米•卡特（仍然健在）和赫伯特•胡佛(31年7个月)之后。

6 2006年11月12日，当超越罗纳德•里根寿命的长度之后，福特发布了他的最后一次公开声明：

与一个人生命的长短相比，家人和朋友的关爱更加重要。感谢上帝的恩赐，让我每天看到日出。更重要的是，感谢他这么多年来一直对我、贝蒂(Betty)及孩子、亲人和生命中的朋友的眷顾。这包括最近几个月无数为我祈祷的美国人。你们的深情厚爱令我感触良深。愿上帝保佑你们，愿上帝保佑美国。

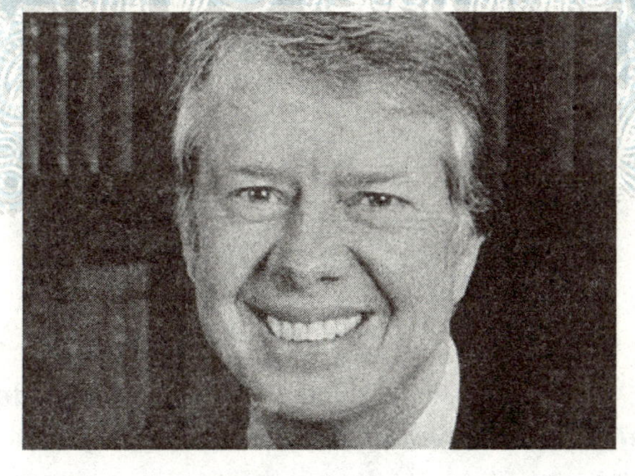

39 The Peanut Farmer — President Jimmy Carter 花生农夫吉米•卡特总统

吉米·厄尔·卡特 总统及第一夫人简介

小詹姆斯•厄尔•卡特(James Earl Carter, Jr., 1924.10.1～)，第39任美国总统(1977～1981)，又称吉米•卡特 (Jimmy Carter)；他与父亲同名，故称小詹姆斯•厄尔•卡特。他早年曾在军队中生活。1955年至1962年任佐治亚州萨姆特县学校董事会董事长，1962年至1966年任佐治亚州参议员。在此期间还先后担任过平原发展公司、萨姆特县发展公司总经理，佐治亚州中西部计划和发展委员会以及佐治亚州改进作物协会主席等职。1971年他开始任佐治亚州的州长。1974年任民主党全国委员会议员竞选委员会主席。1976年代表美国民主党当选总统。在任期间推行能源保护政策。外交方面，卡特积极调停以色列和埃及之间的战争。卡特跟其他国家外交时注重人权保障。1980年，伊朗霍梅尼政权绑架美国大使馆人质，卡特派"蓝光突击队"救援但失败，因此他同年在竞选第二任时，输给了罗纳德•里根。卸任后，他积极参与调停各种战争的斡旋工作，并获得2002年的诺贝尔和平奖。

埃莉诺•罗莎琳•史密斯•卡特(Eleanor Rosalynn Smith Carter, 1927.8.18～)，第39任美国总统吉米•卡特的妻子，与总统育有三儿一女。她13岁那年父亲去世。因家庭生活艰苦，她曾去邮局做工，在家做针线以弥补母亲微薄的收入。她还在当地的理发馆工作过，同时也做些缝纫活。在这期间她仍然保持出色的学习成绩。成为第一夫人以后，卡特经常和她讨论政策，并且重视她的意见。卡特夫人就像在她之前的埃莉诺•罗斯福那样，艰难地克服了本能的羞涩并在大庭广众中发表演说，而且不受总统意见的左右积极地发表意见。她是自罗斯福夫人以后第一位在国会作证的第一夫人。她支持为精神保健计划多拨款项。她还为平等权利修正案大声疾呼，并且反对堕胎。

经典原文
Original Text

1 James Earl Carter, Jr., was born at *the Wise Sanitarium*① on October 1, 1924, in the tiny southwest Georgia city of *Plains*②, near *Americus*③. As the first president born in a hospital, he is the eldest of four children of *James Earl Carter*④ and *Bessie Lillian Gordy*⑤. Carter's father was a prominent business owner in the community and his mother was a registered nurse.

2 Carter is descended from immigrants from southern England (one of his paternal ancestors arrived in *the American Colonies*⑥ in 1635), and his family has lived in the state of Georgia for several generations. Carter has documented ancestors who fought in *the American Revolution*⑦, and he is a member of *the Sons of the American Revolution*⑧. Carter's great-grandfather, Private *L.B. Walker Carter*⑨ (1832 ~ 1874), served in *the Confederate States Army*⑩.

3 Carter was a gifted student from an early age who always had a fondness for reading. By the time he attended *Plains High School* ⑪, he was also a star in basketball. He was greatly influenced by one of his high school teachers, *Julia Coleman* ⑫ (1889 ~ 1973). While he was in high school he was in *the Future Farmers of America* ⑬, which later changed its name to *the National FFA Organization* ⑭,

Words & Expressions

descend [di'send] *vt.* 下降，下来，下去，遗传，祖传，传给

paternal [pə'tə:nl] *adj.* 父亲的，父亲般的，父方的，得自(或传自)父方的

private ['praivit] *n.* 列兵，二等兵 *adj.* 私人的，私下的

serving as the Plains FFA *Chapter Secretary* ⑮.

4 Carter had three younger siblings: sisters *Gloria Carter Spann* ⑯ (1926 ~ 1990) and *Ruth Carter Stapleton* ⑰ (1929 ~ 1983), and brother *William Alton "Billy" Carter* ⑱ (1937 ~ 1988). During Carter's Presidency, Billy was often in the news, usually in an unflattering light.

5 He married Rosalynn Smith in 1946; they have four children.

6 After high school, Carter enrolled at *Georgia Southwestern College* ⑲, in Americus. Later, he applied to the *United States Naval Academy* ⑳ and, after taking additional mathematics courses at *Georgia Tech* ㉑, he was admitted in 1943. Carter graduated 59th out of 820 midshipmen at the Naval Academy with a Bachelor of Science degree with an unspecified major, as was the custom at the academy at that time.

7 Carter served on surface ships and on diesel-electric submarines in the Atlantic and Pacific fleets. As a junior officer, he completed qualification for command of a diesel-electric submarine. He applied for the U.S. Navy's fledgling nuclear submarine program run by then Captain *Hyman G. Rickover* ㉒. Rickover's demands on his men and machines were legendary, and Carter later said that, next to his parents, Rickover had the greatest influence on him. Carter has said that he loved the Navy, and had planned to make it his career. His ultimate goal was to become *Chief of Naval Operations* ㉓. Carter felt the best route for promotion was with submarine duty since he felt that nuclear power would be increasingly used in submarines. Carter was based in Schenectady, New York, and working on developing training materials for the nuclear propulsion system for the prototype of a new

sibling ['sibliŋ] *n.* 兄弟，姊妹，同胞

unflattering [ʌn'flætəriŋ] *adj.* 准确无误的，坦率的，不奉承的

midshipmen ['midʃipmən] *n.* 海军学校学生，见习军官

unspecified [ʌn'spesifaid] *adj.* 未指明的，未详细说明的

diesel-electric submarines 柴油动力的潜艇/柴电动力潜艇

fledgling ['fledʒliŋ] *n.* 刚生羽毛(或刚会飞)的小鸟，新手

legendary ['ledʒəndəri] *adj.* 传说的，传奇般的，口传的

propulsion [prəu'pʌlʃən] *n.* 推进，推进力，推进器

prototype ['prəutətaip] *n.* 原型，原物，样板，模范，标准

submarine .

8 Upon the death of his father James Earl Carter, Sr., in July 1953, he was urgently needed to run the family business. Lieutenant Carter resigned his commission, and he was discharged from the Navy on October 9, 1953.

9 Though Carter's father, Earl, died a relatively wealthy man, between Earl's forgiveness of debts owed to him and the division of his wealth among his heirs, Jimmy Carter inherited comparatively little. For a year, due to a limited real estate market, the Carters lived in *public housing* ㉔ (Carter is the only U.S. president to have lived in housing subsidized for the poor).

10 Knowledgeable in scientific and technological subjects and raised on a farm, Carter took over the family peanut farm. Carter took to the county library to read up on agriculture while Rosalynn learned accounting to manage the businesses financials. Though they barely broke even the first year, Carter managed to expand in Plains. His farming business was successful, and during the 1970 gubernatorial campaign, he was considered a wealthy peanut farmer.

lieutenant [lef'tenənt] *n.* 陆军中尉，海军上尉，（副职、代理、助理）官员

commission [kə'miʃən] *n.* 委任，委托，授权，军衔，委员会

forgiveness [fə'givnis] *n.* 原谅，宽恕，豁免

heir [heə] *n.* 继承人

take to 喜欢，走向，开始从事

read up on 仔细研究，熟读

businesses financials 企业财务

gubernatorial [ˌgju:bənə'tɔ:riəl] *adj.* 州长的，统治者的，地方长官的，总督的

背景知识注释 Background Notes

1. the Wise Sanitarium 怀斯疗养院，当时只有六个床位，由都是当医生的怀斯三兄弟于1921年在普莱恩斯兴建的第一所医院。卡特的母亲在那里当护士。为纪念卡特的母亲，现在该医院改名为莉莲•G•卡特疗养院。
2. Plains 普莱恩斯，它是位于美国佐治亚州萨姆特县的城市。
3. Americus 阿梅里克斯，美国佐治亚州西南部萨姆特县的县治，成立于1831年12月26日。
4. James Earl Carter 詹姆斯•厄尔•卡特(1894～1953)，卡特总统的父亲，他当过农民、花生经纪

人、地方官员，58岁时死于癌症。

5. Bessie Lillian Gordy 贝茜•莉莲•戈迪(1898～1983)，卡特总统的母亲，正式护士，68岁还参加和平队队员到印度工作。

6. the American Colonies 北美殖民地，1607～1775年英国在北美东起大西洋沿岸西迄阿巴拉契亚山脉的狭长地带建立的13个殖民地，从属于英国，但相对独立自治，由英王特许，赋予政治自治权利，但不能占据议会席位。1607～1732年间有16个，由于兼并就只剩13个，它们也就是美国建国之初的13个州。

7. the American Revolution 美国革命，是指在18世纪后半叶导致了北美13州脱离大英帝国并且创建了美利坚合众国的一连串事件与思想。

8. the Sons of the American Revolution （缩写为the SAR）美国革命之子组织，1876年成立于美国加利福尼亚州旧金山。该组织的活动涉及历史研究、筹集资金、为当地提供奖学金和教育奖以及保存与美国革命相关的地点和文件。该组织也对革命战争的殉国者坟墓进行统计和标志，并进行年度鹰童军奖学金计划。

9. L.B. Walker Carter 利特尔•伯里•沃克•卡特，卡特的曾祖父。

10. the Confederate States Army 南部邦联军队，美国南北战争期间美利坚联盟国存在时期的军队，1861年3月6日～9日邦联临时国会立法建立。

11. Plains High School 普莱恩斯中学，建于1921年，在1979年关闭，经过六年改建后成为一个博物馆。

12. Julia Coleman 朱莉娅•科尔曼(1889～1973)，1908年开始从教，50年的教学生涯都为普莱恩斯的学生教授英语，终身未婚。

13. the Future Farmers of America （缩写为FFA）美国未来农民协会，是1928年建立的一种学生学习农业知识的美国国内组织，旨在培养美国的未来农民。今天，FFA已经成为一种动态的青少年组织。在这里，青少年通过接受农业思想、农业技术、农业管理、农业拓展等方面的教育，培养组织能力、个人成长和职场成功技能。除农业教育外、职业启蒙培训、生存技能培训和课堂实践活动等都是训练的重要内容。

14. the National FFA Organization 全美未来农民协会组织。

15. Chapter Secretary 分会秘书。

16. Gloria Carter Spann 洛丽亚•卡特•斯潘(1926～1990)，卡特的大妹，被认为是四个兄弟姐妹中最聪明、最有吸引力、最外向和最有才华的。

17. Ruth Carter Stapleton 露丝•卡特•斯台普顿(1929～1983)，卡特的二妹，洗礼教福音传教士。

18. William Alton "Billy" Carter 威廉•奥尔顿•"比利"•卡特(1937～1988)，卡特的弟弟，曾当过花生经纪人、普莱恩斯加油站老板，活动房屋推销经理。

19. Georgia Southwestern College （缩写为GSW）佐治亚西南州立大学。

20. United States Naval Academy （缩写为USNA）美国海军学院，是美国海军和美国海军陆战队的军官本科教育学校，始建于1845年，位于马里兰州的安那波利斯。

21. Georgia Tech 即Gatech 佐治亚理工学院，是美国一所综合性公立大学，始建于1885年。与麻省理工学院及加州理工学院并称为美国三大理工学院。

22. Hyman G. Rickover 海曼•G.•里科弗(1900.1.27～1986.7.8)，人称“核动力海军之父”，是美国海军上将。

23. Chief of Naval Operations （缩写为CNO）美国海军作战部长，是美国海军军阶最高的军官，是参谋长联席会议成员之一。

24. public housing 公共住房，政府为低收入者所建的住房。

中文译文
Suggested Translation

1 小詹姆斯•厄尔•卡特（又称吉米•卡特）1924年10月1日出生于阿梅里克斯(Americus)附近佐治亚州西南部小城市普莱恩斯(Plains)的怀斯疗养院(Wise Sanitarium)。作为第一位在医院出生的总统，他是育有四个小孩的詹姆斯•厄尔•卡特(James Earl Carter)和贝茜•莉莲•戈迪(Bessie Lillian Gordy)的长子。卡特的父亲是社区一名著名的企业主，他的母亲是一名注册护士。

2 卡特是英格兰南部移民的后裔(他父辈的祖先于1635年抵达北美殖民地)，和他家的几代人一直住在佐治亚州。文献记载卡特的祖先曾参加美国独立战争——他是美国革命之子组织(the Sons of the American Revolution)的成员。卡特的曾祖父，列兵L.B.沃克•卡特(L.B. Walker Carter)，曾在邦联军队服役。

3 卡特从小就喜欢阅读，是位有天赋的学生。上普莱恩斯中学(Plains High School)的时候，他还是一个篮球明星。有一位叫朱莉娅•科尔曼(Julia Coleman)(1889～1973)的中学老师对他影响极大。上高中时，他是美国未来农民协会(the Future Farmers of America)成员，担任普莱恩斯分会的秘书。这个协会后来更名为全美未来农民协会组织(the National FFA Organization)。

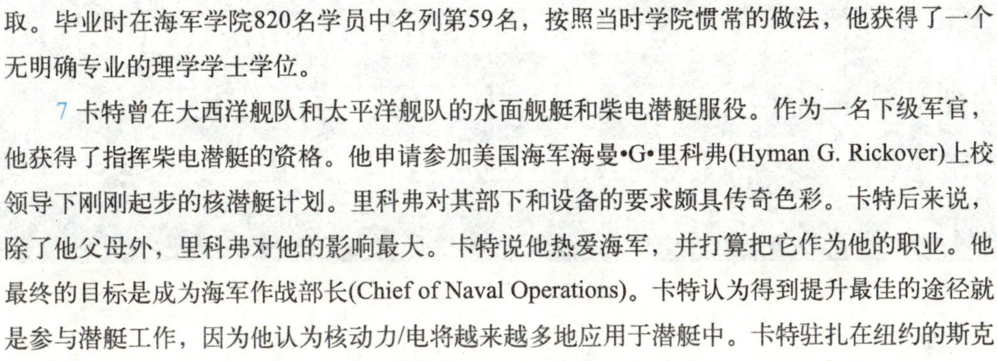

4 卡特有三个弟妹：妹妹格洛丽亚·卡特·斯潘(Gloria Carter Spann)(1926～1990)、露丝·卡特·斯台普顿(Ruth Carter Stapleton) (1929～1983)和弟弟威廉·奥尔顿·“比利”·卡特(William Alton “Billy” Carter) (1937～1988)。卡特担任总统期间，比利(Billy)在新闻中频繁出现，通常造成不良的影响。

5 1946年他迎娶罗莎琳·史密斯(Rosalynn Smith)，与她共育有四个孩子。

6 高中毕业后，卡特在阿梅里克斯(Americus)佐治亚西南学院(Georgia Southwestern College)学习。后来，他报考美国海军学院(United States Naval Academy)。在佐治亚理工大学(Georgia Tech)加修数学课程之后，于1943年被录取。毕业时在海军学院820名学员中名列第59名，按照当时学院惯常的做法，他获得了一个无明确专业的理学学士学位。

7 卡特曾在大西洋舰队和太平洋舰队的水面舰艇和柴电潜艇服役。作为一名下级军官，他获得了指挥柴电潜艇的资格。他申请参加美国海军海曼·G·里科弗(Hyman G. Rickover)上校领导下刚刚起步的核潜艇计划。里科弗对其部下和设备的要求颇具传奇色彩。卡特后来说，除了他父母外，里科弗对他的影响最大。卡特说他热爱海军，并打算把它作为他的职业。他最终的目标是成为海军作战部长(Chief of Naval Operations)。卡特认为得到提升最佳的途径就是参与潜艇工作，因为他认为核动力/电将越来越多地应用于潜艇中。卡特驻扎在纽约的斯克内克塔迪(Schenectady)，致力于编写新型潜艇核推进系统培训材料。

8 1953年7月，他的父亲老詹姆斯·厄尔·卡特(James Earl Carter, Sr.)去世后，迫切需要他打理家族企业。1953年10月9日，卡特中尉辞去军中职务，从海军退役。

9 尽管卡特的父亲厄尔去世时已相对比较富裕，但是赦免了欠他的债务以及他的财产在其继承人之间分摊之后，吉米·卡特所能继承的已经不多。由于房地产市场所限，有一年的时间，卡特一家住在公共住房里（卡特是唯一一位居住过政府为低收入者所建的住房的总统）。

10 拥有科技知识且是在农场里长大的卡特接管了家庭花生农场。卡特上县图书馆研读农业方面的书籍，而罗莎琳则学习记账以管理企业财务。尽管在第一年里他们几近破产，但卡特在普莱恩斯(Plains)还是得到了发展。他的农场经营成功了。在1970年的州长竞选中，他被认为是一名富有的花生农夫。

40 Attack on President Rorald Reagan Changed U.S. Protection Tactics 罗纳德·里根总统遇刺事件改变了美国安保措施

罗纳德·里根 总统及第一夫人简介

罗纳德·里根(Ronald Reagan, 1911.2.6～2004.6.5)，是第40任美国总统(1981～1989)，曾任美国加利福尼亚州第33任州长。在踏入政坛前，里根担任过运动广播员、报社专栏作家、演员和励志讲师，并且是美国影视演员协会(Screen Actors Guild)的领导人。他也是一名伟大的演讲家，他的演说风格高明而极具说服力，他也因此被媒体誉为“伟大的沟通者”(The Great Communicator)。在美国历任总统之中，他就职年龄最大；他也是历任总统中唯一一位演员出身和唯一一位离过婚的总统。

南希·戴维斯·里根(Nancy Davis Reagan, 1921.7.6～)，第40任美国总统罗纳德·里根的妻子，与总统育有一儿一女。她曾经是知名好莱坞演员，并曾与罗纳德·里根在电影《海军悍妇》中演对手戏。她于1951年与时任美国演员协会主席的罗纳德·里根相识，于第二年在洛杉矶位于圣费尔南多山谷的小布朗教堂里与他举行了简短的结婚仪式。成为总统夫人后，她一直致力于“对毒品说不”活动。在1989年所出版的书《轮到我了》中，她描述了自己在白宫的生活。

经典原文
Original Text

Words & Expressions

file ['fail] *vt.* 提出，锉，琢磨，归档

the shift leader 轮班主管，值班领导，领班

brief [bri:f] *vt.* 简报，作…的提要

cliché́d ['kli:ʃeid] *adj.* 陈旧的，陈腐的，充满陈词滥调的

flip a coin 抛钱币决定

lose the toss 掷钱币掷输

the rope line 绳线

take aim at 瞄准，注意到，以…为目标

revolver [ri'vɔlvə] *n.* 左轮手枪

round [raund] *n.* 巡视，一发子弹或炮弹枪炮等的一次齐发

ricochet ['rikəʃeit] *vi.* 弹起，跳飞，漂掠

limousine ['liməzin] *n.* 豪华轿车，大型豪华轿车

speed away 急驶而去

chaos ['keiɔs] *n.* 混乱，紊乱

wrestle ['resl] *vt.* 与…摔跤，与…搏斗

1 *Secret Service*[①] agent *Tim McCarthy*[②] faced a decision on the morning of March 30, 1981—file paperwork in the office or protect President Ronald Reagan on a local trip to give a speech.

2 "So the shift leader rather than pointing to one or the other since we had both been briefed it's probably more clichéd but 'flip a coin' because one of the two of you have to fill that position " said McCarthy.

3 McCarthy lost the toss.

4 On site later that day he recalls scanning the crowd as Mr. Reagan emerged from the hotel after his speech.

5 "I had looked back at the president and all of a sudden *John Hinckley*[③] who is on the left side of the rope line pushed himself forward " said McCarthy.

6 Hinckley took aim at the president and fired a revolver.

7 "I really never put the gun with the person because it happened so quickly." remembered Tim McCarthy. "I could tell by the sound and the smoke that I saw where the rounds were coming from."

8 More shots rang out including one that ricocheted off President Reagan's limousine. As this car sped away and became free of the chaos it was apparent that President Reagan was wounded by the bullet that ricocheted. Once the gunfire ended and officers wrestled Hinckley to the ground three people around President Reagan were also wounded including *Press Secretary*[④] *James Brady*[⑤] and Agent McCarthy."

9 "I was hit in the chest and the bullet went into the lung, liver and diaphragm and the common picture shows me grabbing my abdomen but that's down where the liver was when it went through the liver " said McCarthy. "That's where the pain was at the time but actually I was shot in the chest."

10 Press Secretary Brady suffered serious injuries but survived as did Washington police offer *Thomas Delehanty*⑥.

11 President Reagan also recovered from his wounds but McCarthy says the incident was a wake up call for the Secret Service.

12 "After that metal detectors were used to screen anyone who gets near the president." he said. "Shortly thereafter the legacy is that since that time there has not been another attack on any of our presidents by the historic assassin which is the lone gunman who would simply get close to the president with a handgun and of course attempt to assassinate the president."

13 John Hinckley Junior was found not guilty by reason of insanity. He remains confined to a mental health facility.

14 The limousine that carried Mr. Reagan to the hospital is now on display at the *Henry Ford Museum*⑦ in *Dearborn*⑧ Michigan. The damage caused by Hinckley's bullet was repaired shortly after the shooting.

15 Though the incident occurred over thirty years ago the attack created a lasting bond between the president and his protector.

16 "The President and Mrs. Reagan were more than grateful more than thankful and gracious to me and my

diaphragm ['daiəfræm] *n.* 膈，膈膜

grab [græb] *vt.* 攫取，抓取

abdomen ['æbdəmən] *n.* 腹部，下腹，腹腔

wake up call 叫醒服务，叫醒电话，敲响警钟

legacy ['legəsi] *n.* 遗产，遗赠，传统

insanity [in'sænəti] *n.* 精神病，疯狂

gracious ['greiʃəs] *adj.* 亲切的，和蔼的

family from that day on " said McCarthy.

17 After serving two more Presidents McCarthy retired from the Secret Service in 1993. He now serves as the chief of *the Orland Park*[9] Police Department in suburban Chicago.

背景知识注释
Background Notes

1. Secret Service 即 United States Secret Service (USSS) 美国特勤处，美国联邦政府的执法机构，隶属于美国国土安全部。该机构宣誓雇员分为特工和制服员工。2003年3月1日之前，特勤处隶属于美国财政部。特勤处的主要管辖权是预防和调查对美元和债券的伪造，以及保护总统、副总统、总统当选人和副总统当选人、前总统和他们的配偶(该配偶再婚除外)、大选前120天内确定的总统候选人和副总统候选人、现任和前任总统的未满16周岁的子女和孙辈、来访的外国国家首脑和政府元首及其配偶、总统令指定的个人和国土安全部指定的国家特别安全事件。同时，该处还负责跟踪调查各种金融诈骗犯罪的相关嫌疑人，并为一些地方犯罪的调查提供协助。美国特勤处制服部负责保护各国驻美大使馆、美国海军天文台和白宫。目前还有一些特勤处的任务还处于保密状态。
2. Tim McCarthy 蒂姆·麦卡锡(1949.6.20～)，是伊利诺伊州奥兰公园警察局局长和美国特勤局的一名前成员。他因为1981年用身体挡住小约翰·欣克利射向里跟总统的子弹受伤而名声大噪。乔治·华盛顿大学医院的外科医生成功地取出麦卡锡腹部的子弹，使他完全恢复了健康。麦卡锡于1982年获得了全美大学体育协会(National Collegiate Athletic Association)勇气奖，以表彰他的勇敢。他曾是伊利诺伊大学的足球队员。
3. John Hinckley 在这里指小约翰·欣克利(1955.5.29～)，生于美国俄克拉荷马州，因于1981年行刺当时美国的总统罗纳德·里根而广为人知。1982年欣克利被指控13项罪名。但6月21日，他因查出有精神病而被法庭裁定无罪。此裁决引起美国上下广泛不满，以至于美国国会和很多州议会修改法律，为以后法庭上采信精神病加上了更严格的条件，有几个州甚至废止了精神病可以作为无罪理由的规定。此后欣克利一直在华盛顿一家精神病医院就医至今。
4. Press Secretary 新闻秘书，白宫的高级官员，其主要职责是作为政府的发言人。
5. James Brady 詹姆斯·布雷迪(1940.8.29～)，原里跟政府的白宫新闻秘书和总统助手，1981年头部受重伤致终身残废，以后成为枪支管制的热心支持者。
6. Thomas Delehanty 托马斯·迪里汉提(1943～)，时为哥伦比亚地区大都会警察局警官，当时他也被小约翰·欣克利射出的六颗子弹中的一颗射中颈部，倒在布雷迪身边。

7. Henry Ford Museum　亨利•福特博物馆，始建于1906年。当时亨利•福特开始收集具有历史意义的物品。今天占地12英亩的展览馆主要收集古式的机械、流行文化道具、汽车、火车、飞机和其他物品。

8. Dearborn　迪尔伯恩，是一个有将近98,000人口的城市，位于美国密歇根州大底特律地区和韦恩县，是亨利•福特的家乡和福特汽车公司的全球总部，并且是密歇根大学迪尔伯分校所在地。

9. the Orland Park　奥兰公园，伊利诺伊州库克县的一个村。2006年《货币杂志》授予它“全美最适宜居住的第45个地方”称号。

中文译文
Suggested Translation

1 特勤局特工蒂姆•麦卡锡(Tim McCarthy)在1981年3月30日那天面临着一个选择，要么待在办公室里整理文件，要么在总统去发表演讲的途中保护总统。

2 “包括我在内的两个特工中必须有一人来填补这个位置，而且他们已对我们做了简要的说明，这更像是一种例行公事。当班主管没有指派由谁来执行这次任务，而是以掷硬币的方式来决定。”麦卡锡说。

3 结果是由麦卡锡(McCarthy)参加保护总统的行动。

4 他回忆，在那天的晚些时候当总统结束演讲从酒店走出的时候，他正在现场扫视人群。

5 “我回头看了一眼总统，突然，约翰•欣克利(John Hinckley)从防护绳左边挤到前面。”麦卡锡说。

6 欣克利瞄准总统开枪了。

7 “我没有来得及用枪，因为这一切发生得太快了，但是通过声音和烟雾，我知道子弹是从哪里射出来的。”蒂姆•麦卡锡(Tim McCarthy)说。

8 接着又响了几枪，其中有一枪从总统的座驾上弹开。当轿车加速驶离险境时，显然里根总统已经被一颗子弹打伤了。枪声刚一结束，欣克利就被警察按倒了。总统身边的3个人也受伤了，包括白宫新闻秘书詹姆斯•布雷迪(James Brady)和特工麦卡锡。

9 “我被击中胸口，子弹穿过肺、肝脏和横膈膜，当时照片显示我捂住了小腹——那是在肝脏下边，那时子弹穿过肝脏——也正是疼痛的地方，但事实上我是被击中了胸口。”

10 新闻秘书布雷迪受了重伤，但是他活了下来。华盛顿警官托马斯•迪里汉提(Thomas

Delehanty)也逃过了一劫。

11 总统虽然也伤愈了，但麦卡锡说这次事件给特勤局(the Secret Service)敲响了警钟。

12 “从那以后，金属探测器被用于检测每一个接近总统的人。”他说，“从这次事件得出的教训，使得之后的任何一位总统再没有被过去那一类刺客袭击过。这里的袭击指的是一个枪手带着枪接近总统试图刺杀总统。

13 小约翰•欣克利(John Hinckley Junior)由于精神疾病而被判无罪，但在精神康复机构里终身监禁。

14 运载总统上医院的轿车现在被放在密歇根州迪尔伯恩(Dearborn)的亨利•福特展览馆展出。车上欣克利(Hinckley)制造的弹痕在刺杀事件过后不久就被修复了。

15 尽管事件已经过去30多年了，但这次袭击使总统与保镖之间建立起了长久的友谊。

16 麦卡锡说：“从那天起，总统及其夫人对我及我的家人十分亲切、心存感激、再三称谢。”

17 里根总统之后，麦卡锡又接连为两任总统当保镖。1993年他从特勤局退休，现在他是芝加哥郊区奥兰公园(the Orland Park)警察局局长。

41 Remarks to Schoolchildren at the White House Halloween Party by Bush
老布什总统在白宫万圣节聚会上对小学生的精彩讲话

乔治·赫伯特·沃克·布什 总统及第一夫人简介

乔治•赫伯特•沃克•布什(George Herbert Walker Bush, 1924.6.12～)，第41任美国总统(1989～1992)。由于美国历史上存在过两位布什总统，因此他又常被称为老布什，以便与其同样担任过美国总统的长子乔治•沃克•布什相区别。老布什任内最为人知的政绩莫过于1991年海湾战争。他在任内成功击败伊拉克，并向后者实施经济制裁。但他好战的作风使他对国内经济有所轻视，因而于1992年大选中败给了比尔•克林顿，谋求连任失败。

芭芭拉•皮尔斯•布什(Barbara Pierce Bush, 1925.7.8～)，1945年1月和美国第41任总统乔治•赫伯特•沃克•布什结婚。一年后，第43任总统小布什出生。此后他们又生育了三子二女。芭芭拉是布什的贤内助，她照管全部家务，抚养孩子。他们从结婚到布什当上副总统以来，先后在17个城市居住过，搬家28次，都是芭芭拉操持的。她很少过问政治。有些政治问题她同布什有分歧，但绝少与他争论，更不参与。她性情温和，又柔中有刚。作为第二夫人以及后来成为第一夫人时，她都支持和努力推进基本根除文盲的事业，成立了芭芭拉•布什家庭扫盲基金会。离开白宫后，她仍然继续推动这项事业。

经典原文 Original Text

1 Thank you all very much. And first, let me thank you guys that gave us the *pledge cards*①. You did a good job on that. And my thanks to *Willard Scott*②, the weatherman who got the weather to hold off for us here.

2 And *Barbara*③ and I want to welcome all of you to *the White House Halloween spectacular*④. I want to particularly thank *Marilyn Quayle*⑤, the wife of the Vice President, for being with us right here, and then welcome our daughter-in-law *Margaret*⑥ and the *Turtle*⑦. The Turtle is our grandchild named *Marshall*⑧, going as a turtle. You see how it is? It's on the back there. You've got to see that.

3 How many of you guys believe in ghosts? How many? You know, they say that there's a ghost in this old house. And the most famous one, you know, is Abraham Lincoln. And Barbara and I haven't seen the ghost of Abraham Lincoln walking the halls, but this is our first Halloween in the White House, so maybe we'll see him tonight.

4 But Halloween is a time for ghosts and goblins, for haunted houses and scary stories. But right now I want to talk to you just briefly about a scary story that isn't make-believe. And you know what I'm talking about. I'm talking about illegal drugs and how they hurt people and how they hurt families, hurt kids, some of them just like you.

Words & Expressions

hold off 使不接近，使保持一定距离

goblin ['gɔblin] *n.* 小妖精，小鬼

haunted ['hɔːntid] *adj.* 经常出没的，闹鬼的

scary ['skeəri] *adj.* 害怕的，骇人的，胆小的

make-believe *adj.* 假装的，虚假的，虚幻的 *n.* 假装，虚假，装扮

5 And I get a lot of letters every day as President, a lot of them from children of your age. And I brought along one letter that I want to read today from a fifth grade girl named *Ana Zamora*⑨. She's not here —she lives out in Chicago, but I want you to hear what she's got to say about what drugs are doing to her neighborhood.

6 "Dear President Bush," —here's her letter —"I never go outside because my mom gets scared that I'll get hurt because of the gang fights. President Bush, I've heard that you're pushing for a war on drugs. Please help remove drugs from our neighborhoods. I will do my part by saying no to drugs, and I hope you can do yours. I know this is hard, but you can do it."

7 Well, I want to tell her, Ana, and all of you: We will do our best. And if she keeps doing her part, and if all of you do the same, we're going to stop drugs and keep our schools and our neighborhoods safe.

8 And I know you handed in the pledge cards when you came in, and I know that you got your starfish pins. And last month I went on television to talk about not using drugs. And if you saw me, you already know the story about the boy who saved the starfish. Well, you can read that story on the Halloween bags that we'll be handing out to each of you in just a moment. And I hope you will read it and think about it, too, because each one of you is just as special as the starfish that the boy saves. And just like the boy in the story, you can help someone else —maybe a friend, maybe your own brother or sister—help them stay away from drugs and all the hurt and pain they cause.

9 And so, today I want to tell you the same thing Barbara and I tell our own grandchildren: Drugs are

do one's part 尽自己的职责
starfish [ˈstɑːfiʃ] *n.* 海星
pin [pin] *n.* 针，别针，饰针，背面有别针的徽章、像章
hand out 分发，施舍，把…拿出来

dangerous. You don't need drugs to make you feel good or to be cool or to make friends. And so, if anyone tries to get you to take drugs— even once —you can say "no thanks, I don't do drugs". And if you do that, you're going to make a lot of people who love you very happy, and you're going to be happy yourselves.

10 And now, everyone knows it's Halloween, and it's time for the fun to continue. Thanks for coming, and God bless you, and God bless the United States of America. Thank you all very much.

背景知识注释
Background Notes

1. pledge cards 承诺卡，这里指誓言远离毒品的承诺卡。

2. Willard Scott 威拉德•赫尔曼•斯科特，美国演员、作家、媒体人、小丑、喜剧演员和天气预报员。

3. Barbara 芭芭拉，乔治•赫伯特•沃克•布什的太太，时为第一夫人。

4. the White House Halloween spectacular 白宫万圣节特别活动，许多美国“第一家庭”都曾在白宫与孩子们共度万圣节。时任总统老布什与夫人芭芭拉•布什在白宫接待500名孩子共度万圣节，不仅给他们礼物还告诫孩子们远离毒品。Halloween 即万圣节，为每年的11月1日，源自古代凯尔特民族(Celtic)的新年节庆。此时也是祭祀亡魂的时刻，在避免恶灵干扰的同时，也以食物祭拜祖灵及善灵以祈平安渡过严冬，是西方传统节日。当晚小孩会穿上化妆服，戴上面具，挨家挨户收集糖果。它主要流行于英语世界，如不列颠群岛和北美，其次是澳大利亚和新西兰。但是现在，一些亚洲国家的年轻一辈，也开始倾向于过这个“洋节”。到了万圣节前夕，一些大型外资超市都会摆出专柜卖万圣节的玩具，小商贩也会出售一些跟万圣节相关的玩偶或模型，吸引了年轻人的眼光。

5. Marilyn Quayle 指玛丽莲•塔克•奎尔(1949.7.29～)。美国第44任副总统詹姆斯•丹•奎尔的太太。美国律师、小说家和政治人物。

6. Margaret 即Margaret Conway 玛格丽特•康维，布什第四个即最小的儿子马文•布什的太太。

7. Turtle 马歇尔的绰号。

8. Marshall 马歇尔，马文•布什和玛格丽特的孩子。他们的两个孩子都是在得克萨斯州沃思堡格拉德尼中心收养的。该中心的历史可以追溯到1887年。

9. Ana Zamora 安娜•萨莫拉，1989年万圣节前给布什总统写信的孩子。当年她是个五年级的学生。

中文译文
Suggested Translation

1 非常感谢你们。首先，请允许我感谢你们给我们带来了承诺卡。你们做得很好。此外，感谢天气预报员威拉德•斯科特(Willard Scott)。为了让我们能在此聚会，他让天气持续保持晴朗。

2 芭芭拉和我欢迎各位到白宫参加万圣节的特别活动(the White House Halloween spectacular)。对于副总统的妻子玛丽莲•奎尔(Marilyn Quayle)能光临并和我们在一起，我拟表达特别的谢意。同时我们也欢迎我们的儿媳妇玛格丽特(Margaret)与乌龟。乌龟是我们的孙子，叫马歇尔(Marshall)，走起路来像只乌龟。你看是这么回事吗？他就在后面。你一定看得到。

3 你们中有多少人相信鬼魂的呢?有多少?你要知道，他们说在这个老房子里有一个鬼，而且是最著名的一个，你知道吗？是亚伯拉罕•林肯。芭芭拉和我还没有见过亚伯拉罕•林肯的鬼魂在大厅里行走，但这是我们在白宫度过的第一个万圣节。因此，也许今晚我们就会看到他。

4 但是万圣节是厉鬼恶灵出没以及探究鬼屋等恐怖故事的时候。然而，现在我想跟你简单地讲一个可怕的故事。这是一个真实的故事。你知道我在说什么。我谈论非法毒品和它们如何伤害人们以及如何伤害家庭和孩子，他们中的一些人就像你们那样。

5 身为总统，我每天都收到很多信件，其中许多是你们这样年龄的孩子写的。我带来了一封信，它是一位叫安娜•萨莫拉 (Ana Zamora) 的五年级的小女孩寄来的。她不在这里——她住在芝加哥，但我希望你们能听听她所说的有关毒品对她所在的街区造成的伤害。

6“尊敬的布什总统，”——这里是她的信 ——“我从不外出，因为我妈妈担心由于群殴我会受伤。布什总统，我听说您正在推动一场反对毒品的斗争。请帮助清除我们社区的毒品。通过对毒品说不，我尽自己的一份力量。我希望您也履行自己的职责。我知道这并非易事，但您可以做到这一点。”

7 嗯，我想告诉她——安娜，还有你们所有人：我们将尽自己最大的努力。如果她继续贡献自己的力量，如果你们都这样做，我们将根除毒品并保持我们的学校和社区的安全。

8 我知道你们走进来的时候已经交了承诺卡，我知道你们已经得到了自己的海星饰针。上个月，我在电视上谈论戒毒问题。如果你们看到我，就已经知道那个拯救海星的小男孩的

故事。好了，你可以在我们很快就会分发给你们每个人的万圣节的袋子里读到那个故事。我希望你们读一读并仔细想一想，因为你们每个人都像那个小男孩拯救的海星引脚一样特别。就像故事里的那个小男孩，你们也可以帮助其他人——或许是一位朋友，或许是自己的兄弟姐妹——帮助他们远离毒品以及毒品所造成的伤害和痛苦。

9 所以，今天我同样要告诉你们芭芭拉和我一直告诫我们自己的孙子的事情：毒品有害无益。感觉良好、觉得神气或广交朋友并不需要吸食毒品。因此，如果有人试图引诱你们吸毒——即使只是那么一次——你们都可以说："不，谢谢。我们不吸毒。"如果你们这样做了，将会让很多爱你们的人感到高兴，你们也会为自己感到高兴。

10 而今天，大家都知道是万圣节，该继续尽兴地玩玩。感谢你们的到来。愿上帝保佑你们，愿上帝保佑美利坚合众国。非常感谢大家。

42 Bill Clinton and the Clinton Presdential Center and Park
比尔·克林顿和克林顿总统中心与公园

威廉·杰斐逊·克林顿 总统及第一夫人简介

威廉•杰斐逊•“比尔”•克林顿(William Jefferson “Bill” Clinton, 1946.8.19～)，第42任美国总统(1993～2000)，又称“比尔•克林顿”，曾任阿肯色州州长。克林顿是美国历史上仅次于西奥多•罗斯福和约翰•肯尼迪的第三年轻当选总统，也是首位出生于二战后婴儿潮中的总统。在克林顿的执政下，美国经历了历史上和平时期持续时间最长的一次经济发展，实现了财政收支平衡和国库盈余5,590亿美元。而在第二个任期内，克林顿因伪证罪和妨碍司法罪被众议院弹劾，但最终被参议院否决。克林顿以65%的民意支持率结束任期，创下了55年来二战后美国总统离任最高支持率纪录。此后，克林顿一直进行公开演讲和人道主义工作，成立了威廉•杰斐逊•克林顿基金会，致力于艾滋病和全球变暖等国际问题的防治。2004年，克林顿出版了自传《我的生活》。

希拉里•黛安•罗登•克林顿(Hillary Diane Rodham Clinton, 1947.10.26～)，美国第42届总统比尔•克林顿的妻子，与总统育有一女。希拉里是一位富有争议的政治人物，她当第一夫人期间曾主持一系列改革，曾参加2008年美国总统选举民主党总统候选人的角逐，但最终失败。希拉里并不是第一位参与美国总统大选的女性，但她被普遍认为是美国历史上第一位确有可能当选的女性候选人。虽然希拉里失意于总统宝座，但与其同党的巴拉克•奥巴马成功当选总统之后，提名了她出任美国国务卿，她成为美国第三位女国务卿。

经典原文
Original Text

Words & Expressions

repository [ri'pɔzitəri] *n.* 贮藏室，知识库，智囊团

stem from 起源于，来自

accessible [ək'sesəbl] *adj.* 可接近（或进入）的，可使用（或得到）的

1 In the United States, the presidential library system is a nationwide network of 13 libraries administered by the Office of Presidential Libraries, which is part of the *National Archives and Records Administration (NARA)*①. These are repositories for preserving and making available the papers, records, collections and other historical materials of every President of the United States since Herbert Hoover (in office, 1929—1933).

2 The Presidential library system formally began in 1939, when President Franklin Delano Roosevelt donated his personal and Presidential papers to the federal government. Roosevelt's decision stemmed from his belief that Presidential papers were an important part of the national heritage and should be accessible to the public.

3 The William J. Clinton Presidential Center and Park is the presidential library of Bill Clinton. The center was established by Clinton, the 42nd President of the United States. It is located in *Little Rock*②, Arkansas and includes the Clinton Presidential Library, the offices of *the Clinton Foundation*③, and *the University of Arkansas Clinton School of Public Service*④. It is the thirteenth presidential library to have been completed in the United States, the eleventh to be operated by the National Archives and Records Administration, and the third to comply with *the Presidential Records Act of 1978*⑤.

4 It is situated on 17 acres (69,000 m^2) of land located next to the Arkansas River and *Interstate 30*[6] and was designed by architectural firm *Polshek Partnership LLP*[7] with cxhibition design by *Ralph Appelbaum Associates*[8]. The main building cantilevers over the Arkansas River, echoing Clinton's campaign promise of "building a bridge to the 21st century". the library itself is the largest presidential library in terms of physical area. The archives are the largest as well, containing 2 million photographs, 80 million pages of documents, 21 million e-mail messages, and 79,000 artifacts from the Clinton presidency. The Clinton Library is also the most expensive, with all funding coming from 112,000 private donations.

5 The museum showcases artifacts from Clinton's two terms as president and includes full-scale replicas of the Clinton-era Oval Office and Cabinet Room.

6 The Clinton Presidential Center was dedicated on November 18, 2004. Although it was raining, the ceremony was attended by approximately 30,000 people and included a 20-minute speech made by Clinton, who had recently undergone bypass surgery. It also included performances by *Bono*[9], *the African Drum Ballet*[10] and *the Philander Smith Collegiate Choir*[11], as well as an invocation given by *Floyd Flake*[12] and video tribute from *Nelson Mandela*[13]. Four U.S. presidents (Clinton, Jimmy Carter, George H.W. Bush, and George W. Bush were present; former president Gerald R. Ford could not attend due to health concerns) were on the same stage together. All three other presidents spoke at the event as well. Overall, the ceremony lasted two hours and featured six speakers.

7 On November 17, 2009, the library's five-year

architectural [ˌɑːkiˈtektʃərəl] *adj.*建筑学的，建筑上的

cantilever [ˈkæntiliːvə] *n.* 悬臂

physical area 有效使用面积

artifact [ˈɑːtəˌfækt] *n.* 人工制品，手工艺品，加工品，石器

replica [ˈreplikə] *n.* 复制品

dedicate [ˈdedikeit] *vt.* 致力，献身，为…举行落成典礼（或仪式）

bypass surgery 心脏搭桥手术

invocation [ˌinvəuˈkeiʃən] *n.* 祈祷，符咒

video tribute 致敬视频

health concerns 健康问题

feature [ˈfiːtʃə] *vt.* 是…的特征

anniversary saw Clinton giving a speech to approximately 1,000 people, urging for the passage of health-care reform and the reduction of energy use. He specifically mentioned the center and school as places where discussion on such topics could take place.

8 The library incorporates many aspects of environmentally-sensitive design, in accordance to Clinton's work involving sustainable development. The library's flooring is made of recycled rubber tires and there are charging stations for electric vehicles in the parking lot. In 2007, a rooftop garden was established atop the library, in addition to existing solar panels. The garden collects runoff and is maintained without the use of gasoline-powered lawn mowers and chemical pesticides or fertilizers.

incorporate [in'kɔːpəreit] *v.* 合并，组成公司
environmentally-sensitive 关注环境的
in accordance to 根据
tire ['taiə] *n.* 轮胎
charging station 充电站
atop [ə'tɔp] *prep.* 在…的顶上
solar panel 太阳能电池板
runoff ['rʌnɔf] *n.*(指流入河流中的雨水)溢流
gasoline-powered 汽油发动的
pesticide ['pestisaid] *n.* 杀虫剂

背景知识注释 Background Notes

1. National Archives and Records Administration (NARA) 美国国家档案和记录管理局。它是美国政府独立机构，负责收存所有美国官方历史记录，并负责发布国会的法案，总统文告和行政命令，维护联邦法规的副本。
2. Little Rock 小石城，它位于美国阿肯色州中部，是该州首府和最大城市，普拉斯基县的县府所在地，也是铁路枢纽。
3. the Clinton Foundation 克林顿基金会，是克林顿在作为第42届美国总统第二任期结束的时候建立的。从那时起基金会已经变为一个全球性非政府的组织，在全世界有超过800个工作人员和志愿者。他们的办事处设在纽约市哈莱姆区、波士顿、马萨诸塞州和阿肯色州的小石城。该基金会把重点放在四个重要领域：健康安全；经济权力；领导能力发展和公民服务；种族、民族和宗教的和解。
4. the University of Arkansas Clinton School of Public Service 阿肯色大学克林顿公共服务学院，美国前总统克林顿于2005年创建，是阿肯色大学的一部分，受到阿州政府的资助。
5. the *Presidential Records Act* of 1978 1978年《总统档案法案》，该法案规定所有的总统文件档案和任期内的器物都属于国家。当一位总统离任后，美国国家档案和文件管理局就会增设该总统的临时档案条目；当该总统的图书馆建成并转让给政府后，美国国家档案和文件管理局就会把临时档案撤掉。之后，该总统的档案便可到其图书馆查询。

6. Interstate 30　30号州际公路(Interstate 30，简称I-30)，是美国州际公路系统的一部分。全长590.24公里。

7. Polshek Partnership LLP　波尔谢克建筑师联合事务所。它1963年成立，总部设在纽约，但现由其11位合伙人改名为Ennead Architects LLP。波尔谢克现已82岁，七年前就退出了该所。

8. Ralph Appelbaum Associates　RAA设计公司，成立于1978年，是世界上最大的博物馆展览工程设计公司，以设计大型、永久性的博物馆展览工程而闻名。在纽约、伦敦和北京都有其办事处。

9. Bono　即Bono Vox 博诺•沃克斯(1960.5.10—)，原名保罗•休森(Paul Hewson)，生于都柏林，是爱尔兰老牌摇滚乐队U2的主唱，曾被提名诺贝尔和平奖。

10. the African Drum Ballet　非洲鼓乐芭蕾舞团。

11. the Philander Smith Collegiate Choir　菲兰德史密斯学院合唱团。菲兰德史密斯学院是位于美国阿肯色州小石城市的一所私立四年制本科学院。尽管菲兰德史密斯学院历史上是一所专门为黑人开设的学校，但是现在该校也招收各种民族的学生。不过，菲兰德史密斯学院的学生主体上还是黑人。

12. Floyd Flake　弗洛伊德•弗拉克(1945.1.30—)，1986年至1997年出任联邦众议员，威尔伯佛斯大学校长。

13. Nelson Mandela　纳学尔逊•曼德拉(1918.7.18—)，他出生于南非特兰斯凯一个大酋长家庭，先后获南非大学文学学士和威特沃特斯兰德大学律师资格，当过律师。他成功地组织并领导了“蔑视不公正法令运动”，赢得了全体黑人的尊敬。于1994年至1999年间任南非总统。曼德拉曾在牢中服刑了27年，在其40年的政治生涯中获得了超过一百项奖项，其中最著名的便是1993年的诺贝尔和平奖。他被尊称为“南非国父”。

中文译文
Suggested Translation

1 在美国，总统图书馆系统是一个由13家图书馆组成的全国性网络。这个网络由隶属于美国国家档案和记录管理局(National Archives and Records Administration)的总统图书馆管理处管理。这些图书馆是保存自赫伯特•胡佛(1929—1933年在位)以来每一位美国总统的文件、记录、收藏品和其他史料并对公众开放的资料库。

2 总统图书馆系统的建设始于1939年。那一年，富兰克林•德拉诺•罗斯福(Franklin Delano Roosevelt)总统将其个人以及担任总统期间的文件捐赠给联邦政府。罗斯福认为总统的文献，作为国家遗产的重要组成部分，应当对公众开放。他的决定正是基于上述理念的。

3 克林顿总统图书馆全称为“威廉·J·克林顿总统中心与公园”。该中心由美国第42任总统克林顿兴建。它坐落在阿肯色州小石城(Little Rock)，包括克林顿总统图书馆、克林顿基金会(the Clinton Foundation)办公室、阿肯色州大学克林顿公共服务学院(the University of Arkansas Clinton School of Public Service)。这是第十三座在美国修建的总统图书馆，第十一座由美国国家档案和记录管理局管理与运作的总统图书馆，以及第三座依据1978年《总统档案法案》收藏总统档案的总统图书馆。

4 它位于阿肯色河和30号州际公路 (Interstate 30) 旁，占地17英亩(69,000平方米)。该图书馆主体由波尔谢克建筑师联合事务所设计，而展览部分由拉尔夫·阿贝尔鲍姆设计公司设计。主楼悬臂横跨阿肯色河，呼应克林顿“通向21世纪的桥梁”的竞选诺言。就有效使用面积而言，该图书馆在总统图书馆中是最大的，馆藏也是最丰富的，包括200万张照片，8,000万页文件，21,000万封电子邮件讯息，以及79,000件克林顿总统任职期间的文物。克林顿图书馆耗资亦是最多的，所有资金来自112,000名私人的捐赠。

5 博物馆展示了克林顿两届总统任期的文物，包括以实际尺寸复制的克林顿时代白宫椭圆形办公室和内阁会议室。

6 克林顿总统中心于2004年11月18日落成。虽然这一天正下着雨，但还是有大约30,000名来宾参加了揭幕仪式。尽管克林顿当时刚接受了心脏搭桥手术，但他仍发表了20分钟的演讲。博诺(Bono)、非洲鼓乐芭蕾舞团以及菲兰德·史密斯大学合唱团在庆典上助兴。此外，还有弗洛伊德·弗拉克(Floyd Flake)的祷告和纳尔逊·曼德拉(Nelson Mandela)的祝贺视频。四位美国总统（克林顿、吉米·卡特、老布什、小布什出席；前总统杰拉尔德·R·福特由于健康原因不能到场）同台庆贺。其他三位总统也都在仪式上发言。整个揭幕庆典持续了两个小时，六个人发表了讲话。

7 2009年11月17日，图书馆举行了五周年的庆典。克林顿对大约1,000名来宾发表演讲，敦促国会通过医疗改革和减少能源消耗的法案。他特别提到了中心、学校以及可能讨论这些议题的地方。

8 该图书馆包含多项环保设计，与克林顿所推崇的事业——可持续发展相互呼应。图书馆的地板用再生橡胶轮胎制成。停车场设有可供电力驱动汽车使用的充电站。2007年，除现有的太阳能电池板外，图书馆的屋顶还修建了屋顶花园。花园吸收并储藏雨水，不用汽油动力割草机以及化学除草剂和化肥即可得到养护。

43 Air Force One① and President George W. Bush 乔治·W·布什总统与空军一号

乔治·沃克·布什 总统及第一夫人简介

乔治·沃克·布什 (George Walker Bush,1946.7.6 ~)，第 43 任美国总统 (2001 ~ 2008)，常称 George W. Bush（乔治·W·布什）他在 2001 年 1 月 20 日就职，并且在 2004 年的选举中连任。在担任总统之前，布什于 1995 年至 2000 年间担任第 46 任得克萨斯州州长。布什家族很早就开始投入共和党以及美国政治，布什的父亲是之前曾担任第 41 任总统的乔治·赫伯特·沃克·布什。由于与父亲同样都是美国总统，因此他又常被称为“小布什”，而他父亲就被称为“老布什”。小布什总统任内遭遇了 2001 年的 9•11 事件。在任内布什推行了 1.3 万亿元的减税计划以及对于医疗保险和社会福利体制的改革，同时也推行了社会保守主义的政策，以及反对承认同性婚姻的联邦法案提议。在“美国在线”于 2005 年举办的票选活动《最伟大的美国人》中，小布什被排在美国最伟大的人物的第六位。

劳拉•莲•威尔士•布什(Laura Lane Welch Bush，1946.11.4~)，第43任美国总统乔治•沃克•布什的妻子，与总统育有一对孪生姐妹。劳拉•布什生于美国得克萨斯州米德兰市，这也是她丈夫布什最初做石油生意的地方。劳拉大学本科教育学毕业后，在得克萨斯州的多个城市任教。之后，她又获得了图书管理学的硕士学位，并做图书管理员的工作直至结婚。作为第一夫人，劳拉对教育问题情有独钟，并十分关心妇女的健康问题。在已经过去的日子里，劳拉被认为是一位和蔼可亲、受人尊敬的第一夫人。

经典原文 Original Text

1 Air Force One is one of the most identifiable symbols of the American Presidency. Air Force One is the call sign of any Air Force aircraft carrying the President of the United States. It has become standard practice to refer to the highly customized Boeing 747-200B series aircraft, carrying the tail codes 28000 and 29000, as Air Force One.

2 This aircraft is often referred to as the flying White House. It is equipped with state-of-the-art communications equipment, anti-missile defenses, and furnishings befitting the President. This allows the President and his staff to conduct government business from the air while being protected from attack. The plane is capable of mid-air refueling that can keep the President in the air for long periods of time and allow him to travel anywhere in the world.

3 During his eight years in office, President George W. Bush logged 1,675 flights on Air Force One. He visited every state in the country, except Vermont. He also visited 75 countries during 49 foreign trips.

4 Air Force One has made many memorable flights. Here are two examples from the Bush Presidency:

5 On Tuesday, September 11, 2001, President George W. Bush traveled to *Emma E. Booker Elementary School* [②] in *Sarasota*[③], Florida, where he received news that two planes had flown into the North and South Towers of *the*

Words & Expressions

identifiable [ai'dentifaiəbl] *adj.* 可辨认的，可识别的

call sign 无线电台呼号

standard practice 通常做法

customize ['kʌstəmaiz] *vt.* 定做，定制，按特别订货生产

tail code 尾号

state-of-the-art *adj.* 最先进的，已经发展的

furnishing ['fə:niʃiŋ] *n.* 供应，供给，装备

befit [bi'fit] *vt.* 适合于，为…所应做的，对…适当，与…相当

log [lɔg] *vt.*航行达

World Trade Center[4] in New York City. President Bush was rushed back to the airport where he flew to *Barksdale Air Force Base*[5] in Louisiana. While enroute from Florida to Louisiana, the pilots were told there was a plane approaching. Fearing the unknown plane was hijacked, Air Force One altered its course, but ultimately decided to continue on to Barksdale. (The second plane turned out to be harmless.) The President went from Barksdale Air Force Base to *Offutt Air Force Base*[6] in Nebraska where late in the day he received clearance to return home to *Andrews Air Force Base*[7] in Maryland. Many of the important decisions made that day were made on board Air Force One.

6 On Thanksgiving Day 2003, President Bush was scheduled to celebrate the holiday quietly on his ranch in *Crawford* [8], Texas. Weeks earlier, however, he had asked his staff to begin making plans for a trip to Iraq at the suggestion of White House *Chief of Staff*[9] *Andy Card* [10]. The President and his *National Security Advisor* [11], *Condoleezza Condi Rice* [12], secretly flew on Air Force One from Texas to Andrews Air Force Base, where they picked up aides, military and Secret Service personnel, a few reporters, and changed to a *twin version of Air Force One* [13]. With its lights darkened and window shades drawn, Air Force One landed under a crescent moon at *Baghdad International Airport* [14] using a corkscrew pattern to reduce the chances of being shot. (Just six days before, a plane had been shot out of the sky at the same airport.) President Bush spent two and a half hours in Iraq visiting with the troops and other dignitaries. Take-off from Baghdad International Airport was just as dangerous. Everyone on the plane was told to keep the lights out and maintain telephone silence. Once Air Force One had climbed to a safe altitude, reporters on

enroute [ɔ:n'ru:t] *adv.* 在航，在途中，取道

hijack['haidʒæk] *vt.* 抢劫，劫持

ultimately ['ʌltimətli] *adv.* 最后，根本，基本上

clearance ['kliərəns] *n.* 飞机许可，清除，出清

ranch [ræntʃ] *n.* 大农场，大牧场，牧场工作人员

pick up 拿起，捡起 停下来把…带走

window shade *n.* 遮光窗帘，百叶窗

crescent ['kresənt] *n.* 新月，弦月，蛾眉月

corkscrew ['kɔ:kskru:] *n.* 瓶塞钻，螺丝起子，螺旋开瓶器

dignitary ['dignitəri] *n.* 达官贵人，要人，显贵

altitude ['æltitju:d] *n.* 高，高度，海拔，深（度）

board were free to file reports about the trip.

背景知识注释
Background Notes

1. Air Force One 空军一号，美国总统的专机。这对蓝白相间的波音747飞机已成为美国权力的象征，也成为美国的国际图腾。空军一号也常被人们称为“空中白宫”。将总统的飞机称为“空军一号”是在艾森豪威尔总统时代开始的，主要是为了安全。

2. Emma E. Booker Elementary School 艾玛•E•布克小学，位于佛罗里达州萨拉索塔市，因布什总统2001年9月11日上午正好在该校考察而名声大噪。

3. Sarasota 萨拉索塔，它位于美国南部佛罗里达州萨拉索塔县。

4. the World Trade Center 世界贸易中心，简称世贸中心、纽约世贸、WTC。它是美国纽约曼哈顿的一个建筑群，由七座大楼组成。自1973年4月4日启用以来其双塔即成为纽约的地标之一。这两座分别被称为“北楼”和“南楼”的高楼当时是世界上最高的建筑物，超过了同在曼哈顿的帝国大厦，在2001年9月11日发生的袭击事件中倒塌。

5. Barksdale Air Force Base 巴克斯代尔空军基地，位于美国路易斯安那州博西尔城以东约1.5公里处，隶属于美国空战司令部。

6. Offutt Air Force Base 奥夫特空军基地，位于奥马哈附近，毗邻内布拉斯加州萨皮县的贝尔维尤，是美国战略司令部、空军气象局和空军作战司令部的总部。

7. Andrews Air Force Base 安德鲁斯空军基地。它位于马里兰州乔治王子县，距美国华盛顿哥伦比亚特区8 英里。基地的命名是为了纪念美国空军奠基人之一的弗兰克•马克斯韦尔•安德鲁斯。它是美国总统乘坐的空军一号和直升机的基地。外国元首访问美国，如果正式访问首都华盛顿哥伦比亚特区，其专机通常也在安德鲁斯空军基地降落。这个面积达 4,320 英亩的基地拥有超过 20,000 名的军人、平民雇员和家属。

8. Crawford 克劳福德牧场，占地647公顷，是布什1999年任得州州长时从一位名叫恩格尔•布雷赫特的牧场主手中买下的。布什搬进去后，没有住原来主人的房子，而是另起炉灶、重建新房。牧场内，溪水潺潺，瀑布垂帘。草地上，牛群漫步，小鹿奔跑。布什在牧场内挖了一口鱼塘，养起了鲈鱼。布什认为他的克劳福德农场是块福地。2000年美国大选投票结束后，布什就回到克劳福德静候佳音。布什的夫人劳拉认为，白宫只是她和布什临时的家，而克劳福德牧场才是他们永久的家。

9. Chief of Staff 白宫幕僚长，美国没有“办公厅”这个机构，也就没有“办公厅主任”这个职位，担任类似任务的是“幕僚长”、“参谋长”，也就是领导一帮幕僚/参谋的人。

10. Andy Card　安迪•卡德(1947.5.10～)，老布什政府的交通部长和小布什政府的白宫幕僚长，以及小布什白宫伊拉克小组组长。

11. National Security Advisor　国家安全事务顾问，又称美国总统国家安全事务助理，是美国总统在国家安全相关事项方面的主要参谋。

12. Condoleezza Condi Rice　康多莉扎•康迪•赖斯(1954.11.14～)，美国政治家，前美国国务院国务卿。她是美国历史上就任此职的第一位女性非裔美国人，继克林•鲍威尔后的第二位非裔美国人。

13. twin version of Air Force One　空军一号主备用双机并用模式。空军一号专机事实上是两架鸳鸯飞机，只要运载总统的主机飞到哪里，备用的副机就跟到哪里。如果主机发生机械故障，总统可以随时换乘备用专机。另外，美国总统出国访问时，至少还有1架国家情报局的通讯飞机陪同，目的是监测可能来袭的导弹电波。此外还有两架总统直升机、多架"大力神"军用运输机以及10辆防弹汽车随行。

14. Baghdad International Airport　巴格达国际机场，它是伊拉克最大的机场，位于距巴格达市中心以西16公里的市郊。

中文译文
Suggested Translation

1 空军一号是美国总统最容易辨认的标志之一。它是任何接载着美国总统的空军飞机的航空无线电台呼号。称尾号28000和29000、特别定制的波音747-200B系列飞机为"空军一号"已经成为惯常的做法。

2 这架飞机通常被称为"空中白宫"。它配备了最先进的通信设备、反导弹防御系统，和与总统履行其职责相匹配的设施。这使得总统及其幕僚在空中处理政府事务时能得到保护而免受攻击。这架飞机还能在空中加油，使得总统能在空中长时间飞行以便能够飞往世界任何地方。

3 在8年任期中，美国总统乔治•W•布什共乘坐空军一号飞行1,675次。他视察了除佛蒙特州以外美国的每一个州。在49次国外旅行中，他访问了75个国家。

4 空军一号进行过许多难忘的飞行。以下为它在布什总统任职期间履行任务的两个例子。

5 2001年9月11日(星期二)，小布什总统前往佛罗里达州萨拉索塔(Sarasota)艾玛•E•布克小学(Emma E. Booker Elementary School)。在那里他得到消息称，有两架飞机撞击了纽约市世界贸易中心(the World Trade Center)南北塔。布什总统匆匆赶回机场，从那里飞往路易斯安那州巴克斯代尔空军基地(Barksdale Air Force Base)。在从佛罗里达州飞往路易斯安那州的途中，飞行员被告知有一架飞机正在接近。担心身份未明的飞机被劫持，空军一号改变了其航程，但是最终还是决定继续飞往巴克斯代尔。（那架飞机被证明是无敌意的。）布什总统从巴克斯代尔空军基地飞到内布拉斯加州奥夫特空军基地 (Offutt Air Force Base)。当天晚些时候在得到飞行许可后，才飞回其通常停放的马里兰州安德鲁斯空军基地(Andrews Air Force Base)。那一天所做的许多重要决策都是在空军一号上进行的。

6 2003年感恩节，布什总统计划在得克萨斯州克劳福德牧场(Crawford)悄悄地庆祝这个节日。然而，几个星期前，根据白宫幕僚长安迪·卡得(Andy Card)的建议，他要求他的手下着手制订一项到伊拉克旅行的计划。布什总统和他的国家安全顾问康多莉扎·莱斯(Condoleezza Rice)秘密乘坐空军一号从得克萨斯飞往安德鲁斯空军基地。在那里，他们接上了几位助手、军队和特勤局人员以及几名记者。然后空军一号改为主用机和备用机双机并用的模式。为了防止被击中，空军一号黑灯瞎火，舷窗紧闭沿着螺旋形的轨迹在一轮新月下的巴格达国际机场(Baghdad International Airport)降落。(仅在6天前，一架飞机在同一机场从空中被击落。)布什总统花了两个半小时的时间在伊拉克看望部队和会见其他政要。从巴格达国际机场起飞时一样危险。飞机上的每个人都被告知要熄灭灯火，并严禁使用电话。空军一号上升到安全高度后，飞机上的记者才得以发送这次旅行的报道。

44 Brack Obama and 103 Dollars
青年巴拉克·奥巴马和103美元罚金

巴拉克·奥巴马 总统及第一夫人简介

巴拉克•侯赛因•奥巴马(Barack Hussein Obama, 1961.8.4～)，第44任美国总统(2009～)。他是第一位非裔美国总统，也是首位同时拥有黑(卢欧族)白(英德爱混血)血统，且童年在亚洲成长的美国总统。1991年，他作为优等生荣誉从哈佛大学法学院毕业。1996年，当选为伊利诺伊州参议员。2000年，竞选美国众议院席位失败，后一直从事州参议员工作，且于2002年获得连任。2004年，在美国民主党全国代表大会上发表主题演讲，因此成为全美知名的政界人物；同年11月，以70%的选票当选代表伊利诺伊州的美国联邦参议员，是美国历史上第五位有非裔血统的联邦参议员。2007年2月10日，宣布参加2008年美国总统竞选，并于11月4日正式当选。2009年10月9日，获得诺贝尔和平奖。2011年4月4日，宣布参加2012年总统竞选，并于2012年11月6日正式当选。

米歇尔•拉沃恩•罗宾逊•奥巴马(Michelle LaVaughn Robinson Obama, 1964.1.17～)，是美国第44任总统奥巴马的妻子，与总统育有两女。她成为第一夫人时创造了多个纪录：她是第一位非洲裔总统夫人，也是到目前为止个子最高的第一夫人。她本身也是一名律师，出生成长于芝加哥南部，曾就读于普林斯顿大学及哈佛大学法学院。完成学业后，她返回芝加哥为全美第六大律师行悉尼·奥斯汀律师事务所服务，是芝加哥市长戴利之直属雇员，也为芝加哥大学及芝加哥大学医疗中心服务。米歇尔早在1980年代末期就已结识同于悉尼·奥斯汀律师事务所工作的奥巴马，两人于1992年结婚。米歇尔的父亲于1990年去世，母亲则仍在一家女装直销公司任秘书，米歇尔的兄长在俄勒冈州立大学任男子篮球教练。由于她非常注重自己的形象、举止及衣着品味，因此经常被媒体评为衣着最佳的公众人物之一，更将之与美国已故第一夫人杰奎琳·肯尼迪比较。

经典原文 Original Text

Words & Expressions

Norwegian [nɔːˈwiːdʒən] *adj.* 挪威的；挪威语的；挪威人的

hectic [ˈhektik] *adj.* 繁忙的

crush [krʌʃ] *v.* 压破，压碎

bubble [ˈbʌbl] *v.* 起泡，洋溢着(某种感情)

surcharge [ˈsəːtʃɑːdʒ] *n.* 追加罚款，附加费

desperate [ˈdespərət] *adj.* 绝望的

prized [praizd] *adj.* 被看做最有价值的

1 Mary Menth Andersen was 31 years old and had just married Norwegian Dag Andersen. She was looking forward to starting a new life in *Vestfold* ① with him. But first she had to get all of her belongings across to Norway. The date was November 2nd, 1988.

2 At the airport in Miami things were hectic as usual, with long lines at *the check-in counters*②. When it was finally Mary's turn and she had placed her luggage on the baggage line, she got the message that would crush her bubbling feeling of happiness.

3 "You'll have to pay a 103 dollar surcharge if you want to bring both those suitcases to *Norway*③," the man behind the counter said.

4 Mary had no money. Her new husband had traveled ahead of her to Norway, and she had no one else to call.

5 "I was completely desperate and tried to think which of my things I could manage without. But I had already made such a careful selection of my most prized possessions", says Mary.

6 Although she explained the situation to the man behind the counter, he showed no signs of mercy.

7 "I started to cry, tears were pouring down my face and

I had no idea what to do. Then I heard a gentle and friendly voice behind me saying, 'That's OK, I'll pay for her'."

8 Mary turned around to see a tall man whom she had never seen before.

9 "He had a gentle and kind voice that was still firm and decisive. The first thing I thought was: Who is this man?"

10 Although this happened more than 20 years ago, Mary still remembers the authority that radiated from the man.

11 "He was nicely dressed, fashionably dressed with brown leather shoes, a cotton shirt open at the throat and khaki pants," says Mary.

12 She was thrilled to be able to bring both her suitcases to Norway and assured the stranger that he would get his money back. The man wrote his name and address on a piece of paper that he gave to Mary. She thanked him repeatedly.

13 When she finally walked off towards *the security checkpoint*[④], he waved goodbye to her.

14 The piece of paper said "Barack Obama" and his address in Kansas, which is the state where his mother comes from. Mary carried the slip of paper around in her wallet for years, before it was thrown out. "He was *my knight in shining armor*[⑤]!" says Mary, smiling.

15 She paid the 103 dollars back to Obama the day after she arrived in Norway. At that time he had just finished his job as a poorly paid community worker in Chicago, and had started his law studies at prestigious Harvard university.

16 In the spring of 2006 Mary's parents had heard that Obama was considering a run for president, but that he had

decisive [di'saisiv] *adj.* 果断的
authority [ɔː'θɔriti] *n.* 威信
radiate ['reidieit] *v.* 射出，发散
fashionably ['fæʃənəbli] *adv.* 随着流行，赶时髦地
khaki ['kɑːki] *adj.* 卡其布做的
thrill [θril] *v.* 由于激动而震颤
assure [ə'ʃuə] *v.* 保证，担保
walk off 离开；带走；用散步消除
knight [nait] *n.* 骑士
armor ['ɑːmə] *n.* 盔甲
prestigious [pre'stidʒəs] *adj.* 享有声望的

still not decided. They chose to write a letter in which they told him that he would receive their votes. At the same time, they thanked Obama for helping their daughter many years earlier.

17 In a letter to Mary's parents dated May 4th, 2006 and stamped "United States Senate, Washington DC", Barack Obama writes: "I want to thank you for the lovely things you wrote about me and for reminding me of what happened at Miami airport. I'm happy I could help back then, and I'm delighted to hear that your daughter is happy in Norway. Please send her my best wishes. Sincerely, Barack Obama, United States Senator."

背景知识注释 Background Notes

1. Vestfold 韦斯特福尔德，挪威东南部的一个郡。
2. the check-in counters 办理登机手续的柜台。
3. Norway 挪威，位于北欧斯堪的纳维亚半岛西部，东与瑞典接壤，西邻大西洋。海岸线极其蜿蜒曲折，构成了挪威特有的峡湾景色。自2001年起挪威已连续六年被联合国评为最适宜居住的国家，并于2009年到2013年连续获得全球人类发展指数第一的排名。
4. the security checkpoint 机场安全检查处。
5. my knight in shining armor 在本文中的意思是"我那身穿闪亮盔甲的骑士"。通常被女性用来形容曾经拯救过自己的英雄。

中文译文 Suggested Translation

1 31岁的玛丽•门茨•安德森刚刚和挪威人达格•安德森结婚。她期盼着和他在韦斯特福尔德开始新的生活。但是，首先她必须把她所有的东西运往挪威。那是1988年11月2日。

2 迈阿密机场像往常一样繁忙，在办理登机手续的柜台前人们排着长队。终于轮到玛丽了。她把行李放在行李传送带上，机器显示的信息把她欢快激动的情绪一扫而光。

3 “你若想把这两个箱子带到挪威，必须交103元罚金。”柜台后面的男人说道。

4 玛丽身上没有钱。她的新婚丈夫已先于她去了挪威，而且她也没有其他可以打电话的人。

5 “我彻底绝望了，考虑哪样东西我可以丢掉。但是，对于我的最有价值的东西，我已经做了精心的选择。”玛丽说。

6 尽管她向工作人员解释了她的境况，但他的脸上毫无怜悯的表情。

7 “我开始哭起来，泪流满面，我不知道该做什么。这时，我听见在我身后，有人用温柔友好的嗓音说：‘不要紧，我来为她付钱’。”

8 玛丽转过身，看见了一位她从未见过的高个子男人。

9 “他的声音轻柔、和蔼可亲，而且坚定、果断。我首先想到的是：这个男人是谁？”

10 尽管这件事发生在二十多年前，玛丽还是记得从这个男人身上散发出来的那种颇具权威的气质。

11 “他衣着得体、时尚，穿着棕色皮鞋、敞开领口的棉布衬衫和卡其布裤子。”玛丽说。

12 能带两个箱子去挪威，她激动不已，因此颤抖着向这位陌生人保证说会还给他钱的。男人在一张纸上写下了自己的姓名和住址，递给了玛丽。她再三向他表示感谢。

13 当她终于向安检处走去的时候，他朝她挥手告别。

14 纸条上写着：“巴拉克·奥巴马”，住址在堪萨斯州，那是他妈妈的出生地。在扔掉这张纸条以前，玛丽许多年来一直把它放在钱包里随身携带。“他是我的身穿闪亮盔甲的骑士！”玛丽笑着说。

15 到挪威的第二天，她就把103元还给了奥巴马。那时，奥巴马在芝加哥刚刚结束了他作为社区工作人员的低薪工作，开始在赫赫有名的哈佛大学学习法律。

16 2006年春，玛丽的父母听说奥巴马在考虑竞选总统，可是还没有决定。他们就给奥巴马写了封信，告诉奥巴马他们会投票选他。同时，他们感谢奥巴马在多年前帮助了他们的女儿。

17 2006年5月4日，在一封盖有“美国参议院，华盛顿特区”印章、给玛丽父母的信中，奥巴马写道：“感谢你们所写的关于我的有趣的事情，它使我想起那年在迈阿密机场时的情景。我为那时能够提供帮助而感到愉快，我也很高兴得知你们的女儿在挪威生活幸福。请向她转达我最好的祝愿。你们诚挚的，巴拉克·奥巴马，美国参议员。”

附 录

Michelle Obama's Speech to *the Democratic National Convention*[1]
米歇尔·奥巴马2012年在美国民主党全国大会上的演讲

地点： *Charlotte*[2], N.C.　　夏洛特，北卡罗来纳

时间： September 4, 2012　　2012年9月4日

经典原文
Original Text

1 Elaine, Thank you so much. We are so grateful for your family's service and sacrifice… and we will always have your back.

2 Over the past few years as First Lady, I have had the extraordinary privilege of traveling all across this country. And everywhere I've gone, in the people I've met, and the stories I've heard, I have seen the very best of the American spirit.

3 I have seen it in the incredible kindness and warmth that people have shown me and my family, especially our girls.

4 I've seen it in teachers in a near-bankrupt school district who vowed to keep teaching without pay.

5 I've seen it in people who become heroes at a moment's notice, diving into harm's way to save others … flying across the country to put out a fire… driving for hours to bail out a flooded town.

Words & Expressions

privilege [ˈprivilidʒ] *n.* 特殊荣幸，特权

incredible [inˈkredəbl] *adj.* 难以置信的，惊人的

vow [vau] *n.* 誓约 *v.* 发誓

at a moment's notice 即刻，招之即来，一经通知，随时

bail out 保释，跳伞，往外舀水，帮助摆脱困境

6 And I've seen it in our men and women in uniform and our proud military families… in wounded warriors who tell me they're not just going to walk again, they're going to run, and they're going to run marathons… in the young man blinded by a bomb in Afghanistan who said, simply, "I'd give my eyes 100 times again to have the chance to do what I have done and what I can still do."

7 Every day, the people I meet inspire me… every day, they make me proud… every day they remind me how blessed we are to live in the greatest nation on the earth.

8 Serving as your first lady is an honor and a privilege … but back when we first came together four years ago, I still had some concerns about this journey we'd begun.

9 While I believed deeply in my husband's vision for this country, … and I was certain he would make an extraordinary president, … like any mother, I was worried about what it would mean for our girls if he got that chance.

10 How would we keep them grounded under the glare of the national spotlight?

11 How would they feel being uprooted from their school, their friends, and the only home they'd ever known?

12 Our life before moving to Washington was filled with simple joys: … Saturdays at soccer games, Sundays at grandma's house … and a date night for Barack and me was either dinner or a movie, because as an exhausted mom, I couldn't stay awake for both.

13 And the truth is, I loved the life we had built for our girls. I deeply loved the man I had built that life with, … and I didn't want that to change if he became president.

14 I loved Barack just the way he was.

marathon [ˈmærəθən] *n.* 马拉松赛跑，需要长时间努力或耐力的事件或活动

uproot [ʌpˈruːt] *vt.* 根除，迫使某人迁离 *vi.* 迁离，改变生活方式

15 You see, even though back then Barack was a senator and a presidential candidate... To me, he was still the guy who'd picked me up for our dates in a car that was so rusted out, I could actually see the pavement going by through a hole in the passenger side door. ... He was the guy whose proudest possession was a coffee table he'd found in a Dumpster, and whose only pair of decent shoes was half a size too small.

16 But when Barack started telling me about his family — that's when I knew I had found a kindred spirit, someone whose values and upbringing were so much like mine.

17 You see, Barack and I were both raised by families who didn't have much in the way of money or material possessions but who had given us something far more valuable: their unconditional love, their unflinching sacrifice, and the chance to go places they had never imagined for themselves.

18 My father was a pump operator at the city water plant, and he was diagnosed with multiple sclerosis when my brother and I were young.

19 And even as a kid, I knew there were plenty of days when he was in pain. I knew there were plenty of mornings when it was a struggle for him to simply get out of bed.

20 But every morning, I watched my father wake up with a smile, grab his walker, prop himself up against the bathroom sink, and slowly shave and button his uniform.

21 And when he returned home after a long day's work, my brother and I would stand at the top of the stairs to our little apartment, patiently waiting to greet him... watching as he reached down to lift one leg, and then the other, to slowly climb his way into our arms.

rust [rʌst] *v.* 生锈，荒废

Dumpster [ˈdʌmpstə] *n.* 大型垃圾装卸卡车，垃圾大铁桶

kindred [ˈkindrid] *n.* 亲戚，宗族，血缘关系 *adj.* 有血缘关系的，同宗的，同源的

spirit [ˈspirit] *n.* 精神，心灵，情绪，志气，烈酒

in the way of 妨碍，关于…方面

possession [pəˈzeʃən] *n.* 所有权，财产，财富

unconditional [ˌʌnkənˈdiʃənəl] *adj.* 无条件的，无保留的，绝对的

unflinching [ʌnˈflintʃiŋ] *adj.* 不畏缩的，坚定的，果敢的

pump [pʌmp] *n.* 泵，用（器官）输送

diagnose [ˈdaiəgnəuz] *vt.* 诊断

sclerosis [skləˈrəusis] *n.* 硬化症

in pain 痛苦

grab one's walker 抓住…助行器

prop... up 支撑，支持

sink *n.* 水槽，洗涤槽，污水坑

22 But despite these challenges, my dad hardly ever missed a day of work. He and my mom were determined to give me and my brother the kind of education they could only dream of.

23 And when my brother and I finally made it to college, nearly all of our tuition came from student loans and grants.

24 But my dad still had to pay a tiny portion of that tuition himself.

25 And every semester, he was determined to pay that bill right on time, even taking out loans when he fell short.

26 He was so proud to be sending his kids to college… and he made sure we never missed a registration deadline because his check was late.

27 You see, for my dad, that's what it meant to be a man.

28 Like so many of us, that was the measure of his success in life — being able to earn a decent living that allowed him to support his family.

29 And as I got to know Barack, I realized that even though he'd grown up all the way across the country, he'd been brought up just like me.

30 Barack was raised by a single mother who struggled to pay the bills, and by grandparents who stepped in when she needed help.

31 Barack's grandmother started out as a secretary at a community bank, … and she moved quickly up the ranks. But like so many women, she hit a glass ceiling.

32 And for years, men no more qualified than she was — men she had actually trained — were promoted up the

make it 好转，达到预定目标，及时抵达，走完路程

fall short 不足，缺乏，没有达到目标

a registration deadline 报名截止日期

decent [ˈdiːsnt] *adj.* 得体的，相当好的

step in 介入，插手干预，作短时间的非正式访问

start out 出发，开始从事，雇用

a glass ceiling 无形障碍

ladder ahead of her, earning more and more money while Barack's family continued to scrape by.

33 But day after day, she kept on waking up at dawn to catch the bus, … arriving at work before anyone else, … giving her best without complaint or regret.

34 And she would often tell Barack, "So long as you kids do well, Bar, that's all that really matters."

35 Like so many American families, our families weren't asking for much.

36 They didn't begrudge anyone else's success or care that others had much more than they did. In fact, they admired it.

37 They simply believed in that fundamental American promise that, even if you don't start out with much, if you work hard and do what you're supposed to do, then you should be able to build a decent life for yourself and an even better life for your kids and grandkids.

38 That's how they raised us. That's what we learned from their example.

39 We learned about dignity and decency, that how hard you work matters more than how much you make, … that helping others means more than just getting ahead yourself.

40 We learned about honesty and integrity. That the truth matters, … that you don't take shortcuts or play by your own set of rules. … And success doesn't count unless you earn it fair and square.

41 We learned about gratitude and humility. That so many people had a hand in our success, from the teachers who inspired us to the janitors who kept our school clean — … and we were taught to value everyone's contribution and

scrape by 勉强维持

begrudge [bi'grʌdʒ] *vt.* 羡慕，嫉妒，吝惜，舍不得给

get ahead 获得成功，取得进步，走在前面

integrity [in'tegrəti] *n.* 正直，诚实，真诚

count [kaunt] *vt.* 数，点数，视为，相信 *vi.* 数，有价值，起作用，值得考虑

fair and square 光明正大地，诚实地

gratitude ['grætitju:d] *n.* 感谢，感激之情，感恩图报之心

humility [hju:'miləti] *n.* 谦逊，谦恭

janitor ['dʒænitə] *n.* 房屋管理员，看门人，门房

treat everyone with respect.

42 Those are the values that Barack and I — and so many of you — are trying to pass on to our own children.

43 That's who we are.

44 And standing before you four years ago, I knew that I didn't want any of that to change if Barack became president.

45 Well, today, after so many struggles and triumphs and moments that have tested my husband in ways I never could have imagined, I have seen firsthand that being president doesn't change who you are — it reveals who you are.

46 You see, I've gotten to see up close and personal what being president really looks like.

47 And I've seen how the issues that come across a President's desk are always the hard ones — the problems where no amount of data or numbers will get you to the right answer. The judgment calls where the stakes are so high, and there is no margin for error.

48 And as president, you can get all kinds of advice from all kinds of people.

49 But at the end of the day, when it comes time to make that decision, as president all you have to guide you are your values and your vision, and the life experiences that make you who you are.

50 So when it comes to rebuilding our economy, Barack is thinking about folks like my dad and like his grandmother.

51 He's thinking about the pride that comes from a hard day's work.

triumph [ˈtraiəmf] *n.* 胜利，典范

up close 在很近距离内地

52 That's why he signed the *Lilly Ledbetter Fair Pay Act* ③ to help women get equal pay for equal work.

53 That's why he cut taxes for working families and small businesses and fought to get the auto industry back on its feet.

54 That's how he brought our economy from the brink of collapse to creating jobs again — jobs you can raise a family on, good jobs right here in the United States of America.

55 When it comes to the health of our families, Barack refused to listen to all those folks who told him to leave health reform for another day, another president.

56 He didn't care whether it was the easy thing to do politically — that's not how he was raised — he cared that it was the right thing to do.

57 He did it because he believes that here in America, our grandparents should be able to afford their medicine. Our kids should be able to see a doctor when they're sick, … and no one in this country should ever go broke because of an accident or illness.

58 And he believes that women are more than capable of making our own choices about our bodies and our health care… that's what my husband stands for.

59 When it comes to giving our kids the education they deserve, Barack knows that like me and like so many of you, he never could have attended college without financial aid.

60 And believe it or not, when we were first married, our combined monthly student loan bills were actually higher than our mortgage. We were so young, so in love,

brink [briŋk] *n.* 边缘，边沿，界限

collapse [kə'læps] *n.* 垮台，衰弱

go broke 身无分文，破产

deserve [di'zəːv] *vi.* 应受报答

mortgage ['mɔːgidʒ] *n.* 债权，抵押

and so in debt.

61 That's why Barack has fought so hard to increase student aid and keep interest rates down, because he wants every young person to fulfill their promise and be able to attend college without a mountain of debt.

62 So in the end, for Barack, these issues aren't political. They're personal.

63 Because Barack knows what it means when a family struggles. He knows what it means to want something more for your kids and grandkids.

64 Barack knows the American Dream because he's lived it, … and he wants everyone in this country, everyone to have that same opportunity, no matter who we are, or where we're from, or what we look like, or who we love.

65 And he believes that when you've worked hard, and done well, and walked through that doorway of opportunity, … you do not slam it shut behind you. You reach back, and you give other folks the same chances that helped you succeed.

66 So when people ask me whether being in the White House has changed my husband, I can honestly say that when it comes to his character, and his convictions, and his heart, Barack Obama is still the same man I fell in love with all those years ago.

67 He's the same man who started his career by turning down high paying jobs and instead working in struggling neighborhoods where a steel plant had shut down, fighting to rebuild those communities and get folks back to work, … because for Barack, success isn't about how much money you make, it's about the difference you make in people's

doorway ['dɔːwei] *n.* 门口，门道

steel [stiːl] *adj.* 坚强的，钢制的 *n.* 钢，钢制品

lives.

68 He's the same man who, when our girls were first born, would anxiously check their cribs every few minutes to ensure they were still breathing, proudly showing them off to everyone we knew.

69 That's the man who sits down with me and our girls for dinner nearly every night, patiently answering their questions about issues in the news, and strategizing about middle school friendships.

70 That's the man I see in those quiet moments late at night, hunched over his desk, poring over the letters people have sent him. The letter from the father struggling to pay his bills, … from the woman dying of cancer whose insurance company won't cover her care, … from the young person with so much promise but so few opportunities.

71 I see the concern in his eyes, … and I hear the determination in his voice as he tells me, "You won't believe what these folks are going through, Michelle. … It's not right. We've got to keep working to fix this. We've got so much more to do."

72 I see how those stories — our collection of struggles and hopes and dreams — I see how that's what drives Barack Obama every single day.

73 And I didn't think that it was possible, but today, I love my husband even more than I did four years ago, … even more than I did 23 years ago, when we first met. Let me tell why!

74 I love that he's never forgotten how he started.

75 I love that we can trust Barack to do what he says he's going to do, even when it's hard — especially when it's

crib [krib] *n.* 婴儿床，栅栏，食槽 *vi.* 剽窃

show... off 炫耀，卖弄

strategize [ˈstrætidʒaiz] *vt.* 为…制订战略 *vi.* 制订战略

hunch over 蜷缩身体，弓着腰

hard.

76 I love that for Barack, there is no such thing as "us" and "them" — he doesn't care whether you're a Democrat, a Republican, or none of the above. He knows that we all love our country, … and he's always ready to listen to good ideas. He's always looking for the very best in everyone he meets.

77 And I love that even in the toughest moments, when we're all sweating it — when we're worried that the bill won't pass, and it seems like all is lost — Barack never lets himself get distracted by the chatter and the noise.

78 Just like his grandmother, he just keeps getting up and moving forward... with patience and wisdom, and courage and grace.

79 And he reminds me that we are playing a long game here, … and that change is hard, and change is slow, and it never happens all at once. But eventually we get there, we always do.

80 We get there because of folks like my dad, … folks like Barack's grandmother, … men and women who said to themselves, "I may not have a chance to fulfill my dreams, but maybe my children will. Maybe my grandchildren will."

81 So many of us stand here tonight because of their sacrifice, and longing, and steadfast love, … because time and again, they swallowed their fears and doubts and did what was hard.

82 So today, when the challenges we face start to seem overwhelming — or even impossible — let us never forget that doing the impossible is the history of this nation. It's

distract [di'strækt] *vt.* 使伤心，使混乱

chatter ['tʃætə] *n.* 唠叨，饶舌，啁啾声，潺潺流水声

grace [greis] *n.* 优美，优雅，恩惠 *vt.* 使优美，使荣耀

steadfast ['stedfəst] *adj.* 坚定的，不变的

swallow ['swɔləu] *vt.* 忍受，吞没

overwhelming [ˌəuvə'hwelmiŋ] *adj.* 压倒性的，不可抵抗的

who we are as Americans. It's how this country was built.

83 And if our parents and grandparents could toil and struggle for us, … if they could raise beams of steel to the sky, send a man to the moon, and connect the world with the touch of a button, … then surely we can keep on sacrificing and building for our own kids and grandkids.

84 And if so many brave men and women could wear our country's uniform and sacrifice their lives for our most fundamental rights, … then surely we can do our part as citizens of this great democracy to exercise those rights. … Surely, we can get to the polls on Election Day and make our voices heard.

85 If farmers and blacksmiths could win independence from an empire, … if immigrants could leave behind everything they knew for a better life on our shores, … if women could be dragged to jail for seeking the vote, … if a generation could defeat a depression, and define greatness for all time, … if a young preacher could lift us *to the mountaintop*[④] with his righteous dream, … and if proud Americans can be who they are and boldly stand at the altar with who they love, … then surely, surely we can give everyone in this country a fair chance at that great American Dream.

86 Because in the end, more than anything else, that is the story of this country — the story of unwavering hope grounded in unyielding struggle. That is what has made my story, and Barack's story, and so many other American stories possible.

87 Let me tell you something that I say all of this tonight not just as first lady, … and not just as a wife. You see, at the end of the day, my most important title is still

toil [tɔil] *vi.* 辛苦工作，艰难地行进 *vt.* 费力地做，使…过度劳累

beam [biːm] *n.* 横梁，光线，电波，船宽

righteous [ˈraitʃəs] *adj.* 正义的，正直的，公正的

altar [ˈɔːltə] *n.* 祭坛，圣坛，圣餐台

unwavering [ʌnˈweivəriŋ] *adj.* 不动摇的，坚定的

unyielding [ʌnˈjiːldiŋ] *adj.* 坚硬的，不屈服，刚强

"mom-in-chief." My daughters are still the heart of my heart and the center of my world.

88 But Let me tell you today, I have none of those worries from four years ago. No. Not about whether Barack and I were doing what's best for our girls.

89 Because today, I know from experience that if I truly want to leave a better world for my daughters, and all our sons and daughters, … if we want to give all of our children a foundation for their dreams and opportunities worthy of their promise, … if we want to give them that sense of limitless possibility — that belief that here in America, there is always something better out there if you're willing to work for it — … then we must work like never before… and we must once again come together and stand together for the man we can trust to keep moving this great country forward: … my husband, our president, Barack Obama.

90 Thank you, God bless you, and God bless America.

mom-in-chief 第一妈妈，妈咪司令（是米歇尔奥巴马对自己的称呼）

背景知识注释
Background Notes

1. the Democratic National Convention 民主党全国代表大会，每隔4年在选举年举行。全国代表大会的3个主要功能是：提名总统和副总统候选人；讨论并通过党的竞选纲领；制定党派规则。来自全国50个州、哥伦比亚特区和海外领地的代表、民主党官员以及外国要人都会出席这一会议。1824年，随着推选总统和副总统候选人的党团会议制度变得岌岌可危，民主党内提出举行全国代表大会的设想。1832年，民主党首届全国代表大会在马里兰州巴尔的摩召开，由来自全国各地的代表投票选择总统和副总统候选人。多年来，民主党全国代表制度在本质上发生了巨大变化。由于总统候选人和副总统人选通常在会前已经确定，代表们只是在大会上完成投票形式，而不会改变此前总统预选的结果。2012年美国民主党全国代表大会9月4日在北卡罗来纳州最大城市夏洛特正式开幕，为期3天。约6, 000名代表参与。奥巴马和拜登在6日晚正式接受党内提名，并发表演讲。大会整合了民主党力量，激发支持者的投票热情，为奥巴马谋求连任造势。

2. Charlotte 夏洛特，美国北卡罗来纳州最大和全国第20大的城市，也是梅克伦堡县的县治，位置在北卡罗来纳州中南部、靠近与南卡罗莱那州的边界。夏洛特是以英国国王乔治三世的妻子夏绿蒂王后而名，也因此得到“女王之城”(The Queen City)这个昵称；俄亥俄州辛辛那提和纽约州布法罗同样也有“女王之城”这个昵称。美国独立战争时，英军将领康华利将军(General Cornwallis)在被夏洛特当地居民激烈抵抗后撤出城市，他后来称夏洛特为“叛乱者的一个黄蜂窝”。

3. *Lilly Ledbetter Fair Pay Act* 《莉莉·莱德贝特同工同酬法案》，该法的诞生源于1998年的一个具体案件——莉莉·莱德贝特诉固特异橡胶轮胎公司案。莉莉·莱德贝特诉称，“我在这家工厂工作了20年，但我的工资比相同工种的男工少40%。”经过三级法院的审判，最终由最高法院以时限超出为由终审驳回原告的诉讼。2007年，包括参议员希拉里·克林顿在内的几名民主党国会议员提出了“莱德贝特公平酬劳法案”，旨在消除薪酬歧视，允许雇员在因性别、年龄、种族而遭受歧视待遇后的任何时间对雇主提出起诉。该法案在2008年第110届国会上未被通过，在111届国会上，该法案被再次提出并于2009年1月在参众两院分别表决获得通过。该法案的通过宣告原最高法院的判决无效。

4. to the mountaintop 到山顶上，出自《圣经》以色列人出埃及的典故。摩西带领以色列人摆脱埃及法老的奴役，他被上帝带到山顶上，看到了“应许之地”。马丁·路德·金被暗杀之前的最后一场演讲即名为《I've been to the mountaintop》。

中文译文
Suggested Translation

1 非常感谢，伊莱恩。……非常感谢你和家人所做的工作与牺牲……而我们一直得到你们的支持。

2 过去的几年，借由作为第一夫人的殊荣，我得以走遍了几乎整个美国。所到之处，所遇之人，以及所听之事，让我深深体会到了美国精神的精髓。

3 我的体会来自人们给予我和我的家人，尤其是给予我们的女儿无尽的关怀与温暖中。

4 我的体会来自在一个濒临破产的学区的老师们。他们誓言即便不收分文也要坚持施教。

5 我的体会来自那些招之即来的英雄。他们义无反顾去拯救他人……不远万里地去扑灭大火……驱车数小时去支援即将被洪水淹没的城镇。

6 我的体会来自我们投身军旅的男女军人及其令人自豪的家人……来自那些受伤的士兵的口中：他们不仅要再次站立行走，更要奔跑起来，甚至要参加马拉松……来自一位在阿富汗被炸失明的年轻士兵轻描淡写的话语：“倘若有机会让我做我所做过和所能做的事情，即使千百次牺牲我的双眼也在所不惜。"

7 每一天，我所见到的人们都激励着我……每一天，他们都令我感到自豪……每一天，他们都在提醒我，能够生活在这地球上最伟大的国度里是何等的幸福。

8 成为诸位的第一夫人对我来说，是一种无上的荣幸……但回想四年前我们首次在此聚首时，我仍然对我们即将展开的旅程心存疑虑。

9 尽管对我丈夫心中为这个国家设计的愿景，我信心满怀，……对于他必将成为一位出色的总统，我也深信不疑，……但是犹如所有的母亲，我也曾担心倘若他获此殊荣，这对我们的女儿们意味着什么。

10 身处万众瞩目的聚光灯下，我们该如何让她们依旧脚踏实地，保持本色？

11 让她们离开自己熟悉的学校、朋友和唯一有过的家园，她们会有什么感受呢？

12 在搬到华盛顿之前，我们的生活简单，却充满了快乐：……周六足球比赛，周日则在祖母家……还有巴拉克与我的约会之夜，要么出去共进晚餐，要么出去看场电影，因为作为一个身心疲惫的老妈，我实在没法二者兼顾还不打瞌睡。

13 而说真话，我喜欢我们为女儿们所打造的生活。我深爱着与我一同创造这一生活的男人，……我不想让这一切因为他当了总统而发生变化。

14 我爱的就是巴拉克原来的样子。

15 你们瞧，即便当时巴拉克已经是一名参议员，乃至一名总统候选人了……对我而言，他仍是那个开着辆锈迹斑斑的破车来接我去约会的男子，我甚至可以从后座侧门上的破洞看到外面飞逝而过的路面。……他仍然是那个男子，所拥有最为了不起的东西，是一张从垃圾箱翻出来的咖啡桌，唯一一双像样的鞋却还小了半号。

16 然而，当巴拉克开始向我讲述他的家庭时——就在那一刻，我知道我找到了一个志趣相投的知己，他的价值观和成长经历与我的何其相似乃尔。

17 如你们所知，养育巴拉克和我的两个家庭金钱或物质都称不上富有，但是，家里却给予了我们更为珍贵的东西：毫无条件的关爱，无所畏惧的付出，以及让我们得到他们不敢奢望的机会。

18 我的父亲是城市自来水厂的一名泵站操作员，在我和哥哥很小的时候，就被诊断出患有多发性硬化症。

19 即便当时还小，我也能体会到他每日的痛苦。我知道有许多清晨，即使仅仅是下床对他来说也是一种折磨。

20 但是每天早晨，我看到父亲面带微笑地醒来，抓住他的助行器，用浴室的洗脸池支撑着自己的身体，缓慢地刮好胡须，系上制服扣子。

21 当干完一整天的活之后他回到家时，我和哥哥会站在公寓门口的楼梯顶，耐心地等着迎接他，……我们注视着他弯下腰，抬起一条腿，然后是另一条腿，慢慢地爬上楼梯，迎向我们的怀抱。

22 然而无论多么艰难，我父亲从未请过一天假。他和我母亲决心要让我和哥哥接受自己梦寐以求的教育。

23 而当我和哥哥终于上了大学，我们几乎所有的学费都是来自学生贷款和助学金。

24 但是我父亲仍不得不自己掏腰包来支付其中的一小部分。

25 每个学期，他都坚持按时支付学费账单，哪怕在捉襟见肘的时候，也要去借贷。

26 能送自己的子女去上大学，他感到无比自豪，……他从未让我们因为自己姗姗来迟的支票而错过任何一个报到的截止日期。

27 你们瞧，对我的父亲来说，这是身为一个男人的责任。

28 就像我们中的很多人一样，这就是他衡量生命成功与否的方式——能否靠工作养家糊口让自己的家庭过上体面的生活。

29 当我开始与巴拉克相识相知的时候，我意识到，即使他在美国远隔千里的另一头长大，他的经历与我的却何等的相似。

30 巴拉克是由一位单身母亲抚养长大的。为了支付日常的花销，她苦苦地挣扎着。当她需要帮助的时候，祖父母也会伸出援手。

31 巴拉克的外祖母最初在社区银行当秘书，……很快获得了升职。但是，同其他许多女性一样，她的升职最终还是受到了性别限制。

32 数年间，那些能力不如她——甚至是她亲自培养的男性员工——都被提升到了比她高的职位，挣的钱越来越多，而与此同时，巴拉克一家却依旧只能勉强度日。

33 但日复一日，为了赶公共汽车，她坚持黎明就醒来，……比其他任何人都早上岗工作，……她总是无怨无悔地做到最好。

34 而且，她会常常这样告诉巴拉克："只要你们孩子过得好，巴，这才是真正重要的。"

35 有如许许多多美国家庭，我们俩的家庭都不奢望获取太多，知足常乐。

36 他们不会因为别人的成功而心生嫉妒，也不在意他人比自己拥有更多。事实上，他们对此表现的是敬佩。

37 他们只是相信美国最根本的承诺：哪怕你起步时并无多大的优势，倘若你奋力拼搏，做你应该做的，那么你就能够为自己打造一种体面的生活，甚至为你的子孙后代创造更加美好的明天。

38 他们就是这样把我们养育成人的。我们亦从他们言传身教中学到了许多东西。

39 我们学到了尊严与体面。你所付出的努力要远比你所能得到的重要，……帮助他人要远比自己独自一人一味领先更有意义。

40 我们学到了诚实与正直。实事求是，……不要妄图走捷径或按照自己的一套规则行事。……以及只有在公平、公正的基础上获得的成功才有意义。

41 我们学会了感恩和谦卑。很多人在我们的成功道路上伸出过援手，无论是启迪我们的老师还是保持校园清洁的校工——……我们还学会了要珍惜每个人的付出，尊重每个人。

42 这些都是巴拉克和我——以及在场的许多人——都试图要传承给我们自己孩子的价值观。

43 我们就是这样的人。

44 四年前，站在你们面前，我知道，倘若巴拉克成为总统，我不希望发生任何的改变。

45 那么，今天，在那么多的艰苦奋斗和胜利，以及我的丈夫所经历过的那么多我从未想象过的考验之后，我深切地认识到，当总统并不会改变任何人——它只会提供展示的舞台。

46 你们瞧，我有幸能近距离地亲眼观察当总统是怎么一回事。

47 我发现放在总统办公桌上的各种问题总是那么棘手——那是些无论多少资料或数据都无法帮你得出正确答案的难题。决断所面临的风险是如此之高，容不得一星半点的差错。

48 还有，作为总统，你会收到各种各样的人向你提出的林林总总的建议。

49 但是最终需要做出决定的时候，作为总统，唯一能引领你的是你的价值观、你的视野和塑造今天的你的生活阅历。

50 因此，当它涉及我们经济的重建，巴拉克思考的是有如我的父亲和他的祖母一样的人。

51 他思考的是经历一天辛苦工作之后人们理应获得的自豪感。

52 正是因为如此，他签署了《莉莉•莱德贝特同工同酬法案》，以帮助女性获得同工同酬的公平权利。

53 正是因为如此，他为工薪家庭和小型企业减税，并为汽车行业的振兴抗争。

54 这就是他将我们的经济从崩溃的边缘拉回并使其重新开始创造就业岗位之策——提供人们能够养家糊口的工作，这些好工作就在这里，就在美国本土。

55 至于我们家人的医疗保健问题，巴拉克拒绝听从所有那些要他暂缓医疗改革，把问题留给下一任总统的建议。

56 他不在乎这在政治上是不是一件唾手可得的事情——这不是他所受到的教育——他在乎的是：做正确的事。

57 他之所以这样做，是因为他坚信在美国，我们的祖父母应该能够负担得起自己的医药费用。我们的孩子应该能够在生病时去看医生。……在这个国家里，不应该有人因为一场意外或疾病贫困潦倒。

58 他还相信，女性应当完全有能力对自己的身体和自己的医疗保健做出选择……这就是我的丈夫所坚持的。

59 至于给予我们的孩子应有的教育，巴拉克知道，就像我和你们中的许多人一样，倘若没有助学金，他永远也不可能完成大学学业。

60 而且，你们相信吗？在我俩新婚之时，我们的助学贷款的压力甚至远甚于房贷。当时我们是那么年轻，那么相爱，又是那样的负债累累。

61 正是因为如此，巴拉克竭尽全力提高助学金额度，同时压低利率。因为他希望让每一个年轻人都能大展宏图，不必为了上大学而债台高筑。

62 因此，归根到底，对巴拉克来说，这些并非政治问题，而是个人问题。

63 因为巴拉克知道一个家庭艰难度日意味着什么。他知道想要让下一代和下下一代过上更好的日子意味着什么。

64 巴拉克知道何为美国梦，因为他曾有过亲身的经历。他希望全国的每一个人都拥有同样的机会，无论身份、无论籍贯、无论肤貌和信仰如何。

65 而且他认为，当你努力奋斗，取得进展，并且在跨越了那扇机遇的大门之后，……不应该砰的一声关上身后的大门。……你应该转身伸出援手，给予他人使你获得成功同样的机会。

66 因此，当人们问我，入主白宫是否改变了我的丈夫的时候，我可以坦诚相告，无论是从他的性格、他的信念、他的心灵来看，巴拉克·奥巴马都仍然是许多年前我所爱上的那个男人。

67 他仍是那样一个人，会在自己事业起步的阶段拒绝高薪工作，而走入一个因钢铁厂的倒闭而陷入困境的社区，为社区的重建和人们重获工作而奋斗，……因为对巴拉克来说，成功的标准并不是收入的多寡，而是你给人们生活带来的改变。

68 他仍是那样一个人，当我们的女儿刚出生的时候，隔不了几分钟就急匆匆地查看摇篮，确认她们仍在好好呼吸，并骄傲地抱着她们去找所有的熟人显摆。

69 他至今仍然几乎每晚和我跟女儿一起进餐，耐心地回答她们关于各种新闻和时事的问题，并为她们在学校交朋友的事儿出谋划策。

70 在万籁俱寂的深夜里，我常常看到他仍趴在书桌上，正翻看着一封封人们寄给他的信。有的信来自正在艰难维持生计的父亲，……有的信来自被保险公司弃之不管而命在旦夕的癌症女性，……有的信则来自徒有大志却怀才不遇的年轻人。

71 我能看到他眼里的忧虑，……我也能听出他声音中的决心。他说："你无法相信这些人过的是什么样的日子，米歇尔。……这是不对的！我们必须再接再厉去改变这一切。我们还有更多事情要做。"

72 我看到那些故事——所有那些抗争、那些希望与梦想——我所看到的那一切都是推动巴拉克•奥巴马每一天工作的动力。

73 而从前的我认为这是不可能的，可是今天的我反而比四年前更爱我的丈夫了……甚至远胜23年前我们初次相会时！

74 我爱他，因为他从不忘本！

75 我爱他，因为他值得信赖，会去履行承诺。困难当头、困难重重他只会越挫越勇！

76 我爱他，因为他从不分"我们"或"他们"，对人们一视同仁——他才不在意你是民主党人、共和党人或是无党派人士。他知道我们都深爱这个国家，……他总是悉心倾听，从善如流。他总是乐意去挖掘所遇见的每一个人身上的闪光点！

77 我爱他，因为即便是在艰难无比、令人揪心不已的时刻，法案无法通过，全局似乎皆输了——巴拉克从不让自己被非议和噪声所干扰。

78 就像他的祖母一样，他会重新振作，继续前进，用他的耐心、睿智、勇气和大度！

79 他总会提醒我：我们任重道远，……变革往往是艰难和缓慢的，根本无法一蹴而就。但是总有一天我们会成功，我们一向如此。

80 我们将获得成功，因为像我的父亲，……像巴拉克的祖母，……还有所有像他们一样的人都对自己说过："我没能实现自己的梦想，但或许我的孩子们可以。或许我们的孙辈们可以。"

81 因此，今天，我们许多人站在这里，是因为他们的牺牲、渴望以及坚定不移的爱，……因为一次又一次，他们消除了自己内心的恐惧和疑虑，去战胜困难。

82 因此，今天，当我们所面临的挑战铺天盖地而来——甚至无法战胜的时候——请别忘记，成就不可能之事正是这个国家的历史。我们美国人就是这样。我们的国家就是这么建立起来的。

83 假如我们的父母前辈能为我们艰苦奋斗，……假如他们能修建高耸入云的钢筋大厦，能把人类送上月球，还能轻轻一触按钮就能连接整个世界，……那么当然，我们也能继续忘我牺牲，为我们的子孙后代打造未来。

84 假如那么多英勇无畏的军人可以披挂上阵，为捍卫我们最基本的权益献出自己的生命，……那么当然，作为这个伟大民主政体的公民，我们也可以履行自己的职责来践行这些权利。当然，我们也可以在大选之日通过投票，发出自己的呼声。

85 假如农夫和铁匠都能从一个帝国手中赢得独立，……假如移民们都能舍弃他们所熟知的一切，来我们国家寻求更加美好的生活，……假如妇女们都能冒着牢狱之灾去争取选举的权利，……假如一代人能够战胜经济大萧条，成就一番千秋伟业，……假如一位年轻的牧师能够用他的正义理想把我们引领至山顶，……而假如自豪的美国人敢于正视自己，与自己所爱的人勇敢地做出牺牲，……那么我们一定、一定能为这个国家的每一个人提供一个平等的机会，去实现自己的美国梦！

86 因为归根结底，最重要的是，这就是这个国家的故事——一个关于不屈不挠进行斗争，坚定不移实现梦想的传说。这也成就了我的故事，巴拉克的故事，以及其他许多美国人的故事。

87 今天我之所以这样说不仅仅是因为我是第一夫人，……不仅仅因为我是一个妻子。你瞧，每当一天的工作结束之时，我最重要的头衔还是“一个操心的妈”。女儿们还是我的心头肉，是我生活的中心。

88 但是今天，我不再像四年前那样顾虑重重，不再担心巴拉克和我所作所为是否对孩子们的成长最为有利。

89 因为今天，根据我的亲身经历，我明白，倘若我想要留给我的女儿们、给我们所有的儿女们一个更为美好的世界，……倘若我们要为我们的子孙后代提供一个实现梦想的基础和施展抱负的机遇，……倘若我们要让他们感到机遇无限——让他们相信在美国，只要愿意为之奋斗就一定会变得更好，……那么，我们必须比以往更加努力，……我们必须再一次团结起来，支持这个推动这个伟大的国家继续前进、值得你我信任的人：……我的丈夫、我们的总统——巴拉克·奥巴马。

90 谢谢大家，上帝保佑你们，上帝保佑美国。